ADDITIONAL PRAISE FOR *STICKING TO THE UNION*

"*Sticking to the Union* is a vivid example of history 'from the bottom up.' With admirable sensitivity and skill, Sandy Polishuk allows Julia Ruuttila to share her remarkable story of struggle and resilience, triumph and tragedy, spanning more than eight decades. The result is an intriguing dialogue between memory and history."

—*Bruce Nelson, author of* Workers on the Waterfront

"Sandy Polishuk deftly explores the challenges of history and memory in this fascinating oral history biography of Julia Ruuttila: consummate union, civil rights, and peace activist of the Pacific Northwest. Although haunted by failed relationships, poverty, McCarthyite persecution, and a frustrated writing career, Ruuttila embraced every waking moment of her eighty-four years to struggle for social and economic justice. The story of this extraordinary woman should inspire a new generation of activists."

—*Laurie Mercier, author of* Anaconda: Labor, Community, and Culture in Montana's Smelter City *and Associate Professor of History, Washington State University, Vancouver.*

"Sandy Polishuk offers two gifts: the biography of a fierce local activist whose life bears witness to the fact that ordinary people can effect social justice, and a scholar's journey into the complicated workings of memory. *Sticking to the Union* is a fabulous oral history, Julia Ruuttila a compelling subject, and Sandy Polishuk, a thoughtful scholar who allows Ruuttila's voice to drive the narrative, but who also probes the intersections of ego and memory to present the many truths of Ruuttila's life story."

—*Mary Murphy, History Department, Montana State University*

Palgrave Studies in Oral History

Series Editors: Linda Shopes and Bruce M. Stave

STICKING TO THE UNION

STICKING TO THE UNION

An Oral History of the
Life and Times of Julia Ruuttila

Sandy Polishuk

Sticking to the Union
Copyright © Sandy Polishuk, 2003.
All rights reserved. No part of this book may be used or reproduced in any manner
whatsoever without written permission except in the case of brief quotations embodied in
critical articles or reviews.

First published in 2003 by PALGRAVE MACMILLAN™
175 Fifth Avenue, New York, N.Y. 10010 and
Houndmills, Basingstoke, Hampshire, England RG21 6XS.
Companies and representatives throughout the world.

PALGRAVE MACMILLAN is the global academic imprint of the PALGRAVE MACMILLAN
division of St. Martin's Press, LLC and of Palgrave Macmillan Ltd. Macmillan® is a
registered trademark in the United States, United Kingdom and other countries. Palgrave
is a registered trademark in the European Union and other countries.

ISBN 1-4039-6239-1 hardback
ISBN 1-4039-6240-5 paperback

Library of Congress Cataloging-in-Publication Data
Polishuk, Sandy, 1940-
    Sticking to the union : an oral history of the life and times of Julia Ruuttila / Sandy
Polishuk.
        p.   cm.—(Palgrave studies in oral history)
    includes bibliographical references and index.
        ISBN 1-4039-6239-1—ISBN 1-4039-6230-5 (pbk)
        1. Ruuttila, Julia.   2. Women labor leaders—United States—Biography.   3. Women
labor union members—United States—Biography.   4. Women in journalism—United
States—Biography.   5. Women novelists—United States—Biography.   6. Women
radicals—United States—Biography.   7. Women social reformers—United States—
Biography.   8. Labor unions—United States—History—20th century.   I. Ruuttila,
Julia.   II. Title.   III. Series.

HD8073.R88P65   2003
331.88'092—dc21
[B]
                                                                                    2003049769

A catalogue record for this book is available from the British Library.

Design by Letra Libre.

First edition: November 2003
10   9   8   7   6   5   4   3   2   1
Printed in the United States of America.

*For
Julia
and for Shane*

CONTENTS

SERIES EDITORS' FOREWORD

Oral history, it is often said, allows people to speak for themselves. By putting their experiences into words, so the argument goes, narrators are able to give account of their lives in ways that they choose. In large measure this is true, as Sandy Polishuk's oral biography of labor journalist Julia Ruuttila ably demonstrates. In a series of interviews conducted by Polishuk in the 1980s and early 1990s, Ruuttila recounted a lifetime of activism in the Pacific Northwest, one that embraced many of the major social movements of the twentieth century, from labor organizing by the Industrial Workers of the World in the early years to a broad-based environmentalism at century's end. High points of the narrative include Ruuttila's participation in organizing the International Woodworkers of America in Oregon during the 1930s and her work within unions' women's auxiliaries to advance progressive labor goals.

Underneath the specifics of her story, Ruuttila presents herself as driven by a passion for justice, growing toward a broadly nonsectarian left politics, and uninterested in passing on the details of her personal life. Like many oral history narrators, she is the hero of her own story. Mostly, Polishuk allows Ruuttila to represent herself as she wished; *Sticking to the Union* is an authentic first-person account. But Polishuk also understands that oral history narratives don't entirely speak for themselves, or more accurately, to be broadly accessible, they need the active intervention of an editor. So she has considerably edited the transcripts of Ruuttila's interviews for coherence and flow, has provided important background information to establish context for Ruuttila's stories, and, most importantly, has assessed Ruuttila's account against the extant documentary record. This last point deserves a bit of comment.

Since the publication of Alessandro Portelli's seminal essay "The Death of Luigi Trastulli: Memory and the Event," historians have generally accepted this work's central argument that what is factually inaccurate in an interview may nonetheless offer significant psychological truth. This is an important insight, but, contrary to Portelli's own example, one that has led historians to sometimes rather naively assume that what a narrator says can be taken at face value and that it does not need to be read against other available sources, both written and oral. Polishuk does not make this mistake. Talking with Ruuttila's brother, she learned that her subject might have misrepresented elements of her personal history; checking this against the written record, Polishuk determined that this was indeed the case. Reading other accounts of public events about which Ruuttila spoke, Polishuk found that Ruuttila tended to overdramatize her own role. In all cases she handles these discrepancies in a manner that is respectful of both Ruuttila and the reader, scrupulously pointing them out and explaining them as best she can, while not muting Ruuttila's own strong voice. In the end, Polishuk and Ruuttila demonstrate what is perhaps the most accurate of the truisms about oral history: that it is a fundamentally interpretive exercise.

Thus Sticking to the Union both contributes to our knowledge of twentieth-century social movements and demonstrates self-consciousness about the method of oral history. We are pleased to include it in Palgrave's Studies in Oral History series, designed to bring oral history interviews out of the archives and into the hands of students, educators, scholars, and the reading public. Volumes in the series are deeply grounded in interviews and present them in ways that enable readers to appreciate more fully their historical significance and cultural meaning. The series also includes work that approaches oral history more theoretically, as a point of departure for an exploration of broad questions of cultural representation and production.

Linda Shopes
Pennsylvania Historical & Museum Commission

Bruce M. Stave
University of Connecticut

FOREWORD

In 1966 a photograph in the local paper of Julia Ruuttila, age fifty-nine, being dragged along the street by police at an anti–Vietnam War demonstration piqued the interest of Sandy Polishuk, a young woman activist in Portland, Oregon. Polishuk's fascination deepened as she observed Ruuttila's leadership in the predominantly young, male-dominated left in the Portland community and learned more about Julia's history as a labor activist, journalist, and writer. The years Polishuk spent interviewing Ruuttila and researching her life have produced a rare glimpse into the life and consciousness of a woman whose activism encompassed a half century and benefited a wide variety of progressive social movements.

The collaboration between these two women was the interaction between two different generations of political activists, as Polishuk's feminist interest in the politics of personal life collided with Ruuttila's steadfast insistence that only her public life counted. Blanche Cook has pointed out that, to the generation that came of age in the 1960s and 1970s, "It has become clear that in history, no less than in life, our personal choices and the nature of our human relationships were and remain inseparable from our political, our public efforts."[1] Ruuttila didn't see it that way. Her generation of activists saw only the public arena as the terrain of political struggle. Like other women activists of the 1930s and '40s, her struggle to be taken seriously in a male-dominated union movement led her to regard her personal life as at best irrelevant and at times an impediment to her political work. She often responded evasively and sometimes with irritation to Polishuk's probing about her relationships with men and with her son and her personal struggle to survive. Polishuk worked hard to make sense of the omissions and occasional disingenuousness in Ruuttila's stories, but we are still left with many questions about Ruuttila's private life.

In some important ways, however, Julia Ruuttila's political consciousness traversed generations. Because Ruuttila's activism spans such a long period of time, we can trace both the ways the ideas of later periods echoed those of earlier ones and the ways new ideas interacted with old ones to shape her perspective. The

critique of craft unionism she inherited from her father's Wobbly politics, for example, made Ruuttila an easy convert to industrial unionism in the 1930s.[2] She
abandoned the Wobbly disdain for voting, however, to use electoral politics as a
tool for mobilizing the power of working people. Her Wobbly roots made her feel
less comfortable with what she called the "super-duper" discipline of the Communist Party than with the direct action and anti-authoritarianism of the radical
movements of the 1960s. Like other radicals in the union movement, Ruuttila's
activism was affected by the Cold War and the McCarthy era. But despite occasional nostalgia for the "good old days," Ruuttila remained active and remarkably
open to various forms of protest. Perhaps because she never belonged to either
the Communist or Socialist Parties and was used to functioning independently,
she didn't seem to lose her moorings as much as many other "old left" political
activists did during the 1950s and 60s. While some veterans of the old left were
alienated by the lack of organizational coherence and the countercultural elements of radicalism in the late 1960s, Ruuttila was intrigued and supportive.

The typewriter was Julia Ruuttila's weapon of choice in what she saw as the
war between labor and capital. She used it to write letters to the editor, to com-
pose leaflets and petitions, and to tell labor's side of the story in various labor
newsletters and radical newspapers. Like the better-known woman journalists of
the 1930s and 1940s studied by Paula Rabinowitz and Charlotte Nekola, Ruuttila used columns and news stories in left and labor publications to move beyond
the limited scope traditionally allotted to women journalists.[3] While Ruuttila was
not part of the left literary world, centered primarily on the East Coast, her articles clearly reflected Tess Slesinger's definition of the progressive writer's task as

> the job of seeing the mess in which the plain people had been trapped, of in-
> terpreting it for them, of reflecting their own image so clearly and correctly that
> the plain people themselves would feel a part of life with a voice and a weapon
> and an ally and cease to think of themselves as helpless victims and alone.[4]

Ruuttila's typewriter, her companion until her death, was also a tool in her efforts
to earn a living and, to the disapproval of some of her comrades in the movement, a means of self-expression that revealed her feelings about her life and the
struggles in which she participated. She wrote countless poems and stories based
on her experiences and worked sporadically on the "great proletarian novel."

Ruuttila describes the International Woodworkers of America (IWA) as her
first love and women's auxiliaries as her religion. Barred from becoming a worker
in the lumber industry by policies that discriminated against women, she devoted herself to building union auxiliaries. In addition to the auxiliary to the

IWA, she was active in the International Longshoremen's and Warehousemen's Union auxiliaries in Astoria and Portland, Oregon. Her memories bring to life the activities of the auxiliaries she participated in and illustrate their significance. As several historians have demonstrated, these organizations of workers' wives in predominantly male industries played a crucial but underexamined role in the labor movement in the first half of the twentieth century. Most visible when they were providing critical support during strikes, lockouts, and sit-ins, auxiliaries made important contributions to their unions by building community, providing for material needs, sustaining morale, educating members about the importance of the union, and expanding the concerns of the union beyond the shop floor.[5]

Ruuttila understood clearly how crucial the women's auxiliary was during the lockout of the IWA in 1937 and was proud of the resourcefulness and courage of auxiliary members. Whether they were sitting in at the local hospital to force doctors to fit workers' wives for diaphragms, marching around the courthouse to get the county to grant welfare benefits to woodworkers' families, or throwing a huge party when morale sagged, auxiliary members enabled the workers to hold out for eight and a half months and created an important source of support for each other. Ruuttila's proud descriptions of auxiliary activities demonstrate that, as Ruth Milkman has pointed out, "women's labor activism, much more than men's, extended outside of the workplace and into the larger community."[6] Ruuttila's stories also illustrate the ways that auxiliaries were sometimes pushed beyond the traditional service role by the presence of a few women radical members.[7] In her discussion of the short-lived auxiliary of the Minneapolis Teamsters' union, Marjorie Lasky speculates that auxiliaries that lasted longer might generate "a working-class 'women's culture,' conducive to nurturing women's independence."[8] The Woodworkers' auxiliary that emerges from Ruuttila's descriptions supports Lasky's speculation. For the wives of woodworkers, the auxiliary was a haven; it nurtured their courage, enhanced their self confidence, and cemented ties among its members.

As Polishuk points out, Ruuttila's memories are crafted stories, shaped not only by her experience but by the image she wanted to project. Sometimes differing sharply from the written record and memories of others, Ruuttila's stories are interpretations of her life. The oral history emerges as a self-portrait—one that communicates Ruuttila's view of herself and her relation to the world. Two salient features of this self-portrait were Ruuttila's political and intellectual independence and her unflagging commitment to activism. Ruuttila presents herself as working with a wide variety of participants in the American left and fiercely resisting red baiting. She defined herself as an independent communist and refused to adhere to the orthodoxies of the Communist Party, which she saw as autocratic and humorless, even while married to a party member. From organizing to free Ray Becker, an imprisoned member of the Industrial Workers of the World, to protesting against the Gulf War, or staging a sleep-in to protest rate increases by the local electric company, Ruuttila's commitment to political activism lasted her lifetime, and she achieved her desire to die "as she lived—shouting the system down."

Amy Kesselman
February 2003

ACKNOWLEDGMENTS

Without Julia Ruuttila and her generous gifts of time, memory, and attention, this book would not have been possible. My debt to her is unmeasurable, as is my regret that she did not live to see the completion of our project.

The cooperation and tolerance of Julia's family has been critical to this project. I am continually grateful to Shane Ruuttila for opening his home and his life to me, for his frankness and dedication to telling the truth—even when the material was painful or embarrassing—and his patience with my continuing requests and questions. Also to his wife, Betty Rose, and his sons, Jason and Ryan, for their kindness and generosity.

Lois Stranahan was always ready with answers to my questions. I am grateful to Tom Churchill for allowing me to use the interview with Julia from his novel *Centralia Dead March* and to Bill Bigelow and Elizabeth Patapoff, who shared their interviews with Julia with me.

My thanks to everyone who agreed to be interviewed. Though space considerations allowed me to use very few quotes from these interviews, the insight I gained into Julia and her causes was essential. A full list of interviewees appears in the sources section at the end of the book.

When a project continues for years, as this one did, the debts incurred are many. I am grateful to innumerable people, organizations, and institutions, including the following:

My friends and family who stood by me through the difficult birth of this project, who maintained their faith that I would finish after years of evidence indicating the contrary. Forgive me for not naming you all here, but the list has grown far too long.

The women of the Northwest Women's History Project, who taught me the skills I needed to initiate this project. Without them, this book would not exist.

Cottages at Hedgebrook gave me time, space, confidence, and nurturing in which to discover how one finishes a book. I also thank my fellow writers at Hedgebrook, who listened to and critiqued my early drafts around the wood stove.

Flight of the Mind Writing Workshops for Women provided the atmosphere (and superior teachers) in which I was able to learn the craft of writing. I thank all my teachers at Flight and also at Portland State University's Haystack Summer program and Tillamook Community College as well as my teachers at other workshops.

All my fellow students, but especially the Inkslingers, my writing group, for reading endless drafts with patience and kindness.

Jerry Baum and Sara Halprin read the entire manuscript when it was nearly twice its ultimate length and gave invaluable feedback. Harry Stein served as my personal history adviser, always ready to answer my questions. Matt Kosokoff had a similar role with regard to the Internet.

My many long-distance researchers, who saved me trips and time, included Sarah Cooper, director, Southern California Library for Social Studies and Research; Laurel Lynn Demas, genealogical volunteer; Ed Hedemann and Ruth Benn of the War Resisters League; Jeff Kosokoff, my personal librarian; Tom Neel, library director, Ohio Genealogical Society; Linda Showalter, Special Collections, Dawes Memorial Library, Marietta College; Rickie Solinger; S. L. Wisenberg; Carol Newman; and most of all Gene Vrana, ILWU archivist, who responded promptly and generously to my many requests for information and assistance.

Shane Ruuttila, John R. Godman, and Doreen Labby Carey for the use of photographs. Barbara Gundle for a photo shoot with Julia before her departure for Alaska.

Valerie Taylor and Miriam Kolkin Kelber for the loan of correspondence with Julia.

Librarians and archivists at many libraries and archives, including the Multnomah County Library, Portland State University, Reed College, Lewis & Clark College, University of Oregon Special Collections, University of Washington Libraries, Tamiment Library (New York University), Oregon State Archives, Multnomah County Records Department, Portland City Archives, and the Oregon State Bar. Also to the IWA (now the Woodworkers Division of the International Association of Machinists and Aerospace Workers) and Local 8 of the ILWU for access to their archives. Also the volunteers at the Family History Libraries, Church of Jesus Christ of Latter-day Saints, in Portland. My special thanks to the staff at the Oregon Historical Society Library for their help over the years, especially to Susan Seyl, director of the Image Collection, and her staff, for assistance beyond the call of duty.

Amy Kesselman has been a supporter, reader, friend, and resource for me from the beginning. I thank her for her encouragement and faith in me and the material.

In the changing world of publishing, I feel especially lucky to have had competent, dedicated, and enthusiastic editors. My thanks to Bruce Stave and Linda Shopes for choosing my manuscript for the oral history series; to Deborah Gershenowitz, the history editor at Palgrave early in our process, for her tactful and skillful editing; and to Brendan O'Malley, my ultimate editor at Palgrave, for taking on the project. He and the production editor Erin Ivy shepherded me through the minutiae of publication with patience and kindness. I am especially grateful to Linda Shopes for her constant support, her unfailing confidence in me, her affection for Julia, and her ready words of encouragement throughout the long and sometimes difficult process of transforming my manuscript into a book.

ABBREVIATIONS IN TEXT

ADC	Aid to Dependent Children
AFL	American Federation of Labor
AFSCME	American Federation of State, County and Municipal Employees
ASSK	Astoria Finnish Socialist Club (Astorian Suomalainen Sosialisti Klubi)
CIA	Central Intelligence Agency
CIO	Committee for Industrial Organization, later Congress of Industrial Organizations
CLRC	Coast Labor Relations Committee
CP	Communist Party
CRDC	Columbia River District Council
EEOC	Equal Employment Opportunity Commission
FBI	Federal Bureau of Investigation
FOIPA	Freedom of Information/Privacy Acts
FRBC	Free Ray Becker Committee
HUAC	House Committee on Un-American Activities, popularly called the House Un-American Activities Committee
ILWU	International Warehouse and Longshore Union
INS	Immigration and Naturalization Service
IWA	International Woodworkers of America
IWW	Industrial Workers of the World
NAACP	National Association for the Advancement of Colored People
NIRA	National Industrial Recovery Act
NLB	National Labor Board
NLRB	National Labor Relations Board
NWHP	Northwest Women's History Project
PP&L	Pacific Power & Light Company
SNAP	Society for New Action Politics
UMW	United Mine Workers
WAA	Workers Alliance of America

LIST OF ILLUSTRATIONS

Oh, you can't scare me,
I'm sticking to the union.
I'm sticking to the union till the day I die. ©

INTRODUCTION

I didn't know when I met Julia Ruuttila that she would change my life, but I did know she was special. The first time I saw her she was being dragged by police from an anti–Vietnam War demonstration in front of the Sheraton Motor Inn in Portland, Oregon, where Vice President Hubert Humphrey was speaking. It was only a photo on the front page of my newspaper, but I remembered her. It was 1966; Julia was fifty-nine. I was twenty-six, had two babies, and had moved to Portland—where my husband had started a new job—only a month earlier. I had met few people and had no idea who the local activists were.

Three months later I went to an organizing meeting of the Society for New Action Politics (SNAP). SNAP was to be Portland's New Left organization, an umbrella for progressive activists from the community, high schools, local colleges, and labor unions. We filed into Reed College's wood-paneled chapel: professors, students, workers, housewives, clergy, Democrats, Communists, anarchists, pacifists, anyone wanting to work against the Vietnam War and for civil liberties and human rights. When we broke into committees, I chose one on legal defense. Julia was the chair.

At the time, I was ignorant of Julia's experience in the labor movement and on defense committees. What I saw was a diminutive woman, older than most of the others. I was surprised Julia was running our meeting. This was before the women's movement of the late 1960s began, before liberal organizations even paid lip service to putting women into leadership. But Julia was in charge of our meeting, spoke right up, and knew what she wanted us to talk about and plan. I could see she was a veteran leader.

I soon began to hear many stories about Julia from younger activists in the Portland community. I learned that her father had been a member of the radical labor union the Industrial Workers of the World (IWW, or Wobblies) and her mother had distributed birth control literature when to do so was illegal. I heard how Julia had listened through the keyhole as a child to "Big Bill" Haywood and other labor leaders who had visited her parents' home. I learned about her role in getting a Wobbly martyr, Ray Becker, out of prison and how she was responsible for the anti–Vietnam War resolutions of the ladies' auxiliary of the International Longshoremen's and Warehousemen's Union (ILWU).[1]

The stories I heard were only the highlights of a life lived within the labor and left-wing political movements. Years later when I began to interview Julia, new dimensions of her life emerged: She claimed both black and Jewish blood, suicide was a recurring theme in her family, she had helped organize the woodworkers' union and its ladies' auxiliary in Oregon, she had been a labor journalist for nearly 50 years, she was a poet and fiction writer, she had been subpoenaed by the House Un-American Activities Committee (HUAC).

She was born Julia Evelyn Godman on April 26, 1907, in Eugene, Oregon, the first child of John B. (Jack) Godman and Ella Blossom Padan Godman. She grew up in Eugene and in nearby logging camps and on a remote farm. Julia had a number of names and published at various times under all of them: her maiden name, Julia Godman; her married names, Julia Bertram, Julia Eaton, and Julia Ruuttila; and her pen names, Kathleen Cronin and Kathleen Ruuttila.

Though she told me of only three marriages, she was actually married four times. The first, the one I learned of from her brother only after her death, was to William Clayton Bowen, a sawmill worker. They married six weeks before her seventeenth birthday in 1924. That marriage was dissolved ten and a half months later. Her second marriage was to Maurice "Butch" Bertram on July 6, 1926, in Fresno, California. They lived in California, Oregon, Denver, and Chicago, where her only child, Michael Jack, was born in June 1928. Returning to Oregon in early 1929, Butch got a job at the West Oregon lumber mill in Linnton (now part of Portland) and Julia bought a typewriter. For the rest of her life her typewriter remained a constant companion.

In 1943 Julia divorced Butch and married Ben Eaton, a seaman. She divorced him in 1946. Her only successful marriage was to Oscar Ruuttila, whom she married in 1951 and lived with in Astoria, Oregon, until his sudden death from a heart attack in 1962. They had no children together, but they raised her grandson Shane, who had been born in 1949. Later, Julia's mother came to live with them, too. In 1965, Julia moved her household back to Portland where she stayed until retiring to Anchorage, Alaska, in 1987 to live with Shane and his family.

Though a writer her entire life—writing journalism, poems, novels, stories, speeches, notes for an autobiography—her identity as an activist was just as strong and steady. In 1935 she and Butch helped sign up lumber mill workers for the woodworkers' union and Julia organized their wives into a ladies' auxiliary. The following year Julia created the Free Ray Becker Committee to get the Wobbly martyr, imprisoned since the Centralia Tragedy of 1919, released. In the course of publicizing Becker's case, she began writing for the union's newspaper, the *Timber Worker,* and was, for a time, the Oregon editor. In the next year or so she expanded her outlets to include the *People's World,* a paper published by the Communist Party, though she was not a party member herself; the *Dispatcher,* the ILWU's paper; and Federated Press, a left-wing news service. During the 1930s, she was also part of the army of activists that built the CIO.

In the early forties, before Pearl Harbor, she participated in the movement to keep the United States out of World War II. But once the United States entered the war, Julia got behind her country's struggle, even working for a short time at an army depot. By war's end she was a single mother and a stenographer for Oregon's State Public Welfare Commission. She joined the campaign of Progressive Party presidential candidate Henry Wallace in 1948. After a politically motivated firing by State Public Welfare in 1948, Julia found work again as the secretary to Matt Meehan, the international representative of the ILWU in the Northwest.

When Julia moved to Astoria, Oregon, in 1951 following her marriage to Oscar Ruuttila, she kept her job with the ILWU for a short time and also worked for the Columbia River Fishermen's Protective Union, founded both the Clatsop County Committee for Protection of Foreign Born and an ILWU ladies' auxiliary, and continued writing.

Federated Press went under in 1956, but Julia remained a reporter for the *Dispatcher* and a freelance journalist. After her return to Portland in 1965 she became legislative chair of the ILWU's Portland Ladies' Auxiliary and a Democratic precinct committeewoman, and was active in the anti–Vietnam War movement, several defense committees, and an assortment of campaigns ranging from fighting the storage of nerve gas in Oregon to anti–sales tax organizing.

When Julia turned eighty in 1987, she retired from the *Dispatcher* and moved to Anchorage, Alaska, to live with Shane, his wife Betty, and her great-grandsons Jason and Ryan. There, with the help of Shane and Betty, she self-published her only book, more than 120 poems in a spiral-bound volume titled *This Is My Shadow.* She died in Anchorage in 1991.

Through all the jobs, moves, and marriages, Julia remained an activist, always on the side of the underdog. She stood firmly with the victims of racial prejudice and political repression, but most of all she loathed capitalism and its exploitation of the workers. Belief in the eminence of the working class was her religion; the industrial union her church. Her most consistent prerequisite for a husband was that he be a good union man.

Her best male friends were also from the labor movement: Francis Murnane, an activist first in the International Woodworkers of America (IWA) and later the ILWU; Ramon Tancioco of the Alaska Cannery Union; Frank Pozzi, the ILWU's lawyer; Matt Meehan, her boss at the ILWU. The lawyer Irv Goodman was an exception, but he spent his time defending workers and, as Julia often said, the destitute and damned.

Her closest women friends were married to ILWU members and were cohorts of hers in the ladies' auxiliary—Lois Stranahan, like Julia a tireless activist; Valerie Taylor, the president of the Federated Auxiliaries of the ILWU for many years; Veva Phillips, the vice president of the Federated Auxiliaries; and Clara Fambro, the black woman who became president of the ILWU Federated Auxiliaries when Valerie retired—or were fellow political activists such as Martina Gangle Curl, a talented artist and Communist, and Mary Jane Brewster, who worked with Julia on investigative stories and in political movements for many years.

Though Julia valued her work as a journalist and was especially proud of her investigative reporting, she never abandoned her dream of publishing fiction. A few of Julia's fiction manuscripts survive. While a University of Oregon student, she wrote "A Menace to Our Town," a child's point of view of a Wobbly-led strike that results in the murder of the organizer and the blacklisting of the narrator's father. The instructor in her magazine writing class submitted it to a *Harper's Magazine* contest for college students, where it won an honorable mention.

One of the novels she wrote while living at the West Oregon mill, "The Wolf at the Door," was set in a mill town in the early thirties. FDR's election, the New Deal, the oppressive poverty of the mill town, and the first stirrings of mill union organizing are background, but basically it's a love story doomed by class differences.

At fifty, during the height of "McCarthyism," Julia began her autobiography, "The Bridges of Ce," the title taken from a Louis Aragon poem: "I have crossed the bridges of Cé / It is there that everything began," but she never finished it.[2]

By the time I met Julia in 1966, she suffered from arthritis, asthma, ulcers, and angina, but she was at every antiwar demonstration and on every labor picket line. For those of us who were newcomers to the peace and social justice movement, Julia was a role model of dedication, practicality, and persistence. She had been an activist for over 60 years but never complained that the work should have been done by now, all the victories won. She understood politics was an ongoing battle.

In my interviews with her family, friends, and colleagues, I heard how Julia had passed on labor history to them through both her writing and her personal stories. And I heard praise. Russ Farrell, a Portland Democratic Party activist, described her as a radical: "A liberal is someone who will fight for reforms up to the point of personal sacrifice. Takes a radical to go on from there. And that's what she was her whole life, was fighting for a better world for people."[3]

When Julia was thirty-nine, the FBI reported she was five feet, one inch tall. With age, her height, though not her spirit, diminished. In 1987 her hazel eyes still sparkled, but her dark brown hair was gray. It was coarse and wavy and Julia often tied it back from her face with a red ribbon. With the exception of her affection for red, Julia dressed very much like other working-class women of her generation, in slacks, polyester blouses, and cardigan sweaters. Her shoes were sensible oxfords, her glasses plastic pixie frames. She never lost her elfin smile and her quick and frequent giggle.

I interviewed Julia for the first time in March 1983. The Northwest Women's History Project (NWHP), a group dedicated to promoting the study of the history of women in the Northwest, was searching for a new focus after producing a slide show on women shipyard workers of World War II.[4] I was one of two members sent to ask Julia about the role of the IWA ladies' auxiliary when the union was locked out during a jurisdictional struggle in 1937. We weren't thinking about a project focusing on Julia at the time, but I was fascinated by what she had to say and tantalized by the many facets of her life as a journalist and in the labor movement that I had not suspected.

Though the NWHP did not pursue the IWA ladies' auxiliary project, later that year I hauled my tape recorder back to Julia's apartment for the first of weekly visits that continued into early 1984. Julia agreed because she wanted to tell the story of the unions. And, I like to think, she enjoyed my visits.

It was in her tiny apartment that we did most of our work together. Fifteen feet across and only slightly longer, the room was crammed. Her old manual typewriter, surrounded by stacks of papers and books, dominated the round Formica table. I imagined her eating at that table, shoving aside a pile of papers, moving one stack onto another. Or did she just put her plate on top, eating with care to avoid spilling on an important manuscript?

The adjacent wall served as her bulletin board. Just above eye level, when seated at her typewriter, was a large signed photo of Harry Bridges, the founding president of the ILWU, in profile, chairing his last ILWU convention in 1977, the gavel resting on his shoulder. Higher and to one side hung her favorite painting of Arch Cape, the Oregon beach she and her last husband Oscar had loved. Photos of her great-grandsons and postcards I had sent her from my travels shared the wall. Her friend and fellow Oregon activist Martina Gangle Curl's lithograph, *Storm in the Hopyards,* sat on the bureau. Martina had donated it to an auction to raise money to send an ambulance to Republican Spain in the 1930s. It was left over after the auction and Julia bought it from Martina in installments.

In the most prominent display spot—the entry hall wall that extended a few feet into the main room—she had hung a woodcut depicting the funeral march in San Francisco following Bloody Thursday in 1934, the day two men had been killed by San Francisco police during a Longshore strike. It was a tall picture filled with marching longshoremen, eight abreast for over a mile, the ferry building in the distance. "The artist was from San Francisco," she said, "and her husband was deported—I think to Norway—during the witch-hunts and deportations. She went with him."

Her single bed with its colorful crocheted afghan took up one long wall, a full bookcase the other. Next to the only window stood the television set and the stereo system. The ILWU had taken up a collection to buy them for her. She listened to classical music to bring her blood pressure down. In the middle of the room was the one easy chair.

Before Julia left for Alaska in 1987, I taped a series of follow-up interviews in Portland. The last tapes were made at her grandson Shane's home during my five-day visit to Anchorage shortly before her death in 1991, but the bulk of the work was during that four-month period in 1983 and 1984 when we tried to proceed through her life chronologically. In all, I taped Julia for 33 hours during 17 interview sessions. After she began living in Alaska I wrote to her with questions, mostly to clarify confusing or contradictory information.

The first time I asked Julia a personal question—about one of her marriages—she told me the story was not about *her,* it was about unions. This became an ongoing conflict between us. As a second-wave feminist who had learned in 1960s consciousness-raising groups that the personal was political, I was convinced that her personal life, her feelings, her relationships were crucial to understanding her story.

Julia refused to elaborate on her feelings about much of her personal life; she preferred to talk about the political aspects and ramifications of her experiences. What she remembered of her first abortion was her mother's courage; her son's suicide she blamed on the government.

Even when I succeeded in convincing her to talk about her personal life, the unions were her emphasis. She knew the unions were not perfect—she'd been a victim of their red baiting herself—but she saw unions as the salvation of the working class and she wanted this to be the paramount theme of her story.

When she criticized a particular union's actions, she was quick to point out that that was a long time ago and it was a *good* union now.

Some of her activities she shunted aside or left out completely, such as long-time service as a Democratic precinct committeewoman. She was elected in the 1930s and again after she returned to Portland from Astoria. She was still serving when I knew her in the 1980s. Julia wanted this book to be about unions.[5]

In many respects though, Julia was an interviewer's dream. Not only was her memory clear, but her experience as a writer and her flair for the dramatic meant she knew how to construct a story, how not only to make it meaningful but to build tension as well. My task would be simple, or so I thought. But then I ran up against the complications of memory and motive. Other sources do not always agree with Julia's testimony.

There is no one easy explanation for the inconsistencies that oral historians record. As the oral historian Alessandro Portelli observes, often they tell us more than facts. They can be windows into values, dreams, self-image, and changes in attitude over time. They can assist us in interpreting our interviews and understanding our narrators' characters more fully.

Portelli found it is even possible for stories to be consistent with each other and still be inaccurate. When he interviewed the people of Terni, in central Italy, about the death of steelworker Luigi Trastulli, he found that many of his informants, eyewitnesses among them, agreed: Trastulli died in 1953 in street fighting following the layoff of 2000 steel workers. But the historical record shows Trastulli had been killed in a clash with police four and a half years earlier at an anti-NATO rally. Portelli thinks the unconscious moving of the event tells us about "the interests of the tellers, and the dreams and desires beneath them." This discrepancy, he says, "enhances the value of oral sources as historical documents. It is not caused by faulty recollections . . . but actively and creatively generated by memory and imagination in an effort to make sense of crucial events." The story as retold "merges the two most dramatic events of Terni's postwar history into one coherent story."[6]

Sometimes people come to believe what they wish they did or said. An Austrian research team interviewed World War II slave labor survivors 50 years after their experience. As Michael John, an Austrian oral historian reported, at least three told of the beating and murder of the camp doctor after liberation. Given the doctor's extreme cruelty, their behavior, once they had the opportunity, was not surprising. However, additional research revealed the doctor died a natural death years later.[7]

Not quite so dramatic, but illustrative of what may be the same "wishful" effect, is John Dean's testimony before the Senate committee investigating

Watergate. Ulric Neisser compared the transcripts of the Oval Office tapes with Dean's recollections of the conversations. Neisser concluded that Dean believed his account to be accurate but "[h]is ambition reorganized his recollections . . . he can't help emphasizing his own role in every event."[8]

Many people tend to make themselves the heroes of their own stories and Julia was no exception. This was evident when I compared the official transcripts of Julia's testimony before HUAC and her interview with the FBI with her oral history accounts. Even taking into account that a transcript can tell us only the words spoken by the participants—we miss body language and facial and vocal expression—Julia describes her behavior at her FBI interview as more heroic than the record shows. And Julia's appearance before HUAC was much shorter than she remembered (length being equated with importance). I believe in both cases Julia wanted to have been more important, more effective, and more heroic than the actual facts might imply, but I also think it likely Julia believed what she told me, and that her memory of the events had changed to accommodate her desires over the years.[9]

Memories are creations, they are not necessarily an accurate reflection of what happened. In her research on eyewitness testimony, Elizabeth Loftus has concluded that "postevent information cannot only enhance existing memories but also change a witness's memory and even cause nonexistent details to become incorporated into a previously acquired memory." Over time, she tells us, we may be unable to distinguish between what we ourselves experienced and what we have been told. Surely most of us have "memories" that in truth are stories told to us about our early childhoods, which we "remember" as experiences, perhaps because the story was told so often and was about our favorite subject, ourselves.[10]

There are other pitfalls: Narrators can lie. It may be that they are embarrassed or ashamed of some of their past actions. Perhaps they are afraid the truth will hurt others. Everyone has secrets, including Julia. Furthermore, as Allan Nevins, the "father of oral history," pointed out at the First Colloquium of the Oral History Association in 1966, memoirs and autobiographies can be even more untrustworthy than the stories oral historians collect, since an oral historian's cross-examination might oblige the narrator to stick closer to the truth.[11]

Sometimes Julia changed her story or admitted she'd previously lied or omitted important facts. It was not until our second round of interviews in 1987, when Julia knew me better and trusted me more fully, that she told me her serious illness in California in the 1920s was caused by a botched abortion.

Even as we became closer, some things were not for my ears; I couldn't coax them forth. When she was telling me why she finally divorced Butch, one secret peeked out:

"Well I had become quite interested in another man that I'd met in the union world, but it [the divorce] was mostly over the drinking."

"You didn't tell me about this other man."

"And I don't intend to . . . I knew it was a dead end when I embarked on it. But I did learn a lot from him about how unions function that weren't mass-production unions."

"This other man wasn't in a mass-production union?"

"No."

"What kind of union was he?"

"Well now, that's enough. Subject's off limits."

Inconsistencies showed up as I worked on the transcripts of our conversations, and I would write her for clarification. Once she wrote back, "Some of my errors were intentional. I was embarrassed by your questions. And I did not, and still do not, like to dwell on that painful period in my life."[12]

Everyone, consciously or unconsciously, creates a persona to present to the world, a face that may be different depending on the context and the audience. In his biography of Mary "Mother" Jones, Elliott J. Gorn had to deal with a subject who was "two people, a person and a persona, and the relationship between the two." He states that Mother Jones "polished and honed [her] stories, for they were her tools to teach and motivate." Julia did the same.[13]

Julia's persona, for me and the oral history and at least for some others in her life, was one in which political beliefs—working-class solidarity and antiracism—were primary, and her personal life secondary. Her "official" story of why she left her husband Ben Eaton was that he turned out to be a racist hypocrite, told by way of a terrific anecdote set in a restaurant with a "white trade only" sign. It ended with: "So I just scrambled out over the top of the booth and left. And that was the end of that."

"The end of the meal or the end of the marriage?" I asked.

"Both," she replied.

"You left him then?"

"Sure!"

Later, she admitted the final straw was really a beating she had suffered at his hand. True, but not the image of herself she preferred.

Why had she attempted suicide in 1950? She was unusually hazy on her explanation; it was slightly different each time she spoke of it. She got fed up with the world. She was heavily in debt and bored with life and it seemed she wasn't getting anything accomplished. It was over a telephone bill that she didn't see any possible way of paying, and if she couldn't pay the bill, she couldn't continue to write for Federated Press or the other papers.

Her old friend Helmi Kortes-Erkkila told me Julia's suicide attempt was over a man. "Afterwards she laughed about it, 'Imagine, on account of being spurned by a man, *I* should try to commit suicide,'" Helmi recounted. Was this really the reason? Julia had apparently allowed Helmi to believe she had introduced her to Oscar shortly after her recovery, but I was pretty sure Julia had known him earlier (Helmi obviously had her own doubts, as she prefaced her account with, "I hope it [my version] isn't different"). Was this version of meeting Oscar part of a story of her suicide attempt created for Helmi's benefit? I had no other evidence that corroborated what Helmi told me and it was not the version Julia had decided to present to the world. In every draft of the contents for her unfinished memoir, "The Bridges of Ce," written only half a dozen years after the incident, the chapter on her suicide attempt is entitled "I Cannot Pay My Telephone Bill."

Julia's romantic side, the side she could show Helmi, might confess to a suicide attempt over love, but with me at least she put forward a more independent and self-reliant persona, liberated and dedicated first and foremost to politics.

Yet, Julia did spend time and energy on romance and she definitely romanticized her own life. Betty Wollam was in her early twenties and active in the Communist Party when she met Julia. When Betty asked Julia why her grown son Mike's name was McDonald, Julia gave a fascinating explanation. Betty recounted it to me:

> It was an artist. She said it was in Chicago, that she was quite young and that she was just sort of swept up in this very passionate love affair and was not aware that she was pregnant until she had made her way back to Portland. And she never told the artist. She got together with Butch immediately thereafter.
>
> It was such a romantic story that, y'know, I remember it quite well.
>
> My mother was a radical, but she was a very traditional woman. Julia was something else. A whole new outlook on life, that you didn't have to put chains on yourself. Other people would try to, but you didn't have to accept them. I thought she was such a glamorous older woman.[14]

A fiction, as surely as the stories she wrote for *True Story* magazine. In truth Julia had arrived with Butch Bertram in Chicago, already married, already pregnant. Their child, Mike, attended Portland public schools as Mike Bertram. His name change to McDonald came later. Julia told Betty Wollam what she thought would serve the young woman best as a model.

Those who knew Julia well knew she was "creative" with the truth. Still, I was caught off guard when Julia's brother John R. Godman revealed one secret and led me to another fiction.[15]

While Julia was alive, John Godman refused my requests for an interview and would permit only correspondence, but about ten years after Julia died he began talking to me on the phone. I called one day to confirm the name of Julia's grandfather. He offered to send me the Godman genealogy he'd written. Then he asked me how many times Julia had told me she had married. When I told him three he asked for names. I recited my list: Butch, Ben, Oscar. He seemed a little surprised I knew about Ben. Then he told me she had asked him to put only two marriages in his genealogy, but that she was married four times. I subsequently found the marriage license for the fourth marriage (her first) in the Lane County records as well as the affidavit Julia's mother had had to sign to permit her underage daughter to marry and the dissolution decree only ten and a half months later.

And Julia's brother told more. Their grandfather, John L. Godman, John said, was poor, as his parents had died young—legend says they were killed in accidents on their horse farm in the 1840s—and the children were parceled out to various families. He told me that his grandfather married and lived on his father-in-law's farm. I told him that Julia had told me John L. Godman had married his former slave after the Civil War. John said Julia was determined to find some way to be related to blacks. He said when he showed her that wasn't so, she said they were Jewish on their mother's side.

I had heard Julia say that as well. She surmised it because their maternal grandmother's maiden name was Cone. John said he disproved the Jewish Cone story when he found out that the ancestor in question, Daniel Cone, was Scotch—his original name was MacKoah. But John said Julia ignored it.[16]

I did my own genealogical research at this point. I found a record of her paternal grandparents' marriage. I read censuses. No slaves were listed in the Godman household when Julia's grandfather was a boy. In the next census, 1850, the Godman or Gollman (it had been misspelled in the records) family had disappeared, but two of the children turned up as Godman in a widow's household in the same county, lending credence to John's account. I found the family of her paternal grandmother as well. Her father was listed as a shoemaker born in Ohio. No slaves or "Negroes" in the record.[17]

I thought Julia had used her own life as a basis for much of her fiction, as many writers do, and that many of her stories were exaggerated in order to make them dramatic, exciting, and engaging, but apparently, at least some of the time, she used her fiction as a basis for the stories she told about herself. Julia wrote "Joshua's Daughter: The Story of a Girl Who Passed for White" in the 1950s. I had thought the racial aspect of the story was based on her autobiography, but now I realized it was most likely the reverse.

Julia wanted to be identified with the underdog, the victim, and the perse-cuted. In addition, saying she was black presented an opportunity to educate others about racism. Communist Party activist Susan Wheeler remembers that Julia wanted people to know that she wasn't white. It helped Susan gain "an early understanding of the importance of identifying with people of color. Even though she [Julia] could have passed for white, she didn't want to do that."[18]

Saying she was black allowed Julia to be a role model to Susan and others. It also allowed her to shock people—something she dearly loved to do—and at the same time shake up their ideas. Julia often told me if someone at the retire-ment building she moved to in 1976 said they were glad the building didn't have blacks she would disabuse them of that notion and let them know they were talking to one. At other times she would tell the residents that her very dark friend Clara Fambro was her sister from down south.[19]

When I realized her account of her racial background was untrue, I began to question everything. Had Jack Godman really been a Wobbly? Julia's brother didn't think so. But I had seen the radical books that Julia said her father had raised her on—*Ancient Lowly, Ancient Society,* and *Essays on the Materialist Con-ception of History*—with *Jack* or *John Godman* written on the flyleaves. Shane also remembered holding Jack Godman's Wobbly membership card. And Shane recalled his grandmother Ella, Jack's widow, saying Julia got her politics from her father.

Julia said her maternal grandparents had had a shotgun wedding and never lived together, but the Cone family genealogy, published in 1903, states that Evelyn Cone married Robert Padan thirteen months before the birth of their daughter Ella. Is the genealogy lying about their marriage date to save face? It goes on to say that Evelyn lived in Marietta, Ohio, but doesn't mention Robert. The 1880 census shows Evelyn and her two-year-old daughter living on Evelyn's parents' farm. Julia said Robert was a divinity student when they married. Was he away at college in 1880? The 1890 census was lost in a fire, but the 1900 cen-sus lists Evelyn and Robert Padan married 23 years and living together in Mari-etta. In 1907, Evelyn Padan is listed as the widow of Robert in the Eugene City Directory. Was Julia inspired by the genealogy's silence on Robert to create the story of their never living together? Was a 23-year marriage too boring and con-ventional for Julia's taste?[20]

Much of what Julia told me was indeed true. Her father did receive a bach-elor of science degree, cum laude, from Marietta College in 1897. He was a vet-eran of the Spanish-American War and his widow did indeed apply for a soldiers' pension after his death. Julia's grandfather Godman was a captain in the Union Army. Oscar served in the Navy during World War II. Mike was in the Marines.[21]

Some of the difficulties of truth and memory were resolved by Julia herself when she admitted telling less than the truth and corrected the story. Other times I had to be a detective, puzzling through the chronology and seeking additional documentary evidence. Sometimes, as with her suicide attempt, I could not be sure. Some facts will continue to remain elusive; every life is a mystery to outsiders on some level. Did her father apply for an insurance policy shortly before his death in 1926? No family papers survive; there is no way to know. Many of the vital records, for example, her son Mike's birth certificate, were unobtainable due to legal restrictions. Other information was not retrievable because I lacked sufficient information, or records do not exist. But between my research into the historical record and my many hours spent with Julia, I have mostly sorted out what I believe is true, what is misremembered, what is exaggeration, what is outright creation, and even what most of it means.

What was still left for me to grapple with was how to present the story to the world. Should I change first husband to second in the text? Second to third? Her short teenage marriage changes nothing, I decided. It would just confuse the reader and myself. And so, that first marriage, the one she ignored in the interviews, is mentioned in this introduction only.

Should I ignore what else I learned from Julia's brother and from others and the written record? Should I remove those parts from Julia's testimony that I know are false? Ultimately I could do neither. Julia must be allowed to speak for herself, but at the same time I had to tell what I knew and believed. This is Julia, complex and fascinating, but human, not without faults.

The places where the questions of truth arise are either in the realm of her personal life—ancestry, marriages, affairs, abortions, suicide attempt—or in details that can easily be misremembered; neither interviews with others nor any of the documents I have consulted have raised any doubts about the political activities she recounts, the events involving the unions and other organizations and movements she was involved in. Her views on these events are, of course, her own.

So, in the pages that follow, Julia tells her version of her life. It is Julia's explanation of her suicide attempt and Julia's evaluation of her successes and failures that appear in the text, though I have often noted when the historical record yielded different facts. Though I have removed some of the obvious fabrications, I have left much of her created story of her grandparents and I have done my best to retain the dramatic persona Julia chose to create of herself.

After Julia had moved to Alaska and I was working on the transcripts of the interviews, I decided to ask for her FBI files under the Freedom of Information Act. Julia was interested in seeing her files and was happy to cooperate. In January 1990

I sent in the formal application, but it soon became clear it would take a long time for the files to be released. In fact, she died more than a year before they arrived.

In the meantime, I read an oral history, *Dorothy Healey Remembers: A Life in the American Communist Party*, which used excerpts from Healey's FBI files as well as interviews with coworkers and family to supplement Healey's oral account. Inspired by the format, I started interviewing some of the other people in Julia's story: her family, her surviving friends, people in the unions. I have tried to use the other interviews to present a fuller picture of Julia and the events she described.

In May 1992, I received 479 of the 1236 pages of Julia's FBI files. Over the next two years I would occasionally receive another page or two from another agency. For example, in late 1993 the Immigration and Naturalization Service sent me a copy of a letter Julia sent them in 1953 objecting to a threatened deportation.

Some of the pages are merely photocopies of her writings: articles, letters to the editor, even a preprinted postcard to President Kennedy asking for a rehearing of a Supreme Court decision upholding the registration provision of the 1950 Internal Security Act, which enabled the government to jail Communists. There are newspaper articles covering peace demonstrations she was a part of, several memorial ads Julia had placed in left-wing publications, and even a photo of Julia cut from the *Oregonian* when she spoke as a parent at a community meeting at Shane's high school.

But most of the pages are FBI reports and memos: annual reports on her as a "Security Index subject," memos reporting a new address, lists of participants in demonstrations (the entire list blacked out save for Julia), and narrative reports of organizations and actions of which Julia was a part. I used the FBI material to ascertain dates of demonstrations and when she moved and to further corroborate information I had from the interviews and her papers. I regret we did not have the opportunity to go over the files together.

In editing Julia's narrative for publication, I have rearranged and merged her multiple tellings of certain events and stories with portions of interviews done earlier by others into a single account for clarity and chronology. These interviews include a 1977 interview by Roberta Watts and an interview by Bill Bigelow the same year. Tom Copeland interviewed Julia in 1972 for his book *The Centralia Tragedy of 1919*. Tom Churchill's interview with Julia appears in conversation form in his novel *Centralia Dead March*. Elizabeth Patapoff conducted an exploratory interview with Julia in 1976 for KOAP-TV, Portland, and shared the original reel-to-reel tape with me. Julia's memory was sharper when she was younger, and those interviews yielded details missing from our interviews.[22]

Some of Julia's writings and speeches have also been integrated into her narrative, appearing in the text as if part of the interviews; I have changed a word here and there to more approximate the tone of the interviews. An additional source is Julia's letters.[23]

I have edited out my own questions and remarks from the interviews and therefore sometimes found it necessary to "put a few words into Julia's mouth" in order for the narration to make sense. Sometimes I have changed her word order or added a bit for clarity, as well. The tapes and her papers are in the archives of the Oregon Historical Society in Portland. I believe I have been truthful to the spirit of Julia's story. I've tried hard to maintain her unique voice. What Julia read of it she liked—and if she were alive to see the publication of this book, I think she would be pleased.

(left) John Burwell Godman, Julia's father.
(right) Ella Blossom Padan Godman, Julia's mother.

Chapter 1

THAT'S WHERE I HEARD ABOUT SABOTAGE

Julia Ruuttila was married four times, but she maintained that the great love affair of her life was with a union. Looking back, it must have seemed innate to her; her revered father's love had come laced with anticapitalist and union values.

John Burwell Godman graduated from college in 1897 and then fought in the Spanish-American War.[1] After the war he came west and worked in bridge building and the timber industry, which led him to the radical union the Industrial Workers of the World (IWW), nicknamed Wobblies.

Jack Godman passed on the tenets of the IWW to his daughter, primary of which was a belief in One Big Union—an industrial *union, organizing* all *workers, the unskilled, the woman, the child, the African American, the Asian, the migrant, top to bottom. This was in stark contrast to the American Federation of Labor (AFL), which organized only skilled craft workers. The Wobblies believed in direct action— the strike, not the ballot box.*

Their goal was the abolition of the wage system altogether. The IWW's preamble read: "[A] struggle must go on until the workers of the world organize as a class, take possession of the earth and the machinery of production." They would manage industry for social need, not for private profit.[2]

And it wasn't only her father's heritage that influenced Julia. She accompanied her mother on suffrage marches before she was old enough to understand the arguments. In this fertile ground, Julia grew into a political activist, speaking up, speaking out.

She also grew into a writer—a creator of stories—and created a history of her family that was more romance than reality. Much of what Julia claims about her grandparents Godman is not true. There is no evidence that John L Godman owned slaves or that Julia Pratt was of slave heritage, and there was no "big house" to take her into. Even the age difference between them was exaggerated—she was only six-teen years his junior. I suppose Julia tells us he took her across the river to marry her because she knew Ohio repealed its antimiscegenation laws, but, in fact, Ohio did not do so until 1887, seventeen years after John L. Godman and Julia Pratt mar-ried.[3] She also romanticized her mother's background, imagining her growing up with the hardships of a fatherless home, the product of a shotgun marriage.

My father was an organizer in the IWW. My mother was a great admirer of Eugene V. Debs. My grandfather Godman had owned slaves, but he fought with Grant on the Union side. My grandmother had been a slave on his horse plantation in Kentucky.

My grandfather didn't want to see the Union separated. He was captured during the war and thrown in a Southern prison and, being a southerner and an officer in Grant's army, he really was badly treated. He managed to escape, and runaway slaves helped him to get through the swamp and back to Union lines.

He knew that the North would win and his family owned plantations where they raised cotton—I think this was Mississippi—so he went to Mississippi just before the Civil War broke out and gave manumission papers to all of his slaves and told them to go up North. So I've always wished that I knew more about him because it's very interesting that a southerner would have those ideas. He died many years before I was born.

My grandmother Godman was four years old when the Civil War started; she was about twenty-five years younger than he was. Her name was Julia God-man; I was named after her. I understand she was very attractive. And she was quite light skinned also, in fact, probably an octoroon. Eventually he moved her into the big house, which was falling down by that time because they were all very poor when they got back from the Civil War.

He must have taken her across the river and married her, because, in the days when I was a small child she was getting the pension of a Civil War veteran's widow. When she was working in her yard she wore a bandanna around her head and that was to hide her hair, which wasn't exactly straight. When she went downtown she had a little black hat and a veil and she covered it up that way.

My father got through Marietta College. He graduated magna cum laude with a degree in civil engineering, but when he went back to Kentucky, which was where he was born, the only job he could get was picking worms off tobacco leaves. He came to Oregon to pass for white.

It must have been in the early 1900s because he was in the Spanish-Ameri-can War, where he went hoping to be killed because my mother had told him to get lost. He thought we were down there to free Cuba and Puerto Rico from the tyranny of Spain and then he found out what we were interested in was saving the sugar for the American Sugar Trust. And also he found out—you know they had a rally cry for that war: "Remember the Maine" (that was the gunboat that was blown up in Havana harbor)—*we blew it up* as an excuse to start that war. In 1898—we were doing it that long ago.

He couldn't ever get an engineering job. He always had to take a job as day labor or something and then he'd start all the things he knew how to do. He'd do the work for the foreman, that the foreman didn't know how to do. In later years he worked in logging camps and he set up machinery. That's where he joined the IWW.

The IWW was founded in 1905, two years before Julia's birth. Jack Godman was thirty-one. In the Northwest their focus was on the workers in the primary industry—timber—both in the woods and in the mills.[4]

It was an age before electronic media, when street speaking—the soapbox—was a major avenue for getting the message out to the public and itinerant workers. Wobblies were known for their fiery oratory and drew big crowds. Many cities and towns passed ordinances against street speaking in an effort to thwart them. The Wobblies picked up the challenge and staged a series of spectacular Free Speech Fight campaigns.[5]

The Free Speech Fight grew to be a major organizational tactic from 1906 until 1916. It went like this: A Wobbly would get up on the soapbox and begin with the words, "Fellow workers and friends." Usually before he could say more, the police would pull him off and arrest him (with a few notable exceptions, such as activist Elizabeth Gurley Flynn, all the Wobbly street speakers were men). Then the call would go out around the country for "footloose Wobblies" to come join the fun, ensuring there was always another Wobbly ready to step up to be arrested in turn. The town's jails would fill up; the Wobblies would demand individual jury trials; the city would eventually find the law too expensive to enforce.[6]

You won't find my father's name in any of the books about the IWW. He packed the rigging, as they called it in those times, but never held any official position. "Packing the rigging" was carrying credentials to sign up members in the IWW.[7]

An attempt was made to murder him once, at a camp he was attempting to organize in eastern Oregon, in the short logs, pine country.[8] He said food served him in the cookhouse was poisoned. He lived and returned to Dexter, where we were then living.

When I look back I can see that my mother was really a most remarkable woman, because she was brought up in an orthodox church and she broke away from that and became a Unitarian. That's quite a shift.

She was brought up on her grandfather's farm. He was a member of the landed gentry in southern Ohio. He was quite a moneyed individual. He was the country squire in that area. He was a justice of the peace and a Republican.[9] He was conservative in all his views and she got away from all of those views. She got interested in the single tax, which was a very progressive movement in those days, and eventually socialism. Her name was Ella Blossom [Padan] Godman. My grandson Shane and I refer to her as "Ella B."

They decided that the children should be taught and there should be a schoolteacher, so they brought in this divinity student and gave him a room in the house, but it was separated from the rest of the house. However, he got in on the other side where the family lived. The story that my grandmother told was that she woke up and he was in bed with her but she never went any further than that. And then she didn't tell anyone about what had happened at all, and she must have been about four or five months pregnant when they discovered it.

So when it came out, there was a shotgun wedding. He got fired from the divinity school, but his parents were well-to-do people who owned a shoe factory, so he went to work in the shoe factory. She got a name for her child, but that was it. They never lived together. My grandmother spent the rest of her life single. Her name was Evelyn Padan. Her maiden name was Cone. Many years later, when my mother was teaching school in Marietta, arrangements were made for her to meet her father, but at the last minute she refused to meet him. I think that was very admirable.

So my mother was brought up in the house, on the farm. Well, this farm was some distance from Marietta. There was a country school that my mother went to in the grades, but there was no high school, except in Marietta, so the family went to Marietta and rented an apartment for my mother and her mother. Her mother took in sewing, and they helped them every way they could. In the summers they stayed on the farm.

Then after my mother graduated from high school and became a teacher, which you could if you had a high school diploma, she supported her mother by teaching. She taught for eight or nine years in Marietta, Ohio.[10]

She asked to be transferred to a slum school because she wanted to see how poor people lived. She went to visit in the homes of all of her students and she even wrote a letter about it to the newspaper. I used to have a copy of it, a clipping, in which she found out there was quite a connection between how much children had to eat and their ability to learn. Because if there was no work in the glass factory and the children had nothing to eat, the grades of those children were poor. So she really was able to think on her own.

My parents met in a Sunday School class for adults. My father was an atheist but he had to go to some church because he was going to Marietta College
and it was a requirement. He picked Unitarian out as the least objectionable.

My mother was engaged to another man for six years, but she couldn't forget my father and she always had some excuse and this poor long-suffering man
finally jilted her. She was very annoyed and embarrassed to be jilted; she didn't
realize she had it coming. Then she called up some of my father's former class-
mates who still lived in that area—he meantime had come to Oregon—and
found out where he was, and she wrote to him that she was now a free woman.
So he sent her money for a ticket.

He was working on the Southern Pacific. He built bridges and things like
that. He built all of the bridges and trestles over the Siskiyou Mountains. They
were stationed in Roseburg. So she came to Roseburg and they were married
there.

I was born in Lane County, county seat, Eugene, April 26, 1907. My parents had then been married three years, and my father was superintendent of
three small sawmills operated by the Southern Pacific at a remote company
town, Marcola, on the Mohawk River, northeast of Eugene.

In Marcola, we lived in a tent house—which is a tent fly on a ridgepole,
with a wooden floor and built up wooden sides. Although I was less than a year
old when we left there, I remember this house well, and remember lying in a cra-
dle and the winds blowing the tree branches across the sky. It is my earliest
memory. And I remember riding in a flume held on my father's lap, in a "flume
boat." The flumes carried the lumber cut in the sawmill to the railway siding.
They were built on high trestles, and the boats were "V" shaped, to fit the flume.
My mother rode in the flume boats, too, and her long, black hair, which she
wore braided and pinned in a coronet, but with some soft curls in front, came
loose on one such trip and streamed out in the wind like a banner. Riding in the
flume boats was like flying through the sky. To keep the grade over the rough
terrain, the flume trestles in some places were as much as thirty feet high.

My mother was a much more practical person than my father. He was a very
forceful person and a forceful speaker. My mother was quiet and a low-key type
of person, but she had a good deal of steel and iron in her. I've been able since,
in reevaluating them, to realize in many ways she was the strong person in our
household. She talked about history a lot, but that's funny—she didn't have radical ideas about history and the various countries like my father did.

It was very difficult for her to oppose him, but she became a Socialist when
we were living in Lane County, and, of course, he didn't believe in voting. He
thought it was a pure waste of time; one party was as bad as the other.

I was intrigued with everything my father did. I was very interested in using his tools and making things and I was not interested in the things she tried to teach me to do, such as sewing. Mostly I didn't listen to my mother; I just listened to my father.

My father had built this house in Eugene and we lived there when the logging camps were shut down. That is periodic in the lumber industry. My grandmother Padan came out to live with my parents in Eugene. She was a beautiful seamstress. My father didn't like her, and she didn't like him, and he used to go away and stay in the logging camps months at a time without coming home.

I remember the day my brother was born. I was two years and eight months old. He was born at home. My grandmother said, "Your nose is going to be out of joint now that your little brother is on his way," and that just scared me out of my wits. I remember pushing the chair over in front of the mirror and standing on the chair to see what my nose was starting to look like. I said to my mother, "Why can't we give him away? You gave mama cat's kittens away."

I was a very homely child. My brother was quite handsome. He had curly hair. And he had dark brown eyes and beautiful features. People used to say, "What a pity it is the boy is so handsome and the girl is so homely. She'll never catch a man." It didn't bother me really, I didn't have much use for what I called big people.

I think I must have been about five when my grandmother Padan died. I remember her funeral. My father lifted us up to look at her in the coffin, and my brother said, "Look at grandma lying on her little bed," and I hate to tell you what I said. I must have been a horror when I was a child, a real horror.

Well, not long before this happened a tomcat that came to see our cat had been killed and I had arranged a funeral and buried this tomcat. So when my father lifted us up to look at our grandmother in her coffin, I said in a very loud voice, "She isn't lying in her little bed. She's dead as a doornail like Mr. Thomas Cat." Isn't that awful?

The IWW established a local in Eugene when they were building the railroad to Coos Bay, and they held their meetings on street corners.[11] I went to those meetings with my father and I felt very important because sometimes they let me pass the hat to take up the collection. What I wanted to be, because of going around to those street meetings, was a soapboxer standing on a chair or a box and talking, but then my mother spent so much time drilling me on English and literature that I became a fairly able writer.

The IWW believed in action at the point of production. They didn't think the ballot box would do any good. My mother, of course, was determined to get the right to vote for women and she marched in suffrage parades, and I went with her, walking along and marching. But I didn't know what that was all about because I heard their arguments and I thought my father was right. My mother usually just went ahead on her own and did what she had concluded was proper.

I remember the year that women's suffrage was on the ballot in Oregon. She told my father, "Don't bother to come home unless you register and vote for women's suffrage, because you're not gonna get in this house if you don't." So he went and registered and he voted. I remember him saying, "Well, I see you believe in direct action even if you say you don't." Another time my father voted was when Eugene Debs was running for president from the penitentiary in Atlanta.

All of the Socialists and anarchists and IWWs traveling from San Francisco to Seattle stopped at our house and stayed overnight. I remember Elizabeth Gurley Flynn, and Big Bill Haywood. But the one I clearly remember was Emma Goldman's "companion," Ben Reitman. He's the one that came to breakfast nude. My mother ordered him out of the house. He called her a capitalist-minded prude.[12]

I slept in a bedroom off the living room and was put to bed early, but I was very interested in everything that the big people said and I would take the pillows and the bolster off the bed and get up on my knees and listen through the keyhole to these conversations and I'd hear all these exciting discussions and talks.

That's where I heard about sabotage. The IWW was divided on the subject. There were those that believed in sabotage as part of the class struggle and those that thought that they should confine their efforts against the master class to slowdowns and strikes at the point of production. My father always argued against sabotage. Nevertheless, for some strange reason, sabotage was something that interested me greatly when I was quite small.

My closest friend was a boy named Hiram. I told him that if we could get rid of the capitalist class, our fathers wouldn't have to go to work and could spend more time playing with us. So he asked me how we could get rid of them and I said, "Well for starters, we could blow up a train."

At first what we did was to put rocks and pebbles on the track. But the train went right over the rocks, it didn't do the least bit of good. So I told Hiram that we would have to get hold of some dynamite and blow it up. He said, "Where do you get dynamite?" I said, "Well, first we have to get some money." So we enlisted another child that played with us, and I told everyone they would have to put some money in to buy dynamite. For my share of the money, because whenever I got any money I always spent it immediately for candy, I just robbed my brother's penny bank.

So the three of us went in to this store and asked for some dynamite. The clerk wanted to know what we wanted dynamite for, after all we were so little. I said we wanted to blow up a train. He said, "Do you know anyone that blows up trains?" and I said, "Oh yes, my father has blown up lots of them." I wanted to make it sound like he was important 'cause I thought he *was* important. So he called the chief of police and we were driven home in a buggy by a policeman and the chief of police.

Well, my father must have talked them out of the notion that he had anything to do with blowing up trains, but he had a real bad time of it and that was one time when he was furious with me, just furious. He gave me a long lecture, which I've never forgotten, about you never squeal on your associates, your companions, or anyone you know, and you've got to learn when to keep your mouth shut. He explained it to me in great detail. He started in about some of the labor martyrs and what they'd had to go through and if there hadn't been people that, without realizing it or deliberately, told things about their activities, they wouldn't have ended up in prison or been executed. It was better to keep your mouth absolutely shut unless you knew and trusted who you were talking to. That was one of the most valuable lessons I've ever learned. Stood me in good stead for years and years.

He also explained to me that although you would find as you went on in life that everyone didn't agree with you and it was your duty to attempt to change their views, if they held views that weren't just and kindly, that before you started talking about unpopular subjects—and he went into detail about what they were—you first had to build a base of support. It was very useful to me in different situations I've been in like the Portland Longshore auxiliary. 'Course there come times when you can't let that stop you, you have to speak up, like in that picture on the wall: "To be silent when it is your duty to protest makes cowards of men." Only, of course, it should say, "men *and* women."

My father had a workshop and he had his carpenter tools in there and also some of these books. He used to sit me up on a table when he was making something, and he used to lecture to me or he'd set me to read something and then I'd have to tell him what it was all about.

I was terrified at his not approving of me. I was his favorite child, while my brother was my mother's favorite. I suppose because I was older and would listen to him and my brother was bored by anything he said. My father knew so little about children, he couldn't understand my brother was too young to take in anything he said.

I thought my father knew everything, you know. So naturally his opinions were my opinions and remained so for many, many years. It wasn't until I met the Communists in Denver that I realized that *she* had been right [about voting]. It was such a shock to me one day when I found out I didn't agree with my father. I thought, because you know I'm a really lazy person, "Oh, I'm going to have to do my own thinking from now on," and it petrified me. It doesn't petrify me anymore. I'm used to it.

My mother used to go to the Unitarian church when my father was out working in one of the camps and wasn't home. When my father was home she didn't go to church because he was an atheist and it upset him very much if she went. One time she invited the minister to come to dinner when he was out in camp, and my father came home unexpectedly and the minister was there. Although I was very small, I thought, now this is going to be very interesting to see what happens now. My mother asked the minister to say grace, and he said, "God bless the homemade bread," and that struck my father funny, so he didn't make any of his sarcastic remarks about it.

Those were the days that my mother went on these suffrage meetings and marches. My mother was secretary of the Socialist Party of Lane County.[13] My parents used to take my brother and me to all of these meetings. My mother would put him to sleep on the bench in the back, but I always sat up in the front row and listened. I was interested in what the speaker said. I remember one speaker that had brought some dolls and blocks with him to illustrate what he was taking about. Some of the dolls were capitalists and some of them were the exploited and downtrodden workers, and some of the blocks were the profits. It was quite simple to understand.

My mother took birth control material around in the logging camps and in the poor sections of Eugene. She used to walk up and down the streets with this literature in an egg basket covered with brown eggs, with me, of course, hanging onto her dress and going along. Word would fly down the street ahead of us that the egg lady was coming and they would welcome her.

Dr. Marie Equi [a Portland physician with a general and abortion practice] was quite interested in birth control. That is why my family first became acquainted with Dr. Equi. She sent my mother's name to Margaret Sanger in New York and Margaret Sanger mailed this material to my mother in envelopes that she appropriated from the New York Chamber of Commerce. That was the safest way to send it through the mail so that they wouldn't be opened. It was illegal, you know, to hand around that sort of information.

I distinctly remember the first woman she talked to about "limiting the family," as it was called. This was the wife of a grocery store clerk, who was our washwoman. She had a baby a year, and my mother used to stand on the back porch, where this poor woman scrubbed our clothes, and harangue her about how wrong it was to have so many children, as well as how unnecessary. The woman told her meekly it was the will of God, but my mother soon convinced her it wasn't. She also gave her some money to buy a "douche bag" but the woman spent it for food for her family. She was quite tearful when she confessed what she had done. I remember my mother was so sorry for her she "wrung" the clothes herself out of the bluing water, put them through the wringer, and hung them up.

It was after this woman had still another baby that my mother began trotting around with the egg basket. She bought eggs from one of the neighbors, and when she went after the eggs, she carried a basket which held several dozen. It was flat, with low sides and a stout handle.

The day my mother went after the eggs was the day she took around the leaflets. She would put the leaflets under the eggs. She would say to me, "Now if anyone asks what we have in this basket, we have nice, fresh eggs—I am the egg woman and you are the egg woman's daughter." She meant *anyone on the street*. Because as soon as we rang a bell or rapped on a door, it would be known who my mother was and the lady of the house would run across to her neighbors and say, "The birth control lady is here!" Soon there would be several women in the room, all eagerly listening to what my mother said. She spoke slowly and clearly, explaining and reexplaining. Some of the women could not read very well, so my mother would sit at the kitchen table and write out in very simple words, in her beautiful hand, the "receipt." That's what the information was called, "the receipt." There were several—one had vinegar in it, some women being too poor to buy Lysol.[14] Vinegar was cheap and easy to come by. And if you were too poor to buy a douche bag, you could get douche attachments for your hot water bottle and tell the druggist, if he was nosy, you needed it for "female trouble."

My father always insisted that my mother feed any hobo or transient who came to the door and was hungry. I remember one time when I was about six or seven and she was expecting company on Sunday. She'd gone to a great deal of trouble. She'd cooked a roast on Saturday because she wanted to make her famous lemon pie on Sunday and she just had this one wood stove with a small oven. Then she went next door to borrow something and she sat me down with a fly swatter and told me to keep the flies away from the roast.

While she was away a hobo came to the door so I gave him two of my father's papers, *Solidarity* and some other IWW paper—my father always gave them papers to read—and I also gave him the entire roast. He was quite pleased. My father told our company that I got carried away by the brotherhood of man.

Chapter 2

THE VALIANT NEVER TASTE OF DEATH BUT ONCE

World War I engulfed Europe in the summer of 1914, but the United States maintained neutrality. President Woodrow Wilson was reelected in 1916 on a pacifist platform, with the slogan "He kept us out of war." Nonetheless, under the leadership of former president Theodore Roosevelt and bolstered by the support of newspaper magnate William Randolph Hearst, patriots and munitions interests raised the cry of preparedness. When a German submarine sank the British liner Lusitania *in May 1915, killing 128 Americans, prowar demonstrations and parades increased.*[1]

Along with socialists and others on the left, Wobblies preached against the country's entry into the war, saying it would benefit only the capitalist class; they, as workers, would fight only for industrial freedom.[2] *Meanwhile, even before U.S. entry into the war on April 6, 1917, Europe's war needs had generated an economic boom in the United States. The increased demand for labor led both the AFL and the IWW to actively organize Northwest lumber workers.*

The eight-hour day was becoming the rule in other industries, but loggers still worked ten hours. Additionally, they worked under abominable conditions. They slept two to a bed in crowded bunkhouses, with their work clothes, wet with rain and sweat, hanging on lines overhead, steaming and stinking. Usually there were no mattresses, just straw teeming with bedbugs and lice. No showers. Vile food. One of the loggers' biggest complaints was that they had to carry their own bedrolls from job to job.[3]

The time seemed right to gain higher wages, better conditions, and a shorter workday. In July 1917, both the AFL and IWW lumber workers' unions in the Pacific Northwest struck. The eight-hour day soon became the central demand. Virtually all logging operations were shut down. Washington governor Ernest Lister and Secretary of War Newton Baker asked the employers in the timber industry to

concede the eight-hour day, but they refused even to negotiate. Instead they em-
ployed Pinkerton detectives and enlisted every level of police and government to
end the strike.[4]

The preferred material for warplanes was Sitka spruce, which grew only in the
Northwest of the United States and in the Baltic. To many Americans, to strike now
was treasonous, an attitude cultivated and exploited by businessmen nationwide who
used the war emergency to inflame public opinion, paint Wobblies as guilty of sedi-
tion, and enroll the government in the union's suppression. In September 1917, the
Department of Justice raided IWW halls and headquarters across the country. Using
the Wobblies' own papers to condemn them, the government brought charges of in-
terfering with the war effort and conspiring to defraud certain employers. Soon hun-
dreds of Wobblies were in jail, including most of the leadership.[5]

With their leaders arrested, strike funds running low, the strike at a stalemate,
and fearing their jobs would be taken by scabs if they stayed away, the Wobblies re-
turned to work in mid-September but practiced "strike on the job." They acted like
novices, waiting around for orders and following them to ludicrous extremes. Some
just quit working after eight hours. These tactics hindered production as effectively as
the strike.[6]

In November 1917, Colonel Brice P. Disque, initially sent to the Pacific North-
west in October to "investigate the inadequate procurement of spruce" for airplane con-
struction, brought in soldier-loggers in civilian clothes, organized what would serve as
essentially a company union—the Loyal Legion of Loggers and Lumbermen, the 4L—
and closed the woods to labor organizers. In March 1918, Disque was able to force the
lumbermen into granting improved conditions and an eight-hour day. The Wobblies
claimed it as a victory and burned their bedrolls in a 1918 May Day celebration.[7]

John Godman reacted to the war in Europe and the war against the Wobblies
with paranoia, or perhaps justifiable fear. At least this is what Julia believed
prompted the family's move to the 90-acre farm they had owned on Lost Creek since
July 1915.[8]

My father opposed World War I. He retreated to this remote mountain ranch
about nineteen miles from Eugene. It took half a day to get to the ranch in the
summertime, and even then sometimes you had to get a horse to pull you out
if you got stuck on the road. It was very isolated. My father built barns and re-
paired houses for farmers of that valley, Lost Creek Valley. I must have been
about ten years old.

Persons who had been arrested and put in prison used to come there to rest
up after they got out, and people that were running away to escape arrest for
their views would come there to hide out.

An IWW organizer and agitator named Agnes Thesla Fair stayed there. According to the "capitalist press," she committed suicide in Portland by jumping in front of a streetcar. I think she was pushed—who would choose that way to commit suicide? Then there was Flora Foreman, the schoolteacher fired from her job teaching in Columbia County and sent to a federal prison for opposing World War I.[9]

My father was very interested in everything on that remote ranch. The flowers and the trees. He was not intimidated by the wilderness and my mother was, she was really frightened. She was terrified of the rattlesnakes and she was terrified of the cougars. Sometimes she couldn't bring herself to even go out in the yard. I liked everything about the ranch. I wasn't afraid of the rattlesnakes. I wasn't afraid of the cougars.

Julia identified with her father and probably idealized him. Since he died before she was twenty, she didn't have to develop an adult relationship with him as she did with her mother, who lived into her nineties. Julia complained of her mother's criticism of her choices and her propensity to compare her unfavorably with her more materially prosperous brother, John Godman.

In a May 1992 letter to me, Godman wrote, "I am under the impression that Julia believed that she was closer to our father, and I was closer to our mother. As far as I'm concerned there wasn't any noticeable difference. . . . Our father was a kind of mathematical and mechanical genius, but was somewhat lacking in writing skills and social graces. Our mother was somewhat the reverse of this. . . . [O]ur father decided he didn't like farming very well, and, as a result, was away a lot on construction type work. When at home he didn't mix very much socially with the neighbors and didn't encourage any of us to attend church or Sunday school. This must have been very hard on our mother, as she liked to be around people."[10]

Julia spoke disparagingly to me about her brother. She was particularly appalled at her brother's career in the War Department and even more disapproving when he went to work for the space program with Wernher von Braun, the rocket scientist who started his career working for Hitler but switched his allegiance to the United States after Germany lost the war.

I've never been good at dates and I don't know if it was just before we got into World War I or just afterwards, but there was a great deal of hysteria in Oregon, as in other places, regarding patriotism, so called, quote and unquote, and the war. My father opposed the war as imperialist and urged young men in that valley not to go. The farmers in that area were very conservative and patriotic and my father had had many arguments on the subject with neighbors.

One day the dog was barking and my father looked out the window and he saw the mob coming. They had various weapons, as I recall, including a rope, and guns. Oh, I suppose twenty or thirty people.

Our large yard was surrounded by a fence and there was a stile over the fence, so my father went down and stood on the stile. These people came toward the stile, and when they got there, he was standing on one of the top steps and he'd rolled up his sleeves. I remember that, because he wanted them to see he was totally unarmed. As I learned afterwards, he knew all the people that were in this so-called mob, so he just talked to them and talked them out of it. They were ashamed of themselves. Here they had weapons and here's one man, unarmed with his sleeves rolled up.

But in the meantime, as soon as I saw them approaching with these weapons, I thought they were going to hang him. We had a row of windows in the front of our living room, so we could see everything that happened, and my mother was so frightened that she fell in a faint. My brother, who was considerably younger than myself, went on playing with his building blocks. But I was so frightened I rushed out in the backyard and called our dog and I went into the woods and I didn't come home for three days.

It wasn't the first time I had done that. I had some matches and stuff to make bannock with, which I took from the house. My dog caught a squirrel and ate that and tried to get me to eat part of it. I got so hungry and I couldn't find anything much to eat in the woods, that I finally went home. I planned, if my father was dead, to obtain more food from the house and hike over the mountains on the Indian trail and make my way to Springfield to my grandmother's house.

Of course, my father had not been lynched; my mother had recovered from her faint. My father asked me where I had gone and I said, "I went to save my life." He said, "What about your mother?" I said, "Well, I thought she was dead and you were gonna be dead." He said, "But what about your little brother?" and I said, "Well, I never did like him anyway." Which is an understatement. I never did and I don't now.

My father talked to me awhile and finally he took the blackboard that we had, as my mother was our schoolteacher, and he made me write on it a great many times—it's from Shakespeare—"Cowards die many times before their deaths. The valiant never taste of death but once." I've never forgotten that and I never will. I've never been afraid of anything since. I was thoroughly ashamed of myself for going off.

But this isn't the worst thing that happened during that terrible period. My father's brother-in-law and his older sister had a daughter. She was about six or eight years older than I was, and she got a job as a society reporter on the Eugene newspaper.

She was sitting in the editor's office one day when several businessmen came in the office and talked about they were going to have to eliminate some of the radicals in Lane County. There she sat with her notebook waiting for instructions, what story she was to cover that day. I think women in those days were regarded as part of the office equipment, even reporters, and, of course, her name was different from my father's. So she heard them. They were talking to the editor and one of the names that they read off was my father's. So when she got home from work she got someone to come and warn him.

It was a different type of mob that was coming, composed of Eugene businessmen and other persons, and that wasn't a mob he thought he could talk out of it. That's the time he felt he had to leave home. We were still living on that remote mountain ranch. They were then building Fort Lewis, Army base near Tacoma, Washington. He went up north and went to work at Fort Lewis.

There were members of the IWW that were working at Fort Lewis and the reason they went there was to start a strike and shut it down. They shut it down, but, of course, they got other people to build it. Got it built. And the IWW started strikes in the spruce mills. Spruce was used in the production of planes used in World War I.

Then my father went over to Aberdeen—which was where they were building wooden ships in World War I—and went to work in the shipyards as a ship's carpenter and they managed to get a strike going there and shut the shipyard down. Before the walkout took place, he was accused of being a Bolshevik by a foreman.[11]

"Oh, no, I'm a Zapatist," my father said.

The foreman had never heard of Zapata, and asked, "Is that one of those freak religions?"

"Well, *you* might call it that," my father replied. Thereby saving himself from being fired. He sent for my mother, my brother, and myself.

I never went to school until I was thirteen or fourteen. My mother wanted to send me to school, but my father was afraid I'd get measles and get brainwashed in patriotism and capitalism. She told my father I would grow up to be a social outcast because I wouldn't know how to get along with other people. And in a sense she was right, because I was in continual mischief as a small child. When all my playmates started to school, there I was home alone; my mother's lessons didn't last even half a day.

Truant officers always came to the house. I was a very runty child and my mother used to get some adult book out and have me read them a couple of pages and their mouths would fall open in astonishment and that would be the end of that. But if they had asked me what's two and two or five times five they would have had me.

Then my mother decided I was going to have trouble getting into high school, so she decided to put me in a one-room country school. I had a dreadful time getting used to sitting all day at a desk and to keeping my mouth shut. I found it difficult to get along with the other children, not to mention the teacher.

Julia's brother's recollection of this period is somewhat different. He recalled that she started grade school in the third grade, but left after a short time and was home-schooled by their mother.

> It was said that school made Julia nervous. . . . Julia returned to Dexter grade school for the eighth grade. She was smart and a good student, but also demanded an inordinate amount of help from our parents in the evenings on her school work. And as a result there were many unpleasant episodes. In general our folks found it difficult to handle her. Gradewise the study sessions paid off as she made second place in the County examinations which we were required to pass before receiving a grade school diploma.[12]

My mother taught me to write, I have to admit that. She used to make me sit down and write about rainbows and the cat and all sort of things and look up adjectives and look up synonyms.

What interested my mother was English and history and geography. You had to take this state examination and I barely passed in arithmetic. I got 100 percent in some subjects, but not in history because one of the questions was about the Spanish-American War and, unfortunately, I put some of my father's ideas into the exam.

I argued with teachers. I argued with the teacher I had in the eighth grade. I argued with the teacher I had in high school. I argued with a science teacher over the evolution of man. She didn't believe in it. She insisted I be expelled. The principal, I think, was rather sorry about it. He gave me a copy of John Galsworthy's novel in which he vaguely talks about socialism.[13] He said as I grew older I might learn a tactful way to go about these matters. I went to high school at Pleasant Hill next, and I was kicked out of it for arguing with the teacher, I forget what it was about. I knew a great deal more about history than that teacher did and I hadn't learned to keep my mouth shut.

At Eugene High School I decided to earn some money. I was boarding in a house with a woman and she had a copy of *True Story* magazine which she gave me to read and I thought, "Oh, these silly drivelly stories." And I thought I could sit down and write one right off, so I did. I thought it was better than some of the stories in *True Story.* So I took it to my English teacher and showed it to her and that's when she had me kicked out, because there was so much sin in it. I was quite fond of her and I thought she liked me. I was absolutely crushed at her kicking me out.

The yearbooks of high schools then had what's known as a literary section. After I was expelled from Eugene High School, I had the entire section. I was furious when I saw that because I didn't think they had any right to it. So I went to the principal's office and accused them of stealing my poetry and my story. We had quite a hassle.

Julia's story "The Agate Hunter" and her poem "Brotherhood" were printed in the 1924 Eugenean, *the yearbook of Eugene High School. While her work occupies nearly two pages, the entire section is ten pages; nine other students had work in the literary section as well. The antiracist metaphor in "Brotherhood" of life being a patchwork quilt with many different patterns, "But all woven / From the same spindle of yarn!" is a sentiment Julia would retain all her life. And the agate hunter's depiction of factory work in her story reflects the fear of being a wage slave Julia had learned from her father: "the memory of the subtle ugliness of the automobile factory filled him with horror. . . ."[14]*

Then, the last term I was in high school—I was back in Springfield High School—they had different teachers. I still lacked a year's credits and the students I had started in with, some of whom were still close friends of mine, were getting ready to start to the university. In those days you could take the entrance examination. So that's what I did and that's how I got in. I was there a year.

Julia attended the University of Oregon during the 1925–26 school year. She majored in history, was exempt from English A (popularly known as "bonehead"), she took three terms of magazine writing, and earned an A each term.[15]

I wrote "A Menace to Our Town" when I was going to the U of O. The instructor in my magazine writing class submitted it to an *Atlantic Monthly* or *Harper's Magazine* contest for college students. It won an honorable mention.[16]

The main thing I learned at the University of Oregon was that there wasn't much to learn there in my day. But I'm always glad I went because otherwise I might have felt I'd missed something. Well, I know why I went there and it was not for very good reasons. My mother made it quite plain to me if I didn't I was going to have to get out and earn my living. I didn't want to do that 'cause I had a terrible fear of what my father called the master class. The way he talked about them, I could just see these terrible people—trying to pound the life out of you—that you'd be working for if you were a wage slave.

That year I was in college I worked in restaurants and I worked in a laundry ironing, running white collars through a mangle and ironing apron strings. The aprons went through the mangle but the strings had to be ironed 'cause they got tangled and burned.

I hadn't finished them when the noon break came and here I was standing there at the ironing board continuing to iron these apron strings and this woman came up to me and she said, "You little scabby so-and-so. What are you trying to do? Don't you know that this is the noon lunch break?" All at once I knew the connection between what she said and what my father had talked about.

My mother had rented an apartment in Eugene so that my brother could go to Eugene High School. So I had a place to live. She had decided it was about time she did something about our livelihood. She was going to the university too.

My stupid Republican brother—never did like him. I suppose because he was a very handsome child and I was extremely ugly. He was a very goody-goody boy and I was extremely naughty. He went to Oregon State University. He took engineering. He was determined to be upwardly mobile. And that's where he got brainwashed and ruined. Even before that he had no interest in anything important. You know that he even denies that our father was a member of the IWW.

It's no secret that children in the same family have different stories to tell, different memories of their growing-up years, different interpretations of family members and events. What is remembered and what is forgotten tells us as much about them as it does about memories.

Julia was three years older than her brother, an enormous difference when children are small. Julia remembered sitting in halls listening to Socialist and IWW speakers while her brother slept in the back and missed the lessons. She remembered standing in the crowd longing to grow up to be the soapboxer she was watching. She followed her mother down the sidewalks of Springfield handing out birth control literature. Her little brother stayed at home. Julia was ten when the United States entered World War I and when the Wobblies' decline began. John was only seven. By the time he was ten, his father was becoming an entrepreneur.

By 1920 the Douglas fir on the hills around Lost Creek had become economically attractive for logging, if the lumber could be transported out. Julia's father Jack

*came up with the idea for a flume. With seven others, he formed the Mt. June Flume
Company. Construction began in 1921 and was completed in 1923. The enterprise
was an engineering success, but, during the first years, not an economic one.*[17]

*Julia had warned me of her brother's denial that their father was a Wobbly, but
I was still surprised to read the following passage in a 1993 letter to me:*

> Our father left the flume company in 1923 or 1924, I think, and went to work
> at Westfir, Oregon as a millwright where they were building a large sawmill.
>
> Sometime after Dad left the flume company, the men working for the com-
> pany went on strike. The man who was hired to take Dad's place immediately
> hired a complete new crew. When Dad heard about it, he told our mother, and
> she repeated to me, that his replacement had done the right thing.
>
> Dad remained at Westfir until sometime in 1925 when he returned briefly
> to Dexter. Then, he went up to Bridal Veil, Ore. His original intent was to stay
> only long enough to handle the building of an addition to the existing sawmill
> there. However, the plant manager persuaded him to stay on indefinitely. So,
> it was decided that the family should move up.
>
> This we did when school was out in the summer of 1926. That fall, Dad
> was killed in a mill accident. The plant manager, who had been in the sawmill
> business for many years, was kind enough to say he had never had another man
> working for him in whom he had more confidence than he had in our father.
>
> Does a man who organizes a company, acts as its construction boss, agrees
> with replacing the men who strike against the flume, who gets a compliment
> such as he got from the plan[t] manager at Bridal Veil sound like a man who
> would organize strikes and have a roll with the IWW?
>
> . . . [I]f Dad ever had any sympathy for strikes or the IWW, it would ap-
> pear that such must have been sometime prior to the incidents I have cited.[18]

*Julia and her brother have entirely different memories of their father, different
myths perhaps. It is hard to believe Jack Godman agreed with replacing strikers,
but there is no way to know. The IWW kept no membership records and Godman
wasn't in leadership. But Julia's stories about the radicals, mostly Wobblies, whom
she met in her parents' house, the books her father gave her to read, the meetings
and demonstrations she was taken to, the details she could relate, leave no doubt
in my mind that he was, at least in the days before the IWW's decline, part of that
movement.*

*By World War I's end, virtually all of the leaders of the IWW were out of com-
mission: in jail or awaiting trial, out on bail or fugitives, or deported. Legal defense
was consuming most of the union's money and energy. Government repression was
enormously successful.*[19]

*Demoralized and essentially leaderless, they turned their disappointment in-
ward. They argued, they splintered, but they did not organize. By 1924 they had effectively completed the destruction the government had begun. The locals that were
still viable withdrew from the IWW. A scattering of Wobbly halls remained, mainly
clubhouses where old-timers could gather and reminisce.[20]*

My father was working at Bridal Veil, which is up the Columbia. He was quite
disillusioned after the Wobblies went under. He said they had degenerated into
a bunch of spittoon philosophers, that they'd outlived their usefulness. And in a
way they had. You know, they didn't believe in political action and then they
wasted all their resources in defense funds, because half their membership was
in jail during the Palmer Raids [named for Attorney General A. Mitchell Palmer,
who directed not only the arrests of the Wobblies in 1917 but the roundup of
other radicals in 1919]. Also he seemed suddenly to wake up to the fact that my
brother and I weren't small children anymore and that something had to be
done about our futures. Of course, that's why my mother had decided to go to
the university. So there she was in Eugene and there my father was working up
at Bridal Veil.

I was so depressed when my father told me that about the Wobblies that on
a vacation from the University of Oregon I went on a hitchhiking trip to see if
the things he said about the IWW were true. I went to Centralia and Tacoma,
where there was an IWW local, and Portland. There were two locals in Portland
because the IWW had split into two groups. I went on to Seattle and went to
the IWW local there. And although it was evident to me even then that he was
right, that they had lost their effectiveness, for various reasons I found it very
difficult to accept. So I joined the IWW. As I had a job working in a restaurant,
I put into the food division.

Of course, you know, at that period I was beginning to do my own thinking and so I resisted believing what he told me. He had gotten very discouraged
and disillusioned with the revolution in Russia, something which I couldn't understand at all. I couldn't see anything wrong with it, but I still hadn't got
enough guts or information to argue with him. He was very hard to defeat in an
argument even if you were right and he was wrong. And he'd done my thinking
for so many years.

Chapter 3

I SHED MY YOUTH

After one year as a college student Julia followed Maurice "Butch" Bertram, a transient railroad worker she had met in Eugene, to California and married him on July 6, 1926. Soon she found herself pregnant but dissatisfied with Butch. She became seriously ill from a botched abortion and was still recovering when her father died in September 1926. She and Butch returned to Oregon to assist her mother, but by 1927 they were on the move, stopping first in Denver, then visiting Butch's family in Ohio, and finally living in Chicago where Julia gave birth to her only child in June 1928. Still unhappy with Butch, she returned to Oregon without him early in 1929, but Butch followed shortly after and they reunited and moved to a company sawmill town outside Portland.

While these years were clearly difficult and unhappy ones for Julia, they were also years of political development during which she made a commitment to work for a better world and had her first exposure to Communists.

The apartment we had in Eugene when I was going to the university was on Alder Street, and the railroad track went right back of this apartment house. In those days migratory workers rode the freights. And right beyond there, there was a switching area, so sometimes freights stopped there and I used to look out at them and wave to these migratory workers.

One day I waved to this particular migratory worker and he waved back. He was an extremely handsome man and I was quite taken with him because he made the students at the University of Oregon look like wimps. So I dangled a sign down and I said, "Are you an IWW?" I thought all migratory workers were. Well, he actually *did* belong to the IWW. What he was was a boomer switchman. This was a time when a great many of them were unemployed. He held up his hands and nodded indicating he was. I threw a note out the window. I asked him if he was hungry and I said I would give him food if he was. So he jumped off the freight and that's how I met Butch.

He was quite charming. My mother came while I was talking to him and she thought he was quite nice too. He went on to California and later he wrote me a letter and I began to write to him.

On one of my school vacations Butch came to Eugene. I was on my way to the Washington State Penitentiary in Walla Walla to see Ray Becker, one of the prisoners from the Centralia Massacre [see chapter 6], and I took Butch with me as far as Bridal Veil, but to my amazement, my father didn't like him. So Butch left and I went on to the penitentiary by myself. He said he would go back to Eugene and wait for me, but when I got to Eugene he wasn't there. I felt very badly about my father's rudeness to a migratory worker so I went to California to where he was staying to see him.

I dropped out of the University of Oregon because I wasn't learning anything in the history department. It was all written crazy, quite different from the way history really happened. I went to Fresno, California. Butch was working as a hard rock miner at a place called Big Creek where they were building a tunnel through this mountain. We got married in Fresno and I moved up to Big Creek and lived in this country shack. While I was living there I had an abortion and almost died.

I had decided to go back to school and also I had decided that Butch's ideas about life and mine were two different things, so I didn't want to have the baby. The wife of one of his fellow workers told me about this doctor that did abortions. I went there and had this abortion. It was in a run-down part of town and I was aware he was not a reputable doctor when I saw his office and when I saw him.

Butch came and picked me up with another man that worked where he did who had a car. It was the next day that I got sick. High fever. Hemorrhaging. I went to see a doctor. He put me in the Sample Sanitarium in Fresno. Doctor Sample was the head of that. The abortion had caused septicemia, which in turn caused my intestines to grow together. I had to have an operation. I was in that place two months.[1]

Julia used this experience in an unpublished novel, "The Wolf at the Door," written in the 1930s. She used the novel to propagandize for legalizing abortion.

"There's quite an enlargement of the uterus; you're undoubtedly in a fix, but I can't do anything for you," the doctor said, stripping off his rubber gloves.

"What do you mean?" Bunnie cried, sitting up. "You *must* help me."

He launched into a description of some anatomical irregularity he had found. "If our laws were different, I could take you to a reputable hospital and give you an anesthetic; but as it is, and with the equipment at my command, I wouldn't touch your case for a thousand dollars."

"I'm willing to take the risk."

"I'm not."

"But what can I do?" Bunnie asked desperately.

"You can go to another man less conscientious and take your chance of getting blood poisoning or peritonitis or one of the many other followups, or you can be a sensible girl and go on with this."[2]

When I was in the hospital, I remember thinking that if I live and get out of this place I'm going to live differently. Before that my favorite poem was by an English poet named Richard Aldington. It was a poem about having lived wastefully and sensually, like a butterfly or a sun insect, loving the flesh and the beauty of this world.[3] In the hospital, I thought to myself, "If I get out of here, I'll think about some of the things that my father has said about making a better world."

While I was in the hospital, my father died.[4] Butch quit his job to be near me. And after my father's funeral my mother joined us there. I owed this enormous hospital bill. Of course, Butch, who had very little sense of real responsibility, should have gone back to Big Creek to his job to help pay off these bills, but instead my mother went into a small apartment and Butch moved in with her.

I want to tell you what my mother did. She was really an extraordinary woman. She didn't see how we'd ever get this bill paid. She went to this abortionist and she had a gun with her, my father's automatic. Butch was afraid to go with her. She told the doctor he was going to have to pay this bill. She said if he didn't do it she was going to shoot him. He said he didn't have that much money but he gave her what he had and he said he would send her the rest at so much a month. She said, "Well don't think because I'm going back to Oregon that I won't come back here and kill you, because I will." She said, "You have no conscience, no right to perform abortions which you don't know how to do."

I guess in her long years of teaching school and fighting people over the right of women to vote and birth control that she had gotten a lot of iron determination. And every month, until every penny of that was paid off, we got this check from that abortionist. My mother's enormous courage and determination is what I remember best about that episode.

Well, I didn't go back to school and didn't leave Butch because we had to go back to Bridal Veil so that my mother would have a place to live. At my mother's insistence, my husband Butch was given a job at the planing mill. This permitted her and my brother to continue living in the company house, and Butch's wages provided an economic base for the household. And the company gave my mother a promise that my brother, who was still in school, could have work in the summer.

My mother always tried to get my father to apply for a pension because he was a veteran of the Spanish-American War, but he refused to do so. He said if he took a pension from the government it would interfere with his right to criticize it. But after he died, my mother applied for one and she got it. And then, since she maintained, and his fellow workers publicly maintained, that he was killed in an accident, she got workers' compensation for widows of men killed in industrial accidents from the State of Oregon. So that made her independent.[5]

But I'm sure that what two of my father's fellow workers told me privately was true, that he'd deliberately leaped in front of the lumber jitney that ran over him. He had thought the economic and social revolution was going to happen within a matter of several years. Before he died he was thoroughly disillusioned and discouraged, something that I cannot understand.

What made me believe he did commit suicide is that of all the capitalists that he hated the most, it was insurance companies and he had applied for an insurance policy and been turned down. But the fact that he would apply for an insurance policy when he hated the insurance trust bitterly, in addition to what his fellow workers told me, made me believe that. But my mother chose not to.

Nor did her brother. But Julia had a romantic view of suicide and believed it ran in her family. And Julia wanted to be like her father, identified with him. Perhaps his suicide draws her closer to him and makes her own later suicide attempts and her son's successful suicide 30 years later more bearable. Or maybe she knew him well enough to be right.

Butch was about eleven or twelve years older than I was and he'd been a migratory worker and a boomer switchman for so many years, he couldn't give up the habit of moving on. So after we were in Bridal Veil about a year, he said he wanted to go to Ohio to visit his relatives. By this time some of my dreams about going back to school had vanished and so I said I would go with him.

We left on foot. We hitched rides and stopped off in Denver because we had run out of eating money. I got a job at Penney's department store selling stockings and I made so little money I couldn't pay my room rent and eat so I took a job as a maid because you got a free room and your food. I got as much money working as a maid as I had gotten working as a clerk. Butch was working out on a construction job some distance from Denver and I told this couple I was working for that he was my half brother. So once a month he used to come and see me.[6]

I worked in the home of a reporter on the *Denver Post* who was married to the daughter of one of the coal barons in Colorado. 'Course they looked at me as a very inferior person and they said anything they wanted in front of me because I think they thought I was so ignorant I wouldn't understand anything. I saw no point to disillusion them.

While I was opening bottles of home brew at one of their parties, the reporter came into the kitchen to pick up the tray with two of his friends. He showed them letters he said he had purloined from a secondhand bookstore operated by the head of Denver's Communist Party, William Dietrich.

My employer planned to show the letters to the district attorney. He felt it would get Dietrich indicted and provide him with an exclusive byline scoop. He was planning to get hold of some dynamite and set it off at a post office so that he could get a newspaper scoop and blame it on the Communists. His friends thought this a great idea. The trio was far from sober.

Also mentioned was a rally urging freedom for Sacco and Vanzetti to be held in several weeks on the steps of the federal building. They discussed the possibility of setting off a bomb at the rally and blaming that on the Communists, providing further newspaper copy.

He put these letters under the shelf paper in the pantry off the kitchen, so I stole them. On my Thursday afternoon off, with other servants from that area, I caught the bus for downtown Denver. They were going to the movies—I to Mr. Dietrich's bookstore.

Will Dietrich was the first Communist I ever met. His wife and sister-in-law were Jewish; they worked in the bookstore. They were really wonderful people. They were highly intelligent, well educated. I showed them the letters and he said it was just nonsense, there was nothing in the letters that would, that could, incriminate him in any way whatsoever. He said this reporter was young and idiotic.

They convinced me that my mother had been right, that political action [voting] was quite essential and necessary. I remember one of the examples they used was that you elected sheriffs and people of that sort and then the people that you failed to keep out of office could throw you in jail and do all sorts of terrible things. They could back up all of the things with examples that had happened in the labor world and I could understand that type of thing. Then I began to think back over some of the arguments my mother had used, that I never paid any attention to, and I realized she had been right.

My nostalgic attachment to the IWW ended in 1927 when I met the Dietrichs. Much to my chagrin and embarrassment, they refused to let me into the Party. They told me they didn't take in anyone that was as young and naive as I was. I had a great many things to learn.

Will was the most intelligent and persuasive person I ever met. I've always been very glad I ran into those people. They became my closest friends and I spent all my spare time with them. One of the great coal strikes was going on in Colorado at that time and I used to go out with the Dietrichs to meetings in the coal towns. We also went into the mountains to hunt mushrooms. It was in many ways an interesting summer. It was also the summer they executed Sacco and Vanzetti, and while I was at a memorial demonstration in downtown Denver, the reporter, who was covering the event for his paper, saw me and demanded to know what I was doing there. I was so naive as to argue with him about the case. So Butch and I had to move on.[7]

So then I got pregnant again. The reason it happened, I hate to say this, is we hitched a ride with this man who was extremely interesting and well educated. We rode all day with him, and again I saw that I had made a dreadful mistake in getting mixed up with Butch, that Butch and I really had nothing in common beyond the fact that he had carried a Wobbly card and was a very charming and good-looking man.

I spent a great deal of time talking to this man, and Butch got left out of the conversation and Butch was deeply hurt and extremely jealous by that. In fact, we had arranged to be picked up wherever it was that we stopped at the end of the day. This man had said if we'd be at a certain place at a certain time, he'd take us on. Butch was so upset that he dragged me into the railway station and got a ticket to the next town. So I slept with Butch that night in this town he bought the ticket to. Well, we had condoms but he said he had lost them, which he probably had. He was very careless. Slept with him anyway.

Butch had ten brothers and sisters. I met all of them when we got to Ohio, except the brother who had played ball with the St. Louis Cardinals. They were warm, wonderful people. I got a job in Portsmouth, Ohio, and Butch took off again. Later I joined him in Chicago where he was working for Stewart-Warner Company that made speedometers.[8]

We were in Chicago by the time I found out I was pregnant. I was very upset for two reasons. The doctor in California told me I'd better not get pregnant again for a couple of years. I wrote to him to see what would be the consequences. He said it was okay. Well then I decided to have Mike, and I did.

Maybe I was afraid of all that pain and agony and trying to find an abortionist and not knowing anyone in Chicago.

I didn't like Chicago. When I got there I was very disillusioned, having spent my life in the backwoods and logging camps and small towns. The only thing good about Chicago was the art museum.

'Course Butch behaved so badly in Chicago. He got a job, and it was a pretty good job, and we got a place to live and then he met a man that he had known before. The man had a truck and he was buying produce and selling it to convents and places like that. I found out that what he was doing, if it was produce that was in a bushel basket, he knew how to ruffle up the potatoes or the apples so it looked like it was full and it wasn't. He was continually cheating these places and Butch knew about it and he thought it was great.

Butch quit his job to bum around with the produce peddler. I was furious that Butch had thrown over a decent, reputable job, in which he had a union he was joining, for this kind of a crooked deal.

I can't remember why Butch finally left the produce peddler but we moved to another part of Chicago and lived in a remodeled woodshed, which is where we almost starved to death. I was unable to get a job because I was pregnant. I remember living for three weeks on a sack of rice, which I cooked over an upended electric iron. Then I called up a Catholic charity and they brought me some food. I made several passes at getting work but they weren't successful. My son Mike was born in the charity ward of a Chicago hospital on the south side.

I used to get leaflets from someplace and hand them around the neighborhoods and stuff like that. I meant to get involved with the Communists in Chicago and I had a letter of introduction to two of them from Will Dietrich, but one of them was out when I went to his office, and I forget what happened when I tried to see the other one.

The day in Chicago when I shed my youth was the day I wrote to my mother and told her I'd made a dreadful mess out of my life and I asked her if she would send me the money to come to Portland and I would get a job and try to take care of Mike.

My mother had left Bridal Veil because the mill owner would no longer employ my brother during the summer or let them live in a company house—so much for mill owners. But these bleak facts did not contribute to my brother's understanding of economics or the class struggle. She sent me the money, but when I got to Portland I couldn't get a job because I was going to put Mike in the Fruit and Flower Mission but they wouldn't take children under a year old and he was only eight months old.

Well, Butch arrived by way of the freights from Chicago and appeared one day at my mother's apartment. She welcomed him with open arms. Took him right in. He got a job at the West Oregon mill in Linnton. So I went back to him.

We lived in a company shack for six years. 'Course I don't regret that part of my life with him, because that's where I got my real education, apart from all I had learned from my father and from the Communists in Denver and from my mother when she talked about voting. It takes awhile for what you know to jell into place.

Chapter 4

A BAKING POWDER IN THE MASSES

Though the IWW was effectively incapacitated by government attacks and infighting following World War I, craft unionism—as opposed to industrial unionism—remained still very much alive. A craft or trade union organizes workers according to skill, e.g., electricians and carpenters each in their own union even though they may share a work site, while industrial unions, like the IWW, organize all workers at a workplace, everyone in one union, whether skilled or unskilled. The AFL, which represented mostly skilled craftsmen, claimed close to 3 million members throughout the 1920s.

Nationally, union organizers had formidable opposition. Many companies declared war against unions during strikes by enlisting private armed detectives and calling upon government troops. Suspected unionists were blacklisted and many companies required job applicants to sign pledges that they wouldn't join a union. The courts cooperated in the assault by issuing injunctions against picketing and secondary boycotts. Some employers directly competed by forming company unions.[1]

It wasn't until after the stock market crash in 1929 and the depression that followed that the government came to the aid of union organizers. In 1932, even before the election of Franklin Delano Roosevelt, Congress passed the Norris-LaGuardia Act, which sharply limited the use of injunctions against peaceful picketing. In 1933, the enactment of the New Deal's National Industrial Recovery Act (NIRA) guaranteed workers the right to organize and engage in collective bargaining. It also barred employers from interfering in an employee's choice of labor organization and created the National Labor Board (NLB) to mediate labor disputes. Though the NLB had no power to enforce its decisions, the act spurred union organizing; strikes and unions proliferated across the country.

When the NIRA was declared unconstitutional in May 1935, the National
Labor Relations (Wagner) Act was already in the process of becoming law. It too
guaranteed workers the right to organize and strike, and prohibited many unfair
labor practices. The Wagner Act was more precise than the NIRA, in order to with-
stand constitutional scrutiny. Just as importantly, it gave its National Labor Rela-
tions Board (NLRB) the authority to implement and enforce its rulings.

New Deal labor legislation affected industrial workplaces across the United
States. In Oregon, where the timber industry still accounted for "nearly one-half of
the productive income, employment, and payroll," timber workers, including those
in sawmills, took notice.[2] One such mill was in Linnton, Oregon, where, in 1932,
Julia was living with Butch and their son Mike in a company shack.

We moved to this company house at West Oregon Lumber Company in Linnton. It was a company town. Company owned everything. It was like a town I
had lived in when I was sixteen and seventeen at Wendling where the Booth-
Kelly Lumber Company owned everything, even the church and the store.[3]
There's still towns like that.

In the company towns in those days some of the workers were no better
than serfs. They really weren't. They were usually in debt to the company store.
It was intolerable.

The West Oregon and Clark & Wilson companies called a meeting in the
community center and all of the slaves were ordered to go with their wives. The
speaker was a man named C. C. Crow. He was the editor of *Crow's Pacific Coast
Lumber Digest* and the workers all called him "Carrion Crow."[4] He came there
to explain why we shouldn't vote for Roosevelt, but for Hoover. He said if Roosevelt got in, they'd take the tariff off on lumber, and cheap Canadian lumber
would come down here and our wages would be forced down and we'd all be
working for fifty cents an hour. And the screaming thing was that at that time
they were getting twenty-two and a half cents an hour.

Although everybody that was in there knew they shouldn't do it, they
couldn't suppress a titter. It just ran all over this crowd of people. And finally
they just were laughing out loud. It was so funny. I think that things began to
change—at least it did in Linnton—after this silly thing happened at the community center.

So I suddenly began to see the value of getting Roosevelt elected. I began
talking to the people in that sawmill camp out there and everybody that would
listen to me on the subject.

Then the owner of the mill, his name was E. D. Kingsley, he had a mock
election at the time clock. Before you could punch out, you had to vote, the day

before the real election. Well, I heard later that he almost had a stroke of paralysis because the Communist Party candidate that year got more votes than Hoover did. But the only reason that he got any votes was so it would be a slap in the face at the mill owner. They weren't Communist, might as well be frank and tell you that. All the men, all the people in the mill, about 96 percent, voted for Roosevelt. You see, they were ready to vote to rebel.

The purpose of the New Deal was, of course, as I look back, the saving of the capitalist system. By the time Roosevelt took office, it was near collapse. Yet, the New Deal was in a very real sense a people's movement. Under the National Industrial Recovery Act, wages went up. At West Oregon they jumped from twenty-two cents an hour to forty-two and a half cents an hour, low. Working people regarded the election of Roosevelt as the second coming of Christ.

But there was still no union security; you could be fired if the foreman did not like the color of your eyes or considered you an agitator—or, at West Oregon, if you refused to wash his car on Sunday.

Part of the time the mill was down, so I was forced to take a job at the Wildwood Golf Course, where I sold green fees, rented clubs, and waited table and washed dishes. My son was four years old, as I remember. It was three miles from where we lived. I used to hitchhike to work and I had to take him with me. If we didn't get a ride and he got tired, I carried him. I got a dollar seventy-five cents a week. I also did ironing for people in their homes.

Butch did lumber loading on the sidetrack. That's one of the hardest jobs there is in the mill and he wanted to become a tallyman, which is a much better paid job and not so hard on your muscles. He applied for the tallyman's job and, to his surprise, he was given it. So he said to me, "Now you have a little education, you teach me how to tally lumber. I know the grades."

I'd been brought up in sawmills and logging camps and had most of my education back of the sawdust pile, so I knew a lot about lumber grading and I thought there must be some simple way of figuring this out because it took several years to learn all of the dodges and things you had to memorize to tally lumber. So finally I figured out a simple mathematical equation that could be used. So I told my husband, "You don't need to know why this works." He'd only gone to the seventh or eighth grade and had never had algebra or higher math. I said, "It doesn't matter why it works, it does. Just sit down here and memorize it and let's see how you are on your fractions."

The next morning—we were up all night with this stuff—he went to work and tallied lumber and he became one of the best tallymen that they had in the plant. So several of his coworkers, who loaded lumber on the sidetracks, said, "How did you learn to tally lumber overnight?" And he said, "My wife taught me." So four of them came to the little school I had for tallymen and three of them got through the course.

So a couple of years later, it occurred to me, what am I sitting around here for still working my feet off in restaurants when I could be tallying lumber myself. So I went down to the mill office and applied for a job as a tallywoman, and they told me, "Oh no, women can't do that kind of work. What makes you think you can tally lumber?"

I said, "Just give me a chance, I'll prove it."

"Nothing doing. We don't hire women tallymen. We're not going to have any women working in this sawmill."[5]

Some of the people that worked in that mill lived in Linnton on the hillside. They were the better-paid workers. The lowest of the low workers lived down in these dreadful little shacks. They were duplexes made of No. 4 common, with knotholes so big you could look through into the next apartment and see your neighbors quarreling over which bills to pay, or even reach through with a stick and snag a piece of bread off their table. They had no hot water and they had a toilet in a sort of a clothes closet and a kitchen sink. They were three-room affairs.

That's where I met the Japanese. Although they lived in some of these same places, they were so clean and they had little flower gardens and even flower boxes on their roofs of their little shacks. So I insisted we move from where we were living up near the tram into the mill, and move down with the Japanese. Some of them were quite well educated. The ones that joined the union—after we started organizing the union—were the best union members that we had.

All the big mills were in Portland. They've since all moved down into southern Oregon because the timber has been cut off in this end of the state. There was one in downtown Portland, Eastern-Western, and there were two at Linnton: Clark & Wilson and West Oregon. And there were a couple out in St. Johns: Inman-Poulsen and Portland, and another one, Jones, out in southwest on the river.[6]

My husband worked at West Oregon in Linnton. When they first started to organize the union, a man approached him and Butch said, "Ah, hell with it." He said, "Trade unions aren't any good." You know, that's what the Wobblies thought in those days, they thought they were formed so that one craft, y'know, would always scab on another. And that usually had held true.

I didn't have the slightest interest in the AFL efforts to organize the mills either. I thought they were a scabby craft outfit because I was brought up in the IWW and that's what they thought of craft unions. But then, in 1934 the Longshoremen went on strike in Portland.

Although the International Longshoremen's Association was founded in 1892, it had virtually disappeared from the region. But in 1933, fueled by the passage of the NIRA, longshoremen began flocking into the union. In 1934 they went on strike for union recognition up and down the Pacific Coast.[7]

Longshoremen's working conditions were nearly unbearable. The longshoremen wanted a closed shop and control of the hiring hall. This latter demand made a lot of sense, given the infamous shape-up, where foremen chose the lucky few who more than likely had slipped them a bottle of liquor or other bribe. The men would show up at six in the morning for work that started at eight on the chance of getting picked. Sometimes they would be told to show up at three or four in the morning only to wait for a ship that didn't come in. And if it didn't come, they were not paid. When they did get work, they could be forced to work round the clock until the job was done, to utter exhaustion. And since 1929, there was less work and income for nearly everyone.

Even before they went on strike, the Longshoremen were preparing for a long battle. They expected the strike to be lengthy and they knew they couldn't do it alone. In Portland, they went to the unemployed council and to college students to explain the coming strike and to ask them not to scab. They went to neighborhood grocers, small farmers, and the churches across town to educate them so they would be ready with donations when the time came. They also opened a commissary with food, donated by farmers and grocers, and supplies they'd bought with money donated by other unions.

The Longshoremen emerged victorious, in July 1934, after striking for nearly three months. The Pacific Coast waterfront would never be the same again. Once they won, the Longshoremen helped the other unions. They would no longer unload a truck if the driver couldn't show his union card (the Teamsters grew nearly tenfold as a result) and they wouldn't eat in a restaurant unless it had a union waitress. So all the unions benefited because, as longshoreman Louis "Frank" Young said, "We wouldn't touch nothing that wasn't union."[8]

Butch had no use for the strike because Longshoremen were AFL at that time, and he was still an IWW. But then came the day in the 1934 dock strike when four men were shot over at Pier Park in Portland by the police. The police chief had put armed policemen on gondolas on the railroad tracks that led into Terminal 4. That's where they had all of their scabs concentrated. They were trying to take hot cargo in to be loaded on the ships and they had a lot of college students from Oregon State that were acting as scabs. That's where they got their goddamn scabs.

And there was a huge mass of longshoremen because the railroad men said they would not move the trains—they belonged to the railroad unions—they would not move the trains into Terminal 4 if there were people on the tracks. So a great many longshoremen rushed out there, and sat on the tracks. And they were all up and down the right-of-way and the police fired, and four men were shot. None of them were killed, though in the same strike in Seattle and San Pedro [Los Angeles] and San Francisco, men were killed. I think two hundred men were shot in San Francisco, but only two were killed.[9]

The wife of an Italian millworker got the motes out of my eyes. The day after the shooting, she came to me and said she and her daughter and husband were going to go over to St. Johns and see what was going on up there. By the way, the foreign-born people at West Oregon were the only ones that took any interest at that time in the longshore strike. They knew a great deal more than the rest of us about what it was really all about.

What I saw over there changed the entire course of my life.

This longshoreman's son said he'd take us down the trail onto the railroad camp so we could get a real good look at what was going on down there. Before he took us there he took us up to the place where the four longshoremen had been shot. There was still blood there. Some of it had sunk in and the railroad ties were red. Longshoremen had a large wreath of red roses there in their honor and they had it roped off.

And we saw the trees in the park that were pockmarked, literally pock-marked, with bullet holes. Some of the men, to get away from the shooting, had run up to the fence around the park, and it wasn't very far from the play area where a great many children had been at play, and they thought that was fire-crackers, and they got off the swings and teeter-totters and all ran down that way. Why they weren't all killed I've never been able to figure out. For years, you could go out there and dig lead out of the bark of those trees.

We went up on this bluff where the strikers were set up. You could look down from there into Terminal 4. They had the scabs headquartered on a ship that was tied up there. The terminal was like an armed camp. They had barbed wire fence around it; they had sandbag huts inside the fence with gun emplace-ments; they had machine guns down at the gate into the terminal; they had an armored truck running around in there. The strikers had their soup kitchen up there on the bluff and they had fires going with mulligan stew cooking. They had their arsenal of weapons. What do you think their arsenal consisted of? Slingshots and a couple of boxes full of pebbles. Slingshots against machine guns.

And while I was standing there with my three Italian friends looking down into the armed camp, and it *was* an armed camp, a whole bunch of deputized thugs, is what they were, swarmed out of this one sandbag hut and ordered us off the tracks. This Italian millworker said, "You don't have any authority here. This is railroad property. You can't order us off." So they knocked this striker's son down on the ground—he was quite slender—and began kicking him in the stomach. We tried to stop them and they pulled their guns, and I really expected to be shot. I was so frightened that I couldn't move. I hung on to this Italian woman or I would have fallen down. She stood like a rock.

Just then a longshoreman came from behind one of those little yellow railroad huts. He was a big tall man about six feet tall and had his hand in his pocket bulged out like this. I realized afterwards it was his hand and not a gun. You see these things in the movies and you think what a bunch of baloney. He said, "If you're looking for trouble, you're going to get it. Now get back down where you came from and move right now." And they slithered off the track and back down the bank, through the barbed wire fence, into their stupid huts, and we were left alive.

As we walked along, Mrs. Tenderelli kept saying: "You with your machine of writing could do much."

I typed a petition on my beat-up, thirdhand Underwood, demanding the removal of that police chief—his name was Colonel B. K. Lawson—for the shooting of unarmed men near a park where children were at play. Many people signed the petition and that triggered off quite a wave among various groups throughout Portland, and "Bloody Shirt Joe" [the sobriquet they hung on Mayor Joseph K. Carson after this incident] had to fire him. It was the first conscious, planned, political action of my life.

By the time I got home, I was convinced that the longshoremen were on the right track and, whatever kind of a union they belonged to, there was nothing wrong with it. So I told Butch, "We've been quite wrong about this strike and about the AFL longshoremen. This isn't the ordinary craft union. This is industrial war. It's the real thing and we belong in it."

The 1934 strike of the longshoremen was sort of a mainspring for everyone else that wanted to organize in the industrial type of unions. There always had been crafts around this area, you know, but there was nothing much for the industrial workers or nothing that amounted to anything.

This man had tried to get Butch to sign up in the federal union of the lumber and sawmill workers that had a federal charter under the Carpenters and Joiners. They were trying to organize the mill and had about ten people signed up, that was all. There were three hundred fifty people worked at West Oregon and seven hundred at the other mill out there. I said, "You gotta get in and join the Carpenters and Joiners and help to organize the workers at this mill and I'll help you."

Well, it was a more or less industrial type of union, but it was one without any democracy because you paid your dues and you paid your per capita tax to the Carpenters and Joiners, you could send delegates to their conventions and conferences, but you didn't have any vote. They call it a federal union, federal charter.

Federal unions were a temporary solution for the AFL to the problem of industrial unionization. They were essentially storage vessels. A local would be chartered directly by the AFL but be expected to be abandoned quickly as its members were parceled out to the various international unions with jurisdiction over them.

In practice it wasn't so simple. Most industrial workers were semiskilled or unskilled; there weren't unions to transfer them into. The craft unions wanted the right to skim off the few skilled workers in each factory. But the workers saw the advantage of one union, one bargaining unit, one date for the contract for everyone in the plant, one strike, one negotiation, no opportunity for management to play one group off against the other.[10]

Federal union dues were kept lower than those of craft unions. The federal Sawmill and Timber Workers' Union, which had been chartered in 1933, was turned over en masse to the jurisdiction of the United Brotherhood of Carpenters and Joiners in March 1935. Lumber workers paid only 25 cents a month per capita tax instead of the 75 the carpenters in construction paid. But the carpenters didn't consider the sawmill and timber workers equals and would never absorb them into the union with full rights and benefits of the skilled union members.[11]

Still, the longshoremen's struggle and victory had convinced Julia to work for the union, even if it was a federal union and part of the AFL. Butch joined along with workers at camps and mills all over the Northwest. Like the longshoremen, the woodworkers had to strike for union recognition. Their strike involved men throughout the Douglas fir region—the area west of the Cascades in Oregon and Washington and a small area in northern California. At one point, it was estimated that 90 percent of all operations in the region were shut down.[12]

So Butch joined. And then he and I set about getting other people to join. Well we used to go around to people's houses and talk to them about the desirability of doing what the longshoremen had done and organizing. We didn't have any job security. If the foreman in the mill or the boss or the superintendent took a dislike to you, they could fire you and there was nothing you could do about it. Nevertheless, at the time that the woodworkers strike started in 1935, we only had about seventeen people, as I recall, signed up in that mill. In some of the mills, they had a lot more. But we were down on the picket line with applications, and before the day was over, we had the rest of them all signed up. Now the day that we put the picket line up was May 5, 1935.

They called a strike to get wage increases and other conditions, but it was mainly to get union recognition. And it was also an organizational strike, because a great many working men, even if they haven't got to the point of going on strike themselves and joining the union, they won't go through a picket line, and there was a picket line there. So we just signed everybody up when they came down. When they saw the picket line, they wouldn't go through. Just a handful of real scoundrelly people went in to scab.

My brother was gonna be hired by some New York company in the engineering department, but the Depression came on so they didn't need him. So Butch got him a job punching pigeon holes at West Oregon. He would very much like to have scabbed but he was afraid to. He was afraid the strikers would beat him up, which I'm sure they would have. He wouldn't picket. They used to go up there and drag him down on the picket line. He caused so much commotion that they finally gave it up.

People had got sick and tired of being slaves. I can look back clearly and see West Oregon. There was a tram that led from the highway down into the mill, and on both sides of the tram, the company shacks stretched along the highway where the people lived. Before the '34 strike, when Kingsley, who owned that mill, would be coming by in his car, the workers would line up at the edge of the tram and take off their hat and bow. I mean, it was really degrading. Then after the longshoremen won their strike and different people knew longshoremen and saw how much better off they were, I think people began to think. Nevertheless, the fact remains that it was sort of like a baking powder in the masses. All this is sort of ferment that works. You can get driven down just so low and then you begin to rebel.

At Bridal Veil, a mass picket line went up and the governor of Oregon sent the sheriff deputies to arrest the mass picket line. They marched them at bayonet point the twenty-four miles from Bridal Veil to the Multnomah County Courthouse. Men were killed in Eureka and several other places on picket lines. The state and city government and the employers and the newspapers were all against the working people. There was no way that you could get your side of the story across in those days.[13]

The company sent around letters to the people that lived in the company houses at West Oregon and told us if our husbands didn't return to work by a certain date we'd have to move out in a week's time. So the union attorney sent me and another wife of a striker to go from door to door and get a list of names of all the people that had been ordered out. When we got to the house at the end of one of the rows, we didn't know until that day that this man'd been sneaking in and, in effect, scabbing. We didn't know until this particular time.

He ordered us off his porch and I said, "You talk like a scab." He went into a rage and banged the screen door at me and it threw me off balance and down the steps—the mill houses at that end of that row were built up high—threw me off the steps. He jumped down and started beating me up.

I learned a great deal out of that encounter. I learned that if you're as small as I am, you'd better not tangle physically with a man who is six feet four inches tall and weighs over 200 pounds. I managed to get to my feet and I started to hit him, but all I was able to do was to tear the pocket off his shirt. He threw me down on the walk and really started beating me up. The last thing I remember, before I passed out, was his huge foot coming toward my chest.

Now the woman with me, Jennie Hilkey, was his sister-in-law. The guts and courage of that woman! She told me later, she reached down and picked me up and ran down the road with me under her arm, like a sack of meal. He was running behind us screaming, down at the place where the tram came out from the mill, where the pickets were and also a couple of police cars and cops. He ran after her screaming, "Arrest that woman. She called me a dirty son-of-a-bitching scab."

She saved my life. I got two front teeth knocked out and I got my ankle and foot busted, which is why today I have to wear shoes like this in order to walk, because the foot wasn't set right. When I think about that woman. You know, she could have been frightened off, because he would have set on her next.

The cops came next day and served a warrant on me. In the meantime I had been to the company doctor, Dr. [Cecil E.] Brous, who was a friend of mine, and had obtained crutches. So I was on crutches when I appeared in police court. My body was covered with bruises and two of my front teeth were missing. I was tried for—what'd they call it—disorderly conduct.

The union attorney told me to deny that I had used "bad language" after he threw me down the steps, but I had been brought up by a mother who not only was a Socialist, but also she was sort of religious, and she had taught me never to tell lies. So I told the truth and I got fined ten dollars. The man who beat me up, John Hilkey, was fined fifty dollars for "the more serious misdemeanor." His fine was suspended, as was mine, because we had no previous police records.

As the strike went on, Abe Muir, who was the top brass in this area for the Carpenters and Joiners, came out here and tried to sell the strike out. In other words, he was interested in getting a bunch of per capita payers, and he wasn't interested in getting a really militant union going that would take care of the workers' rights. He made every effort to get us to go back to work without any strong guarantees that we'd have union recognition, just on the five cents an hour. We won the strike, but the only wage increase we got was the five cents. Of course, we got union recognition and that was the most important thing of all.

And another thing that was very important, particularly to sawmill workers, was to get our self-respect back, because before this strike, if you wanted to be sure of getting any work in the mill shutdowns, which were frequent, you had to wash the superintendent's car and make rabbit hutches for his wife and cut her grass and a whole bunch of stuff like that. And a lot of sawmill workers lived in company houses, and they were just deplorable, simply deplorable. You were practically serfs. In fact, I couldn't see much difference.

Where there were company stores, after you paid your debt to the store and they took the rent out of your check and the wood out of your check, you were lucky if you had enough money left to buy a couple of postage stamps in actual money. In Linnton there was no company store, but you were in debt to the two groceries that were there. You never got out of debt. You could never leave there because you could never get any money to get away. There wasn't much difference between them and slaves on the old plantations in the South. Really, there wasn't. So we had a great deal at stake.

After we won the strike in '35, my husband and I moved out of that company house and moved over to St. Johns. Lots of us did. Butch became a committeeman. They call them job stewards in some places, but we called them committeemen, and he was one of the three committeemen in that mill. Of course, my husband was extremely good in those days. He had a lot of charm and magnetism and he didn't look down on other people. He'd only gone to the eighth grade himself, but he did read. He read working-class papers. And he believed in the preamble of the IWW, which I still consider a great document:

> The working class and the employing class have nothing in common. There can be no peace so long as hunger and want are found among millions of working people and the few, who make up the employing class, have all the good things of life.
>
> Between these two classes a struggle must go on until the workers of the world organize and take over the machinery of production.[14]

I still believe that, though I got over thinking that you shouldn't vote.

The strikes on the waterfront, in the camps and mills and other mass production industries in the thirties all had this factor in common: We won them, and we were no longer timber beasts, sawmill stiffs, and waterfront bums. We were the people who loaded the ships and sailed them, who made the head rigs turn and the green chains run. We were the workers of the world. Without us there would be no world.

The AFL in the mills turned out to be largely a company union and that was obvious to most of the people who worked in the mill and to some of their wives, that it was little better than the 4L, which was *really* set up by the employers.[15] That was during World War I to stop the IWW, to break the IWW strikes. (Of course, I hate to say these things now because it's very important that all labor should get together.) So the Woodworkers didn't leave the Carpenters and Joiners, but they set up a Federation of Woodworkers.

I started writing for the lumberworkers' newspaper. It was sort of accidental. When the strike started in 1935, I was the only person connected with the lumber and sawmill workers in the state of Oregon who had a typewriter and it was very useful. So I got called on to do this and do that. And then very soon they started a newspaper. It was first published in Aberdeen. It was called the *Timber Worker*. It's now the *International Woodworker*. In about 1936, they set up an office in Portland and I was in charge of the Oregon office of the newspaper. Before that I was trying to write the Great American Proletarian Novel. Wasted my time. Then in 1937, when we went CIO, we were locked out for eight and a half months. That was a real postgraduate course.

Chapter 5

I HAD A TYPEWRITER

There had long been an industrial-union minority in the AFL advocating to organize workers in mass-production industries, the skilled and unskilled together, and in the early 1930s they increased the pressure. But the old-guard craft union advocates held fast. The comments of John P. Frey, president of the AFL Metal Trades Department, were indicative of the views of many labor leaders: "To mingle highly skilled and lower skilled into one organization is as impractical as endeavoring to mix oil and water, for the oil will persistently seek the higher level."[1]

The independent, autonomous unions that constituted the AFL jealously guarded their territories. They were the elite and they wanted to stay that way. They didn't want to lose any of their potential members to an industrial union. Moreover, they didn't want less skilled workers joining their craft unions, potentially outnumbering them and outvoting them.

John L. Lewis was president of the United Mine Workers (UMW), one of a handful of industrial unions in the AFL. In 1933, Lewis and the presidents of a few other industrial unions (and one maverick, Charles P. Howard, president of the Typographical Union) urged the AFL to accommodate to the times and change its attitude toward industrial unionism. Finally, in November 1935, impatient and frustrated by the AFL's refusal to modify its position, Lewis organized a committee within the AFL, the Committee for Industrial Organization (CIO).[2]

CIO organizers said their intention was to organize new industrial unions and bring them into the AFL. Nevertheless, the AFL leadership demanded that the committee dissolve. When Lewis and the CIO refused, the AFL asked all the affiliated unions to withdraw from the CIO. When this failed, the AFL suspended and ultimately expelled them. Eventually the CIO would be transformed into the independent Congress of Industrial Organizations, chartering its own independent unions.[3]

The Woodworkers were in the middle of this battle. They felt like second-class union members in the federal union the Carpenters and Joiners had formed for them. They wanted a union that they, the rank and file, controlled, one in which their voices were heard and heeded. And Julia, as the president of the ladies' auxiliary of the woodworkers' union and wife of a union activist, understood the woodworkers' union members' feelings of powerlessness within their AFL union and was firmly on their side.

The union had gotten tired of being taxed, taxation without representation, of having to pay per capita tax on its membership but at conventions of the Carpenters and Joiners not having any voice and vote.

Speakers from the CIO had been before our various meetings. It was the CIO that organized the woolen mills and many other mass-production unions. The AFL was a craft setup, it wasn't interested in the mass-production unions. In other words, they really weren't interested in what we considered to be the legitimate working class. We wanted a union that could fight for your basic rights and was interested in organizing the unorganized in the mass-production industry, that would support you in time of beefs and not sell you out.

So at a convention of the Federation of Woodworkers in Tacoma in the summer of 1937, delegates to the convention—I was there—took a vote and overwhelmingly, it was almost 100 percent, they voted to go CIO. Then that recommendation was taken back to the affiliate locals.

The Federation of Woodworkers, an unchartered, unrecognized, unaffiliated organization attempting to reform the United Brotherhood of Carpenters and Joiners within the AFL, metamorphosed at that convention into a chartered union: the International Woodworkers of America (IWA)-CIO.

The AFL did not meekly relinquish its Sawmill and Timberworker locals. The jurisdictional struggle between the AFL and the IWA centered in Portland, where the AFL's Building Trade Council set up picket lines around the major mills. The Carpenters and Joiners refused to build with CIO lumber and Teamsters refused to haul it. The mills shut down in response.[4]

When the IWA filed charges with the NLRB in October 1937, it alleged a lockout at six Portland sawmills, insisting that there was "collusion between the lumber operators and the A. F. of L. to break the C. I. O. and form A. F. of L. unions in the mills." But the NLRB was unsuccessful in getting the AFL to agree to an election or to recognize its decision to certify the IWA as the bargaining agent in the mills where it held a clear majority.[5]

The employers claimed neutrality. The mills said they couldn't operate until they were assured of a peaceful situation and, additionally, the market was bad and they couldn't afford to stay open. While the poor market did work in the employers' favor by providing an excuse to close, there was also evidence that the IWA's claims were correct, that the employers favored the AFL.

Julia had been raised with the antiemployer precepts of the IWW. She didn't expect the company to support her cause and she had no illusion of employer honesty. The plants were shut down and the IWA was shut out. The employers might deny it, but, with the IWA members and their supporters, she knew it was a lockout and always referred to it as one.

The employers have their various organizations and they're quite powerful. All the big mills were in Portland and on the Columbia River bend and all of the workers in those mills were locked out for going CIO. They never tried to negotiate, they just locked us out. If they had to have a union, they preferred that we were still hitched to the Carpenters and Joiners. They wanted to force us back into the AFL. They couldn't maneuver the CIO like they did the AFL. They were terrified of the CIO. In those days, they were equated with the Bolsheviks.

The lockout lasted eight and a half months. The Malarkey Plylock plywood workers had their own local. They were locked out two years and eight months. That's a long time for families to do without a paycheck.

We immediately set out picket lines at all of these places because it was quite apparent to almost everyone that what the employer would do next would be to try to bring scabs in to run the plant. At some of the places, they were fairly successful, but I think we only had about seventeen that worked West Oregon.

Watching his family's suffering during a strike or lockout is a strong incentive for a worker to cross the picket line or to vote to give up the struggle. As Matt Meehan, a Longshore union organizer at the time, said, "Feed the belly of the striker and he'll fight to win. But you gotta keep his belly full and also you have to keep their families full because many strikes are lost when the wife forces the man back on the job. Even the best union man just can't stand up under that kind of pressure."[6]

The best way to counteract that impulse is to involve the wives, make them allies with their husbands. The Woodworkers already had a ladies' auxiliary but it took on a new importance once the lockout began.

I was one of the two women that organized the woodworkers' union auxiliary. It was a huge auxiliary with hundreds of members. We once had a letter from the head of the CIO at that time, John L. Lewis, saying we had the largest women's auxiliary in the CIO. Now that was in the day when not many women, wives of workers, had jobs of their own, so the auxiliary was extremely important to them because it was something they could belong to. We weren't welcomed in the PTAs and clubs that other women found activity in. We were the wives of lowly workers and lived on the other side of the tracks. So it really meant a great deal to us to have that auxiliary. It was a special focus of our lives and we used to do all sorts of things.

We had two meetings a month, and one of them we had in the daytime at the time when the local met, and one of them we had in the evening at the time when the local had an evening meeting. Our husbands used to come over after their evening meeting and we used to have cake and coffee, and we used to sing songs out of the old IWW *Little Red Songbook.* Of course, we had it mimeographed, but that's where I got the songs.

Let me explain what the auxiliary meant to its members by relating what two of them did after their husbands crossed the picket line. One woman was very upset because we banned her from auxiliary meetings. She said that had nothing to do with her being in the auxiliary. It was the only thing she had and she loved coming to meetings. But we escorted her, weeping, out the door.

The second woman packed up her clothes and left her husband (and twelve-year-old son who had refused to leave his father) because he had finally gone in to scab. Her husband had a top job in the planing mill and they were buying a house in St. Johns, but he belonged to the union. He'd been all over Oregon looking for another job and couldn't get hired. He was blacklisted. He held out until he was threatened with foreclosure, so he finally went in.

She came to the house and she said she couldn't live with a scab or without the auxiliary, it meant everything to her. She asked if she could stay with Butch and me. I said, "I want you to go home, because I don't consider he's an ordinary scab. He was a foreman and he held out for five months, and this will be over some day, but the union will be in a weakened condition and they will have to take in the scabs." And that's exactly what happened. I said, "I don't want you to leave your son and your husband. He's a pretty decent guy." I said, "He's not an ordinary scab. There's scabs and scabs."

When that thing started out, if anyone had ever told me that I could say there's scabs and scabs, I would have called them a liar. But those are some of the things you learn along the way. There are people that you don't want to antagonize and you don't want to unfairly call them things they're not, because eventually they'll be with you again. And if you can't win a fight today, you may win it tomorrow, because the fight continues one way or another. It keeps going on. 'Course, I wouldn't have got up publicly and said that.

I had served two terms when it was AFL and, when we went CIO, I served a term under the CIO. So this is the story of how we got through the lockout. I've always felt that women had more imagination and guts than men, I really believe that.

We had no treasury; we had no strike benefits. We were too new. Very few people had any savings. Very few people owned their own homes. We had endless difficulties. We couldn't get on welfare, because welfare told us if our husbands would go through the picket line, they'd have work and we'd get food. We were not about to let our husbands go through the picket lines. We realized when the lockout went on and on that if we were going to win the lockout, our people would have to get fed.

My parents were highly educated people and my mother had been a teacher and I had been to university and I had a typewriter. And I didn't have too much in common—that's what I thought when all these strikes started—with the other people because they had very little education. I was a person that didn't understand anything except by the book.

But after the big struggle came along—in fact in the 1935 strike is when I got a good education about what is really brains and education—I began to see that these women, including one of the brightest women I've ever met, who'd only gone to the third grade, knew far more than I did. And I think they looked down on me because I didn't know how to do anything useful. I couldn't can fruit or crochet or sew or anything. So we sort of looked down on each other. But after these troubles started, we began to appreciate one another. I could type up strike bulletins. I could write letters of protest. And they were marvelous at organizing the soup kitchen and the clothing depots and at all of these things that kept us going.

At the beginning of this lockout, the auxiliary had run a clothing depot where you could go and get clothes and the union had run a place where you could go and get groceries. Soon it became necessary to open up soup kitchens. When we were going around begging food and money to keep the soup kitchens going and the clothing depots going, we went to a great many places to ask for help.

We went to Fred Meyer's and we took with us a logger's wife who had known Fred Meyer before he became a rich man with his supermarkets. In fact, I think he'd had kind of a crush on her from what she said. She was a very handsome redheaded woman. Fred Meyer gave us a case of canned vegetables. That was the extent of his support. And the dairies shut off all our milk, although all of us had always paid our bills before this. We went to Meier & Frank's [local department store], because we'd all been customers, and they gave us twelve pairs of stockings for children that didn't match.

I had a few friends in the community who weren't from my side of the tracks, but they were people who read books, like the librarian in the branch library and the company doctor, whom I liked to talk to, and a woman whose husband was an executive in an oil company. When I was taking a petition around after these men were shot in the Longshore strike I thought these people would sign the petition too, but they wouldn't. So I saw then where my real friends and my real allies were.

I think it was during the 1937 lockout that I started writing "true stories" to make money. I sold the first one I wrote. The company doctor, who was a friend of mine although he deplored my politics and I deplored his, came to the house and he said, "What are you doing with that old typewriter?" I told him I was writing a novel.

He says, "Well, what makes you think that you can break into the publishing world?" He said, "Why don't you try writing for a magazine. If you want to know which one would be the easiest to break into, go to the drugstore and see where the biggest stack of magazines is. Buy one of those and familiarize yourself with their style and content."

I did and it was *True Story* magazine. I thought, "Oh this is really stupid stuff, I can do better than this." I went home and wrote one and mailed it off and they bought it. I still remember how much I got: $165, which was like a fortune. It took me about three and a half hours to write it. Butch had been enraged when I took "good money" to buy stamps. I wrote a number of them and used some of the money for our bills and some to buy food for the soup kitchen and the commissary. But I finally got so caught up in union activities and writing for the union paper and the Ray Becker case that I didn't have any time for that "true story" stuff anymore.

We ran a huge soup kitchen in St. Johns during the lockout, simply enormous. We must have fed hundreds and maybe thousands of people. The loggers' hiring hall also served food bought with donations from the Longshoremen.

I was there once with an auxiliary committee and they were having what we thought was beef. Since many of us were subsisting at that time on cornmeal mush, we were furious and protested loudly. It turned out to be venison. Two loggers had gone into the woods and shot a deer, although it was not deer hunting season.

Women used to go around to meetings of other locals and unions to beg money to keep these places going. Of course, it was a bit difficult because, since we had left the AFL, there were only a certain number of unions that we could go to, mostly the seamen's unions. Most of the unions in Portland *were* AFL and were no longer willing to help us. So we had run out of money and that's why we were out of food.

I remember one day a man named Ernie Young came to the house. He was on the plant committee at Eastern-Western Mill, it was one of the big mills, and he was on what they called the mooching committee, the committee that went around trying to get food to feed the people.

We were going to have some macaroni with a little salt and pepper on it; it was all that we were able to get at the union commissary the day before. He came to the house and he had a quart of milk. I said, "Where did you get that milk?" He said that the mooching committee went around in the affluent neighborhoods early in the morning and took milk off of people's porches. Then he gave me a sliver of cheese. I said, "And where did you get the cheese?" and he said, "Don't let's go into that."

After a while, in spite of all that we could do, people started getting their gas and water and electricity turned off, and they would be ordered out of their rented houses. Their furniture would be taken away. I remember, for instance, after we had organized the unions and got the wages up, my husband and I had bought some furniture and almost everybody else had done the same. And after the lockout started, we had no money to keep up the payments, so they were always coming and repossessing our furniture.

One day word was rushed to me down the alley, the repossessors were coming after my furniture. So I jumped into bed with all my clothes and shoes on. I'll pretend to be sick, at least maybe I'll save the bed. But all they did was to lift me up in the blankets and lay me on the floor and they took the bed. And then they went out in the kitchen and started to take up the linoleum, but one of the men looked ashamed of himself. He said, "You can't do that, because see what's she's gone and done. She's put down molding and the molding belongs to the house. You can't take it up." So I saved the linoleum, that was all. They forgot to take two pie pans I had bought when I got the other furniture. So I took the two pie pans and I ran out in the street and threw them after the truck. What good were two pie pans? No stove to put them in.

Well I never thought you should give up on a good cause. One of the great shocks in my life was when Harry Bridges, international president of the ILWU, came to Portland at the time we were locked out. Down at West Oregon the Longshoremen were refusing to load a ship with lumber. That had been going on for a long time, and not to load the ship was a violation of the contract the

Longshoremen had. But, nevertheless, they wouldn't load the ship because we were picketing.

Bridges came to Portland and said at a meeting, where I was, that he thought we would have to give up the struggle to remain in the CIO and that later we could make a comeback. But no one would give up and we won.

After the onset of the Depression, with millions unemployed, various groups on the left began organizing the unemployed. In 1935 the Socialist Party launched the Workers Alliance of America (WAA). In 1936 the Communist Party's Unemployed Councils, under the influence of the Party's newly adopted Popular Front line, joined the WAA and became its dominant political force.[7]

The organization used ingenuity to meet the needs of its members. For example many of the unemployed couldn't pay their bills, so utilities would get shut off. Dirk DeJonge, an activist in the Oregon chapter of the WAA (called the Oregon Workers' Alliance), explained, "Well, the unemployed council . . . would simply go and turn on the water. . . . [S]ome people would pour fresh concrete over the meter and over the valve that was used to turn off the water. And the same with light. In those days we had some clever people, people who could fix the people's electric wires in such a way that they would constantly operate but would not register on the meter. It was the same way with natural gas."[8]

We knew in a vague way about the Oregon Workers' Alliance. A great many people belonged to it because this was a period in which there were many people who were unemployed and in desperate straits. And we had heard that they had had luck in getting people's lights and water turned back on.

So the auxiliary had a meeting of its executive board and we decided to go down to the office of the Oregon Workers' Alliance and talk to their top officers about how they had solved some of the problems of their members. Now, there were two cochairmen at that time. One of them was William K. Patrick, he was a member of one of the railroad brotherhoods. The other one was Trent Phillips. From having worked as a reporter on the Woodworkers' paper, I had found out I could find things out about people. I have always been naturally curious. I knew that Patrick was not a member of the Communist Party (CP) but that Trent Phillips was. I also knew from talking to people who were active in the Workers' Alliance that Trent Phillips was the one who had the imagination and brains.

You know when you can't beg any more money from the unions that are friendly—they've given you all they possibly have—when your children are starving and being sent home from school because the school nurse said they had the mumps, only it turned out that their glands were swollen from malnutrition, and when they are going to school in the snow with bits of inner tube tied around their bare, chilblained, little feet because you can't half sole their shoes anymore—there isn't enough shoe left to have soled—you don't much care about labels. I said to the ladies' auxiliary, "I should tell you that he's a Communist." And they didn't give a hoot.

So we went to see Trent Phillips. He really was a great guy. He told us we should go to the Panama Building—that's where the welfare was headquartered in those days—and we should sit down on the stairs, in the landings, and stand up and sing out the window of the stairwell and make a commotion. He said we should sit in the welfare office and don't leave and take a few children with us, sit down on the floor. He said the welfare would listen to us. So maybe fifty or sixty or seventy of our members went there, and we did exactly that.

So we got some of our worst cases taken care of, and we got our water turned back on, and a few things like that. It was really only the tip of the iceberg. But it didn't even take the edge off the trouble and poverty. We still didn't get any grants to buy food.

So we went back to see Trent Phillips and said, "What should we do now? We got our water turned on, but we haven't got any food." So he said, "Well, you'll have to get the union itself, and all of your members in Portland, including the men in the union, will have to join in. You'll have to take all your children out of school and you'll have to march around the [county] courthouse."

So we were really afraid because, naive as we were, we realized that some of the leaders in the local union would be terrified at the thought of doing something that Trent Phillips said and we thought maybe that was too radical an action. Nevertheless, we were really desperate. So we decided we had to do it.

We set up a committee of women to go and talk to the executive board of the Woodworkers local in Portland. Now, I cannot remember, it's so long ago, whether we told them that it was Mr. Trent Phillips of the Workers' Alliance who had given us this advice, but I do remember telling them that the Workers' Alliance had had success in getting on welfare. And we did say the Workers' Alliance had had success with demonstrations, and we did outline this type of demonstration. And they agreed it was a great idea and they voted, I believe unanimously, to support the demonstration. They set up committees to help us. We spent a lot of time making signs.

We went to the courthouse. We marched. Our husbands marched with us too. There were more than five thousand of us marching round and round the courthouse with our signs. Made quite a commotion all these woodworkers that reported. Pictures were taken which later appeared in the press. After a couple of hours of this the county commissioners sent someone out to say that if we'd set up a committee, they'd negotiate. I think they said there could be ten people on it. We held an election out in the street. I was quite pleased to be on the committee that was elected to negotiate with the county commissioners. And before the day was over, we were all on welfare. And that is how we lived the rest of the lockout![9]

Their success at the county commission was not matched at the city council. When Julia, representing the auxiliary, went there to request police protection for IWA members who were being shot at by the employers' thugs, she was told by Portland mayor Joseph K. Carson that protection could not be given as "it would cost too much and the city was broke." She said that "[w]hen we protested this attitude, citing the fact that the year before during an AFL truck driver's strike, policemen had been placed in the cabs of all scab trucks, Mayor Carson said, 'That was different, private property was involved and had to be protected.'"[10]

But most of the women's energies were not directed at protesting—they were devoted to basic survival.

One of the hospitals in this end of town threw out a woman who had just had a baby right after the baby was born because they didn't have money to pay on the bill in advance. So, we made a layette for that woman—I shouldn't say *we* because I can't sew—and someone went to her house and nursed her until she was on her feet. And we took food to her. We did a great deal of that type of thing in the Woodworkers' auxiliary.

Then we got the idea that we should have someone come and speak to our auxiliary meetings on birth control because it was no time to be bringing any more children into the world when we couldn't even feed the ones that we had. I think I must have gone to see Dr. Equi to find out who we could get—that's probably the first time I met her. She was a wonderful person and she gave me the name of Dr. Lena Kenin. So I went to see her and she agreed to come and speak at a meeting on different methods of birth control, something that most of our members knew absolutely nothing about. It was the largest meeting that we ever had. We advertised it in all areas where the workers lived. It was just absolutely jammed.

Well, she advocated the use of diaphragms to be used with some kind of cream; however, they had to be fitted. So she volunteered her services. I think she agreed to fit diaphragms to a large number of women, maybe twenty. But we realized to get all of our people covered and to get those diaphragms bought, we were going to have to get other doctors interested. So we sent a committee up to the medical school.

What a fight that was! The head of the medical school was a Catholic. Well, we had a sit-down up there. That's right! So they finally agreed to fit the diaphragms. We had a tussle with the welfare to make them buy the diaphragms, but we won that one too. How many years ago that was. Portland was very backward in those days.

Father Jackson was the priest in North Portland. I began going to Mass at that church because a great many of the woodworkers, especially the ones born in the old country, were Catholics, and I went to their funerals and weddings.

The first time I talked to Father Jackson seriously about problems was after the lockout started. A great many of the students went to Catholic high schools in another part of the city and they had no carfare to get to school. So I went to see Father Jackson about what could be done, and he said, "Why didn't their parents come and talk to me?"

I said, "They're embarrassed that they have no money, but you are the priest of this parish and it's up to you to arrange something. This is a poor parish, but there are parishes in Portland that aren't poor."

He said, "You're right. I'm glad you told me."

He raised the money for the carfare. So after that we used to talk a good deal about the different problems connected with the people. He became a very good friend of mine.

You know if you're out of work that long there comes a time when some of your members will go back in to work and that had happened in several of our mills. But it didn't happen at any of the mills where we had a lot of people that belonged to the women's auxiliary, because we used to send committees to their plant meetings and at the proper place in the meeting the committee would get up and say, "The women are behind you. Stick it out!" We didn't lose a single mill in which we had a large membership, not one! Because the women thoroughly understood what it was all about, that we for a short time had been in control, more or less, of our own lives and destiny.

We didn't want to give up this union that had real guts and democracy. We not only had better wages, but we cut down the overtime without pay. We had gotten our self-respect and independence, so they weren't about to give that up even if they didn't understand all this theory and the history of the struggle of the masses.

When you are involved in a huge mass struggle like that, you have so many immediate problems to take care of. You try and get people to do things they've never done before, such as marching on the courthouse, so you don't have time to get up and say, "Well now, the reason that we're involved in this is really because we need a different social and economic system." You talk about the immediate thing.

Well, a few loggers' wives were already radicalized because they were married to men who had been in the IWW and perhaps several others got radicalized, like one woman who'd been a teacher and was a reader. But a great many of the women could only read what they called the big words, you know, the newspaper headlines, the big words. And an awful lot of *men* couldn't read and write. We could tell, because we used to hand out copies of the *Timber Worker* and the guys would hold it upside down. I mean, that's pitiful. It's hard to radicalize people if they can't read. In fact, we set up classes to teach some of the men how to read.

We wanted to get everybody registered to vote, because there were a few people in office we wanted to get rid of, like Major General Charles H. Martin, who was governor of Oregon during some of these troubles.

Now there were other things that we did to help win the lockout. I remember one desperation point when some of our own members in the auxiliary began to say, "Maybe we better think this over and quit trying to beef up our men because I think we're gonna lose this and we better go back." I think we'd been out about six months then.

So I talked to some of the women that were on the executive board of our auxiliary and we decided that the best thing to do was to take the little bit of money we had left in our treasury out and to have a huge party for all of our members, and the union members too, to get their courage up. So the women that could cook, we had them bake cakes in washtubs. We took copies of the old AFL charter and cut them up in small pieces and passed those pieces around for souvenirs. We had gallons of coffee and we sang union songs like "Solidarity." That seemed to greatly revive everyone's courage.

Another time when things were very low, we got two movie houses out in the working-class end of town to give us a free movie. We always tried to think of things like that that we could do when people's spirits were flagging.

Of course, the neighborhood I lived in was occupied almost entirely by millworkers. We were all in the same boat. Practically all of the children went to school there. The PTA had always looked down on us and none of us were welcome at PTA meetings, but we decided to have a meeting in the school and explain, invite all the teachers and the PTA ladies to come and tell them that they had to join us.

We had several demands. We wanted to get free bus passes purchased by the PTA or by the school board so that our sons and daughters who were high school age could get to high school. And we thought they should help us get shoes. We had gone to the Sunshine Division—I've never had any use for them ever since— and they gave one boy a pair of shoes. The soles fell off before he got home.[11]

So we organized this big meeting and, much to my surprise, most of the teachers came to it and the PTA ladies came. They all signed a resolution that we had about what the lockout was all about and that the children shouldn't be punished over this and join us in our demands. Our demands were kind of meek and mild, but we got a good deal of publicity that way. So gradually the support widened out. By this time, a great many of us had got a pretty good education in doing the best we could to get help.

We also used to go out on the picket lines. I remember going on the picket line at West Oregon and you could see all of our seventeen scabs working in there, working on the green chain.[12] They were poor workers and I remember one of them ran the jitney off the dock because he didn't know how to operate it. We used to stand on the railroad tracks beyond the sidetrack and we used to scream, "Scab," and other words at our seventeen scabs.

There was another factor in winning this lockout and getting our members back to work. That was the National Labor Relations Board hearings that were held on our charges of unfair labor practice. Now at that time the NLRB, which was set up under the Roosevelt administration, was a very fair outfit. I well remember the hearing that was held in the case of West Oregon. I went there so I could write it up for the union newspaper.

The hero of the lockout was a Japanese woman. There were a lot of Japanese workers there. Well, maybe not a lot, but sixty or seventy. And several of them had wives. One of these women, Mary Itoyama, got up and testified that one of the top foremen at the mill had come to the house where she lived with her husband, who worked on the green chain at West Oregon, and said if he didn't go through the picket line and go to work they would both be deported.

The company had their representative at the hearing and this man got up and denied that he'd ever done such a thing. She got very angry. She stood up and she shook her finger at him and said, "He's a no-good, no-truth man." She couldn't think of the word "liar." I'll never forget that woman. "No-good, no-truth man," that's what she said.

We won that one. It was really terrific.

According to the hearing transcripts, Harry C. Duncan, the yard foreman who was in charge of the green chain (all of whose workers were Japanese), was not accused by Itoyama or anyone else of threatening to deport Japanese. However, Itoyama did testify that Duncan "always scare the Japanese boys all the time, because they haven't any citizenship." The record also shows that Itoyama said, in reply to being asked when she first suspected that Duncan was "double faced," that "he was always that way. Front of face he say may be truth, but back a different story. All Japanese boys know."

Julia's husband Butch testified at the NLRB hearing that there was *a rumor that Duncan "had said that, 'the dirty son-of-bitches ought to be deported,'" but the source of that rumor was unknown. Duncan denied telling the Japanese crew that they could be deported if they didn't join the AFL, though he knew such a statement had been made but didn't know by whom.*[13]

The employers *had* threatened to deport the Japanese unless they went in as scabs [i.e., sign an AFL card]. Not a single one did. Nope, the Japanese were among our best members. The Italians were terrific, the Hungarians, the Austrians, all the foreign-born were. So we won the hearings at most of the mills, but I think we lost at three.[14]

The local never forgot the loyalty of its Japanese members. In World War II when the lumber barons tried to drive them off the job, the union kept them working and stood up to the mayor and the governor. It wasn't until the feds moved in, under the president's executive order, that our Japanese members, including Mary Itoyama and her husband, were taken, first to the Portland Livestock Center and then to a concentration camp in Idaho.

That was one of the worst mistakes that the Communist Party ever made, they refused to fight for the rights of the Japanese. Well, several years later, they recognized their mistake and admitted it, but, in the meantime, the Japanese had spent two years in concentration camps. I belong to the Japanese American Citizen's League because I think it was terrible that we took them into the concentration camps in World War II.

The people that I had known as a child, when my father was in the IWW and my mother was a member of the Socialist Party, they were the leaders of the intelligentsia among those two groups, so I had never really, until I went to live at that mill, lived right down at the bottom of the heap. It was a wonderful education, the six years I lived in that sawmill camp. Terrific. I learned a lot that you couldn't learn on any campus or out of any book.

When I look back at the courage of those women who had never read the books that I had read, that were written by leaders in the IWW and the feminist movement of that time, you wondered about the tremendous strength that women do have to understand what's basic, especially poor women. When I think about some of those women it's all I can do to keep from crying, when I think about the courage of those people.

'Course, some of the men had a lot of guts too. When we won the NLRB hearings at the different mills, the employers at West Oregon said they would take all of the men back to work except the three who were on the plant committee. One of them was the husband I had at that time, Butch Bertram. But you know those people had been through so much. They had lost their second-hand cars, their furniture. Eight and a half months is such a long time to be without any money. They were willing to stay out until they took the three committeemen back. I was proud of the three committeemen when they urged them to go back anyway. So they went back to work, but as soon as they had had one payday under their belts they sat down. And those three got back too!

And so the millworkers were able to stay in the CIO, where Julia described herself as having "found a home." Unfortunately, it did not remain a happy home for her. Anticommunism reared its very ugly head.

John L. Lewis, head of the CIO, was strongly anticommunist, but the Communists were the most effective and the hardest-working union organizers available, and he accepted them. To those who questioned the policy, he is reputed to have said, "Who gets the bird, the hunter or the dog?" He would make use of the Communists and discard them later.[15]

In the IWA, as in the larger CIO, the activists were not of one mind politically. The president of the IWA, Harold Pritchett, was a left-wing Canadian. The first International leaders were all left wingers, but the leaders of the Columbia River District Council (CRDC), which included Portland, were more conservative. The president of the CRDC, Al Hartung, was a dedicated anticommunist.[16]

The Portland local introduced its first anticommunist resolutions at the second convention of the IWA in the fall of 1938. By 1940, in addition to Hartung and the CRDC, the left leadership was contending with Adolph Germer, a strong anticommunist, whom John L. Lewis assigned to lead the IWA's organizing drive. In addition, the Immigration and Naturalization Service (INS) and the State Department were harassing Pritchett.[17]

The defeat of the left leadership of the IWA that followed was a preview of the CIO's purge of Communists and Communist-dominated unions after World War II.

I decided that the union movement was great and for many years I felt I'd found a home in life in the CIO. I really thought they would change the country. I thought the CIO was the answer to everything at that time, but, of course, the employers never give up.

When they hadn't been able to starve, beat, shoot, and kill the workers into submission, they started another tactic to divide and split. They started out the red scare within the union. And this always goes on. I've seen the red scare used for many, many years. Looking back, I can see that it was the employers, the

FBI, and the INS—the Immigration and Naturalization Service—that caused all the trouble.

The split happened almost right away. Two sections grew up in the woodworkers' union, the right and left wing they were called. Of course, by this time there were all these rivalries between people that had ability and wanted to be in top office in the union and they sometimes would fall for this stuff. There were a lot of extremely ambitious right wingers in the Oregon area and they were more interested in consolidating their power in the union than in organizing the rest of the unorganized woodworkers.

I remember being at a district council meeting of the woodworkers' union when a lot of red baiting was going on from the floor. A delegate from the local in Seaside got up and he said, "If a war ever breaks out between the reds and the nonreds, here's one that's going red." All the loggers that were in the meeting just clapped and roared with approval when he said that!

The left locals were mostly in the state of Washington. The Portland local had a number of left wingers in it, most of them ex-IWWs, but there were a lot of right wingers. Needless to say, the faction I was specifically with was the left faction.

For a long time, we had a very large and very active women's auxiliary, and the women's auxiliary was quite progressive. I was the president for three terms. The right wing came into an auxiliary meeting and said they were taking over and they ordered us to hold another election and get rid of me.

Well, it's to the women's credit that they told the men it was none of their business. They had got very well educated and organized during the strike and the lockout. In fact, they helped to win the lockout. They held an election and I was reelected by one vote. But, considering that the men had come in and demanded I be got rid of, it was quite a victory in a way.

I was the head of the *Timber Worker* office in Oregon then too, doing all the Oregon news. The Ray Becker articles led to it.

These two jokers from the Portland local, Ernie Young and Ted Andrews, prominent members of the right wing and the Columbia River District Council—at *this* point, the right wing was in control of the Columbia River District—came up to my office and they said, "We could arrange so that you could always work for the *Timber Worker.* We like what you write." (Well, you know, I always corn things up a bit and put human interest things in. I don't see why a labor paper has to be so damned dull.) "You give us just a little bit of help in telling us which ones belong to the CP."

Actually, at that time, I only knew of one man who did belong, but I certainly wasn't going to give his name over to them. So I told them, "Well to hell with answering a question like that. I'm not a snitch and never have been one. And to hell with you. Get out of the office. You can't fire me because I've already quit."

I loved that job dearly, on the *Timber Worker,* writing the Oregon news. This was 1940, the struggle between the right and left wing of the IWA in Oregon and Washington had become intense.

These two guys that came up there and made that proposition to me worked at the Eastern-Western Mill. They had been very active in the 1935 strike and had gotten a great deal of food to feed the people with. They had been very dear close friends of mine, especially Ernie Young. He and my husband had been on committees and he and his wife had been many times in my house.

He came back into the office about an hour later where I was picking up my possessions to leave. He was crying and he says, "How can you? You've been our sister." And I think he used the word comrade, though he was the opposite of a Communist. He says, "How can you say goodbye to us like this?" And I felt bad too and I started to cry also.

You know, people that you've been through a strike with—the lockout lasted eight and a half months and the strike lasted three months—the ties and the bonds you form then are stronger than any others you could ever have in life. You never forget it. And there am I, a left winger, and there's Ernie Young, a right winger, and we're both crying.

But that was it. I loved the woodworkers' union and it's still my favorite union. Leaving the union was harder than leaving Butch. It was the great love of my life.

Many of Julia's colleagues in the union movement were not native born. They were particularly vulnerable during the red scare.

Well, the Immigration and Naturalization Service started in putting deportation proceedings against left wingers. They deported some to Canada and some to other countries, including the Scandinavian countries. This is before World War II.

The point came [in 1940] when Harold Pritchett, the president of the woodworkers' union, couldn't get back in from Canada. The Department of Immigration, which has always worked with employers to smash up the organizations of the working people, wouldn't let Harold Pritchett in anymore.

So the leadership of the union passed from liberal and left-wing lines to right-wing lines. It got so bad that they put a deal in their constitution that if you had ever been a Communist—and to be a Communist usually meant to be *suspected* of being a Communist—that you couldn't hold office in the IWA.[18]

They kicked some people out of the union and two of their leaders in the state of Washington were sent to that awful prison on McNeill Island, framed and charged with being Communists. Those were very unhappy times for me because I don't believe in that sort of stuff.

The red hunt within the unions was not instigated solely by conservative union leadership and the INS. The Labor Management Act of 1947, better known as the Taft-Hartley Act, passed over President Harry Truman's veto, effectively removed radicals from union office. Section 9 (h) required that in order for a union to have the right to use the National Labor Relations Board, each of its officers had to sign an affidavit that he or she was not a member or affiliate of the Communist Party and did not believe in, was not a member of, nor supported any organization that believed in or taught the overthrow of the U.S. government "by force or by any illegal or unconstitutional methods."[19]

In 1952 or somewhere about then, I was sitting at the press table because I wrote for Federated Press, and some joker from Forest Grove, which was always the right-wing IWA local, got up and said, "There's a woman sitting at the press table that's a Commie pink," or something like that, and he moved I be thrown out.

Quite a few people got up and talked against it. Some man I didn't know at all from the Middle West District got up and defended freedom of the press. He was damn good. Because that's what was at issue there really, not me. I was sitting at the press table beside the *Oregonian* reporter, and he was a good guy. He was completely apolitical, but he was a goddamn good objective news writer, just was after the story. He asked me a great deal about my connections with the woodworkers' union. I told him how I got my teeth knocked out on one of their picket lines and a few other things and he started to write all this stuff up.

Well, then it came to a vote. Al Hartung—he was president of the union at this time and I really think he was in favor of kicking me out, but as president he didn't say that—he just merely took the vote and the overwhelming majority voted I'd stay in.

So this joker from Forest Grove got up and he objected. He said, "I've got to have the floor on it again. They've got to rescind that and throw her out, 'cause I don't think people realize just what she is."

I thought Hartung would break his gavel, he beat it so hard on the podium. He said, "Shut up. The rank and file has spoken. Sit down." That was good, I really enjoyed that. Nevertheless, I was deeply hurt because after all I felt that I had grown up in the IWA.

The next time I saw Al Hartung was during the height of the Vietnam War. He was already retired as international president. I had helped form, with members of the Amalgamated Clothing Workers and the ILWU, a Labor for Peace Committee. We had sent invitations to come to our meeting to a great many union locals and union officials and Al Hartung came to the meeting. When I walked into the room and saw him sitting there, I didn't know what to do. I was afraid my presence there would cause him to withdraw from participation. I thought his participation was far more important than mine. But I sat down quietly by the door and he got up and said, "Aren't you going to speak to me?" So we became friends, although he had been a bulwark in the right wing, though not one of its instigators.

Ray Becker (in hat) and Irvin Goodman.

Chapter 6

FREE RAY BECKER

Julia had known about Ray Becker since she was a girl, when her father would ask her to write to Becker in prison, but it wasn't until 1936 that she decided to try to get him out. Ray was a Wobbly. He'd been arrested in 1919 along with other Wobblies in Centralia, Washington.

The Centralia Tragedy, or Massacre, as it is more popularly known, occurred on November 11, 1919, the first Armistice Day, the first anniversary of the end of World War I, when the Wobblies of Centralia defended their hall from an attack by the American Legion and in the process killed four legionnaires.

Julia was only twelve in 1919 at the time of the Centralia events, which she later referred to as the "frameup." It took place in the context of nationwide labor unrest when, the challenge of World War I over and faced with inflation after war price controls were removed, workers initiated a wave of protest and were striking more than ever before. A general strike in Seattle in February, called in support of striking shipyard workers, led businessmen to fear the coming of a Bolshevik revolution, an attempt to wrest away their power, as had happened to Russia's elite so recently. One response was the government's creation of a General Intelligence Division in the Justice Department with a mandate to investigate domestic radicals, with the young J. Edgar Hoover at its head. The IWW, with its rhetoric of worker control, was perceived by many as part of the Bolshevik menace.[1]

The history of the IWW in Centralia, Washington, had been one of conflict and expulsion. A thriving town in southwest Washington, about halfway between Seattle and Portland, it was a hiring center for loggers for the nearby forests and therefore a logical site for Wobbly organizing. But local lumber baron Franklin B. Hubbard wanted the town to be Wobbly free.

In April 1918, during the parade culminating Centralia's Red Cross fund drive, someone called out, "Let's raid the IWW Hall!" as the marchers neared the Wobblies' hall. The crowd rushed forward, smashed windows, carted off furniture, auctioned some of it right there in the street, and made a bonfire with the rest. Then they grabbed the Wobblies they'd found inside and dumped them over the county line.[2]

But the Wobblies returned to Centralia in the fall of 1919 and rented space down the street from their former hall. Within a month, Hubbard called a meeting at which the town's businessmen formed the Centralia Citizens Protective Association "to combat I.W.W. activities in this vicinity." After the newly formed American Legion post announced a parade for November 11, the first Armistice Day, the Protective Association called a meeting, after which a secret action committee was formed. By early November a raid on the IWW hall was being talked about openly in town. Britt Smith, the local Wobbly organizer, visited Elmer Smith, the only lawyer in Centralia sympathetic to the IWW, who advised him the Wobblies had a right to defend their property.[3]

As the Wobblies feared, the Armistice Day parade halted in front of their hall. When several legionnaires ran to the front door and began kicking it in, the Wobblies, who had been waiting inside and in two buildings across the street, started shooting.[4] Three legionnaires, Warren Grimm, Arthur McElfresh, and Ben Cassagranda, were mortally wounded in the crossfire. A mob quickly armed itself and went after the Wobblies. Some were found hiding inside the hall. Others tried to escape. Wobbly Wesley Everest ran out the back door and was chased into the nearby river, where, stopped by the swift current, he turned and shot his closest pursuer, Dale Hubbard. Everest was captured, dragged back through town, nearly lynched on the way, and finally taken to jail, where he joined several other Wobblies and lawyer Elmer Smith. As news of the deaths of all four legionnaires got out, a roundup of Wobblies and suspected Wobblies commenced, until 22 men crowded the jail. At 7:30 that evening the lights in Centralia went out. A mob broke into the jail, dragged Wesley Everest out, drove him to a bridge, and lynched him.

Ten Wobblies were indicted for conspiring to kill Warren Grimm, one of the legionnaires shot at the door of the hall. Lawyer Elmer Smith was indicted with them. They stood trial from January 25 to March 13, 1920. Witnesses for the defense were threatened and told what to say beforehand by legionnaires. Some who persisted in testifying for the defense were immediately arrested for perjury. Prosecution attorneys coached at least one witness with the prosecutor in attendance.[5]

The jury wasn't allowed to visit the scene of the incident. They were told a large band of IWWs was hiding in the hills. Several jurors claimed juror Harry Sellers had said, in essence, "They ought to be hung whether they're guilty of murder or not." Other jurors felt the defendants were innocent but were afraid to acquit them. As

juror Carl O. Hulten put it, "One man had been lynched; they might lynch others."
These jurors could have hung the jury, but fearing the next jury might be less sym-
pathetic, they settled on a conviction of second-degree murder for seven defendants
and acquitted two, so the two could work for the freedom of their fellows.[6]

Though the jurors weren't allowed to see the statute book to determine the sen-
tence for second-degree murder, they signed a petition for leniency and believed the
defendants would get two to five years.[7] But Eugene Barnett, John Lamb, Bert
Bland, O. C. Bland, James McInerney, Ray Becker, and Britt Smith were sentenced
to 25 to 40 years. As early as 1922 some jurors had signed affidavits that they be-
lieved the defendants were not guilty. In August 1925 seven jurors petitioned Wash-
ington governor Roland H. Hartley for the immediate release of the prisoners. The
following month jurors called on the governor. This was followed by letters from six
jurors pleading for a pardon, all to no immediate avail. McInerney died in prison in
1930; five accepted parole in the early thirties. Finally only one man remained in
the Washington Penitentiary at Walla Walla: Ray Becker.

Becker was still imprisoned because he refused parole; he wanted a pardon and
nothing less. Over the years there had been considerable public support for the pris-
oners through the Centralia Publicity Committee, the International Labor Defense,
and the Centralia Liberation Committee, but by 1934, only the American Civil
Liberties Union was still involved with Becker's case.[8]

As soon as the mills all were organized in Portland, I decided that there were
enough ex-IWWs in that union that we might be able to get Ray Becker out of
prison if we organized a Free Ray Becker Committee (FRBC). I said to Butch
that we had got to get the Woodworkers to pick up that case.

So we went before the executive board and they agreed to help set up a defense committee headquartered in Portland. We had quite a large committee,
the Free Ray Becker Committee. There were educators, lawyers, labor leaders. I
went around and solicited all these people to be on the committee. The man
who was then an official in the Association of Firefighters and at one time was
the vice president of the AFL State Federation of Labor and was an ex-IWW, S.
P. Stevens, was the chairman of that committee and I was the secretary.

We were asking for a congressional inquiry into the case. However, that was
merely a device to get publicity, because we believed that publicity was the key
that would unlock the jail cell doors.

As much as she wanted to see Becker free, Julia also wanted to expose the frameup
that had sent him to prison. She felt his case was "representative of the tactics used
by all operators who connive with unscrupulous public officials in time of labor

disputes, to frame innocent men. . . . a congressional *investigation of this case would set a valuable precedent in labor defense work."*[9]

Julia took advantage of the IWA's newspaper, the Timber Worker, *to inform the union about Ray Becker. In August 1936 Julia wrote a news story for the* Timber Worker *reporting that the Portland local of the Lumber and Sawmill Workers had endorsed the call for a congressional investigation. The Columbia River District Council and the Portland Central Labor Council had done so earlier. She used every article to educate the woodworkers on the case and its relevance to the union movement.*

> The stand taken by Becker and his comrades . . . was a stand against the unwarranted raiding of union halls all over the Northwest, a stand for constitutional rights of free speech and free assembly, and a stand for the inherent right of workers to organize into unions of their own choosing.[10]

The committee sold *Ray Becker* buttons and horsehair belts that Ray made in Walla Walla. Members of our committee who were good speakers, like Stevens, went before union groups and made a pitch for support. Resolutions were passed and money collected to hire lawyers and pay traveling expenses of investigators the committee sent to Centralia and elsewhere.

I was one of the investigators. I was driven about Lewis and Grays Harbor Counties [Centralia is in Lewis County. The trial was moved to Montesano in Grays Harbor County] by the late L. L. Dietz, a former Wobbly from Grays Harbor. We went to the law office of the man who had been Elmer Smith's law partner during the last years of Elmer's life. He refused to let us remove the files from his office. We saw it would take several weeks to go through them and put them in order. They weren't doing any good there collecting cobwebs so, when he went out to lunch, we loaded the box in the back of Mr. Dietz's truck and took off.

There were many leads in there. There was the complete list of the lynchers of Wesley Everest. There were many tips about people that knew things that were pertinent to the case. So after I had waded through all those papers, I went to Centralia and moved into a very cheap hotel. I stayed there for some weeks interviewing all the people that were mentioned. I found that many people having knowledge of the case remembered vividly the persecution and ostracism to which they had been subjected in 1919 and 1920 and that they still lived in what might be described as a state of terror. Some of these people refused to say a word about the matter; others spoke to me in confidence or with the greatest caution and reserve; still others talked freely but refused to sign affidavits for fear of reprisal from "the other side." Several of the affidavits I did secure contained what they admitted were only partial statements of the fact. I repeatedly found people not at home, in spite of the fact that I had made appointments to see them. On several occasions, persons who had previously promised to make statements declined to do so, saying they had been "advised or warned to keep quiet."

I followed this procedure during my trips: I would recontact friends and good contacts made on the last trip, letting it be known I was back in town, staying at my cheap hotel, that I would be there with my rented or borrowed typewriter between certain hours each day, writing up my notes. It was surprising how many persons came to see me, or left unsigned notes under my hotel room door. The rest of the day I would go out, trying to verify reports, interviewing people, checking, rechecking, and cross-checking stories told me.

I shall always remember my surprise at the impact time has upon the personalities of the people; how the part individuals had played, when they were younger—cruel, brave, criminal, or merely weak—had colored their lives, their family relationships—and the pity I felt (unwillingly, it is true) for several who had once played very discreditable roles.

One man asked me again and again to try to understand why he could not sign an affidavit admitting what he himself had done and what he "knew," because of the suffering and shame this would bring to a family he had not had at that time, and who knew nothing of his connection with the events.

Even more moving, of course, was the courage and dignity revealed in some of the stories told me, as those who had been participants in another way in the tragedy, who had been beaten, lost jobs, been jailed, related their accounts of those happenings.

Some were what are known as very simple people. Of all the jurors, I was most deeply impressed by Mr. Hulten. As I recall, he had come down from his remote place of residence at Lake Quinalt, by prearrangement to meet me in Aberdeen. He insisted on taking me into the dining room of the best hotel for lunch and on paying for the lunch. He was very simply dressed but he had immense dignity, and I shall never remember anything as moving as his saying to me: "Saying he is afraid is not what a man can say—it would take a long time to say to yourself; if you were a man you would know this." Then he looked at me, while I sat at the table with its dazzlingly white cloth and fine silver, hardly breathing, and at last he said, "I have said it to myself and now it can go on your paper."

He was not a man who possessed what is sometimes glibly described as "political understanding," as P. V. Johnson was (the man who almost hung the jury, and who knew exactly what it was all about). It must have come to Mr. Hulten slowly over the years: the fear that he had been afraid, the gradual perception of what actually had happened in Montesano.

I have no idea what was his financial situation; he was solid, heavy, and dark, very simply dressed. He looked like a farmer or fisherman; I thought perhaps he was part Indian. He seemed to derive great pleasure from buying me such a fine and expensive lunch. I shall remember him always, with his knarled, weather-darkened hands moving with grace over the white cloth; his almost courtly manners in such contrast to his appearance and the careful way in which he spoke, as if he had thought out every word in advance.

P. V. Johnson was the juror I came to know best. He suffered more from guilt than anyone I have ever known. It had caused him to leave Grays Harbor County and go to Portland, but even there he sometimes fancied people "might know he was the one who sent them all to prison" (since he had finally given in on the jury), so he had retreated into an almost inaccessible spot in the forest, far from any road, between Scappoose and Vernonia, Oregon. There he had carved out a sort of homestead in the wild, packing in on his back things he could not make.

I sometimes thought P. V. Johnson would gladly have traded places with Ray Becker, finding what he considered his proper penance in so doing. He had been brought up in the Lutheran faith, and much of it was still with him. He had been a union member and was also, I suspected, a Wobbly sympathizer. He had tried in vain to think of "what he had done" in hanging the jury for such a long time as a noble action; and still had moments of insisting to himself, or so he once told me, that "this was what saved them from first degree." To me he was a Hamlet in a red plaid shirt.

It all hinged on whether the hall was raided, which it was, before there was any shooting. Two of the men who had testified for the prosecution—and one of them at the time he signed an affidavit for the defense committee was a state representative at Olympia [Clyde Tisdale]—signed affidavits admitting their testimony was not true. Witnesses that I interviewed changed their testimony.

One of the most interesting pieces of evidence we got onto was this young man who had been out at the bridge where they lynched Wesley Everest. He was quite young at the time. He had participated only indirectly in the lynching; he didn't actually hang him off the bridge or shoot him full of holes. He cried as he was telling the story. He was at this time a member of an IWA local in Centralia.

He was terrified if he signed an affidavit testifying all that went on at the bridge that his local union might find out about it and he might be kicked out. I assured him that we wouldn't use his affidavit unless it was necessary. Privately

I had so little faith in the courts that I didn't think we were ever going to get Ray Becker's case into the courts.

We also got an affidavit, and it was a first-class affidavit and one of the ones I didn't get because we considered it was too important for a novice like me to be writing it up, so we sent Cliff O'Brien, a Portland attorney, to the California town where I had traced this man was living, so he could reinterview him. He was in the car that took Wesley Everest out to the bridge. It was a very strong affidavit.

One of the names [in the files] was of the young IWW [Tom Morgan] who at nineteen had turned states' evidence. I traced what had become of him. He was living in Eureka, California. I found him and persuaded him to sign an affidavit admitting why he had done it and that he regretted it very much and things he'd testified to in court weren't true.

Morgan told Julia that while he was in jail "he was subjected to a 'third degree.' That a group of legionnaires . . . twisted his wrist and threatened him with hanging" if he didn't say what they wanted him to say. If he cooperated, "he understood . . . he would be released from jail and that he would not be tried, with the I.W.W.'s, for murder." In his affidavit he said he was also told by one of the prosecuting attorneys that a conviction would be better for the Wobblies since otherwise they would be lynched.[11]

Morgan told me that during the past four years he had kept moving, in the hope that he could finally throw that gang off his trail. During our drive from Eureka to Arcata to the lawyer's office to sign the affidavit, he appeared to be very nervous and seemed to think we might be "taking him for a ride." He quieted down somewhat after he had signed the affidavit and said, "I'm glad to get that off my chest" but expressed the belief that "they'll learn about this and get me no matter where I go."[12]

One of the affidavits that we had, which was very damaging to the prosecution, was from a man who was a veteran of World War I. He was in uniform when he heard there was going to be this meeting at the Elks Club—that was after the lynching—and he went to this meeting. They were drilled by C. D. Cunningham, who acted as the attorney that prosecuted the men at the trial, in where they were to say they stood when these events happened.

I interviewed all of the living jurors. They were the most impressive affidavits, admitting how frightened they were and that they didn't believe he was guilty at the time, but they were afraid to do anything else but bring in a verdict of guilty.

P. V. Johnson, the last juror to hold out for acquittal, said he finally gave in "because he believed he would be endangering his life if he held out any longer . . . he believed in fact that he would be lynched by the legionnaires if he held out for such acquittal."[13]

Ray Becker took up a strategy of reopening his case through habeas corpus proceedings. Five jurors, including Johnson, went to Walla Walla on February 2, 1936, to testify at one of his habeas corpus hearings along with lawyer Irvin Goodman, Julia, Communist Party member Dawn Lovelace, and—unbeknownst to the others—an undercover National Guard spy. At the hearing the next day the judge refused to hear the habeas corpus proceedings, accepting the state's argument that there was no proof the jurors were intimidated during the trial.[14]

P. V. Johnson went with us to Walla Walla to visit Ray Becker. That was quite a meeting between the two. For P. V. Johnson it was as if he was getting forgiven for all of his sins, and Ray Becker was very forgiving.

Ray wanted to come out and sue the State of Washington and that's why he refused to come out on parole. He wanted complete vindication. Of course, he was right, but that was very idealistic, which he was, of course. He was the son of a minister. He was such an idealist it was hard to deal with him.

We hired attorneys. Every time we got an attorney, he would go over and talk to Ray, and if things didn't move fast enough, Ray would demand that attorney be fired. He fired the committee, you know. He didn't fire me or S. P. Stevens, the chairman of the committee, but he fired the Ray Becker Committee. We did file an appeal in one of the Washington courts, but just as we had thought, it came to nothing. There were still many people in the state of Washington that didn't want all that stuff to come out.

In April 1936, two months after the ill-fated court appearance, attorney Irvin Goodman wrote Ray to explain the FRBC's analysis and strategy of organizing "a broad united front" to pressure the governor to release him. He told Ray he was a political prisoner and that his "case belongs to the working class . . . the working class must procure your release."[15]

Ray remained adamant, his strategy unchanged. That summer he wrote Julia reiterating that he was unwilling to accept anything less than complete vindication. A year later, in May 1937, when a particular judge wasn't available for a month for a habeas corpus hearing Ray demanded, he wrote Julia an angry letter accusing the committee of playing him for a chump for accepting a postponement until the judge was available and disowned the FRBC.[16]

Frustrated by his lack of cooperation and confidence in the committee, Julia sent Ray a letter of resignation. However, by the following October Ray seems to have for-

given Julia, as he sent her gifts he had made in prison. At the same time he wrote her he had fired another of the lawyers the committee had found for him. He was tired of his "stalling tactics." In the meantime, Julia and the FRBC continued to work for Ray's release.[17]

I'll never forget the day that Steve [S. P. Stevens] and I went to see the lieutenant governor, Victor A. Meyers. We went up in the cupola, I guess you'd call it, of the statehouse with him. You could look out over the city, and up there's when we told him what we were gonna do, for him to take back to his superiors—because he was a liberal, but the governor was not. We showed him some of the affidavits and we told him we had much more material and we were going to make them all public and a lot of heads would fall. And he agreed to take that message.

It wasn't too long after that that they commuted Becker's sentence. He was unhappy about it and they had to drag him out of prison. Commutation was better than getting paroled because a commutation of sentence doesn't say either way. But what he wanted was a full pardon. Then he wanted to sue the people who had put him there. You know it was completely unrealistic in terms of what the politics were like at this time. All together he was in for twenty years, because I remember that "Twenty Years in a Stone Cell" was the title of one article I wrote about him.

On September 20, 1939, Governor Martin commuted Ray Becker's sentence to time served: eighteen years and three months; however, counting from the time of his arrest, Becker was imprisoned over nineteen years and ten months.

Washington state senator Mary Farquharson, who had been working for Becker's freedom through the American Civil Liberties Union, and the Reverend Fred Shorter, minister of Seattle's Pilgrim Congregational Church, picked Ray up at the prison in Walla Walla. Shorter had been a member of one of the earlier defense committees, the Centralia Liberation Committee, a Seattle committee in which labor and religious leaders were active in the 1920s. Farquharson was nervous about how Ray would receive them and was relieved when he told her he was planning to go to New York. He wanted to visit friends in Portland first, so the three of them traveled to Portland by train. Julia was among those waiting there.[18]

I remember the day that Ray Becker got off the train. This same afternoon there was a meeting of the large Portland local. Quite a large committee of loggers that belonged to the IWA were down at the station. We took him over there to the union hall where the meeting was held. The loggers hiring hall was only a short distance. As we're walking down Sixth Street from the station—he'd been in there all those years and the traffic frightened him so—he ran down an alley. He was just terrified, like a frightened animal.

Ray was taken by the loggers into the meeting. I can still see him walking down the aisle to the platform escorted by two of the officials of the local.

He had a great deal of courage because he went before all of the union groups, including the Portland Central Labor Council—which had supported his release and even ponied up some dough towards paying the bills—and spoke and thanked them. There was money left in his defense fund and he donated that to the organizing fund of the IWA.

We held a banquet to celebrate Ray's return, but the bitterness between the AFL and CIO was so great that Paul Gurske, an official in the FRBC, was the only AFL official that would come to the banquet. The others were afraid.

Ray stayed with Butch and me for several months. He had learned various trades in prison, including the making of jewelry and leather goods. We had no car, so he set up a shop in our garage. He taught my son Mike, who was then maybe ten or eleven years old, how to do some of this work that he did.

There was this wealthy man in New York, Robertson Trowbridge, that had become interested in the IWW at the time they were sent to Leavenworth for opposing World War I. He'd contributed to the old Centralia Defense Committee. He'd become interested in Ray and they corresponded. He had sent Ray a great many books. He invited Ray to come back and stay with him. So Ray went back and stayed with Trowbridge for three or four months.[19]

You know, Ray Becker took my novel, "The Wolf at the Door," back to New York with him and the rich man showed it to the editors of Random House. Bennett Cerf wrote a letter. He said he had set up all night reading it. He said he and two of his editors that he'd gotten to read it decided that it was too long and should be edited. He didn't think I was an experienced enough writer to do that but he urged it be sent to other publishers and probably one of them would publish it. By the time I got this letter, I'd lost all interest in it.

Then Ray came back to Portland and that's when he set up his store over in Vancouver, Washington, and sold these belts and things that he made. Well, then he bought a log cabin on a little piece of land south of Portland and had set himself up in business there, making the stuff he made and he died out there. He was found dead [in 1950].

He just really had nothing left when he didn't have his case. His whole life had been spent in the effort to get out, so he just had nothing left to hang on to or be interested in.

Jail had an extraordinary effect on him. It does on most men. He could never get out of the habit of collecting bits of string, he had a big roll with him all the time. And he had an awful time with money. The police claimed that when they found his body there was over $700 in cash in the house, which they described as unbelievably filthy, the money strewn about.

His real name was Ralph Burgdorf, and just prior to the incident in Centralia he'd done time for resisting the draft. I think, in fact, he'd escaped. What was so special about him was that, looking at him or talking to him, you'd never believe he'd done these things.

His family had nothing whatever to do with him when he was in prison, but after his death—of course, it was in all the newspapers—his brother appeared to claim his money. His brother had always known he was in prison, but he'd never done anything. His brother took charge of the body and also of his little bank account. We tried to insist that we be allowed to give him a public funeral, but all the brother would agree to was that his body could lie in state in the undertaking parlor and we could go over there to visit him.

So I took a red rose over there. I went with the secretary of the woodworkers' union and some other IWWs and I put this rose in his buttonhole, because in the old IWW and Socialist funerals over the years, they always put a red rose in their button hole.

Chapter 7

YOU CAN'T TELL ABOUT PEOPLE

Julia didn't have the best luck with husbands; she was divorced three times. She didn't tell me about her first marriage, when she was so young her mother had to sign her acquiescence, and asked her brother to leave it out of the family genealogy. She never denied her marriage to Butch Bertram—her child and her involvement with the woodworkers came out of it—but she said she soon recognized it was a mistake, though they didn't separate permanently until 1940 after fourteen years of marriage. Her third marriage, to Ben Eaton, was also omitted from her brother's genealogy, at her request, but she admitted it to me, though it was short-lived.

My father said it would be perfectly ethical to steal from a banker because they are the biggest thieves in the country. "But," he said, "no one but a fool tries to rob a bank. They're always caught." And he said, "I never want to think I've raised up a daughter to be a fool." That always was stuck in my mind. My father also had taught me that the worst kind of stealing was to steal from your fellow worker. That was absolutely unconscionable.

When we were living in Linnton, there was a woman named Mrs. [Nora] Olsen that ran a small family grocery store. During the lockouts and layoffs, she extended the credit of her customers. I was in the store with Butch one day when there was no work at the mill and when we came out of the store he showed me some items he had stolen.

I tried to get him to take them back, but he wouldn't. I took them back and had them added to our bill. I said, "When my husband took his things, I'm not sure that he told you to put them on the bill. He was in a big hurry." She said, "Well, I'm sure that he must have and I forgot to do it because he's one of the nicest men I have ever met." That's how he was: charming.

And he took to drinking. He became an alcoholic. Well, he had done a good deal of drinking in his life, but you know we had prohibition. Anyway, he got so he would go down to the Japanese bunkhouse. Very few people at West Oregon would associate with the Japanese except Butch and myself, because the IWW—at least he had learned that much—they didn't discriminate.

The Japanese made rice wine, sake, and he took to drinking with them. He just drank more and more. And then he got so he wouldn't go to work if he was drunk or he'd go to work drunk. He was always very popular with the men and they would hide him back of the lumber pile and do his work for him until he sobered up.

We had moved to St. Johns. You had to live at the mill before the union, but after we won the strike in 1935, you didn't have to live in those dreadful company houses anymore. I found out that when he was drinking and didn't come home on weekends, he sometimes went to . . . he was so good-looking women were just crazy about him. So I thought, "My God, I'm gonna end up catching gonorrhea or syphilis." I just told him to leave [in 1940].

Then in 1943, he was arrested in connection with a disturbance that he caused trying to get into the house in which I was living. The neighbors called the police and when they looked up—you know they got all those stupid police files—they found out that he was wanted in connection with an unsolved murder in Michigan.[1]

Dr. Equi read about Butch in the paper and she called up her personal private attorney—I think his name was Charlie Robison—and she sent him down to get Butch out of jail. She did this because he was an ex-IWW and because she was sympathetic to people who were being framed. And she felt that he was being framed.

So Robison went down there and in the meantime Butch had confessed that he had shot this man in an argument in a card room. The man was cheating at cards, so he had shot him and subsequently this man died. All the evidence, so called, had disappeared because the courthouse in Miles, Michigan, where this had happened, had burned down. So Robison got him out. Butch was very grateful to Dr. Equi. He used to go up there a great deal and see her.

Sometimes I think I would have left Butch before I did but I'd fallen in love with the IWA, his union, and I had started to work for their newspaper. So I don't regret the last part of my life with Butch. I learned a great many things from him before he became an absolute alcoholic, and he was a good union man.

In 1952 Julia learned from her son, Mike, who had stayed in touch with his father, that Butch had remarried and was living in Washington State. He died in Portland in 1975.[2]

Julia rarely mentioned Ben Eaton and if she did it was to explain what a hypocrite he was. She disliked even the memory of him, so much so that she usually referred to him as "my second husband," avoiding his name altogether.

Julia and Ben were married in May of 1943, the same week as her divorce from Butch was granted. In November 1946, at their divorce hearing, Julia testified they had been separated a year and a half. Julia usually said they separated after two or three months, but the divorce record implies two years.[3]

I met Ben at the old Governor Building, which was CIO headquarters. He was a seaman when I first met him. He belonged to the Sailor's Union of the Pacific. He was an intellectual and he was very interesting to talk to and he was tall. Since I was so short, I always liked tall men. And then, as he was spending a great deal of time out on ships, I didn't see him very often. After we got married, he came ashore to work. He had good ideas and he was a great reader, but he was absolutely a terrible person. We were married a couple of months when I began to see it was a dreadful mistake.

During World War II in order to get meat you had to have red stamps, and when you used up your red stamps you couldn't get any more meat. Now this man was of English descent—one reason why I've always disliked the English is because I was married to him—and they need their meat. One time he heard of a place where you could get meat even if you didn't have any red stamps. So I went there with him and with his mother and stepfather to eat.

We'd been served when I noticed this sign that says "white trade only" on the wall back of the cash register. So I said, "We'll have to leave."

He said, "Well, I'm not going to leave until I finish this food."

So we were sitting in a booth, the four of us, and it was the booth nearest the door, so I just scrambled out over the top of the booth and left. I left without him. Hypocrite. He thought it was pretty silly when we'd already ordered the food and some of it had been served. He thought we should have eaten it and I shouldn't have made a scene. You can't tell about people.

This incident was the only story about Ben Julia readily related. And she told the story with the implication that she not only left him and his mother and stepfather in the restaurant, but that she left the marriage at that time as well. In fact, when she first told me this story in March of 1984, after she said she scrambled out over the top of the booth and left, she said, "And that was the end of that."

I asked, "The end of the meal or the end of the marriage?"

"Both," she said.

"You left him then?"

"Sure."

"Really, right then?" Even for Julia, this was very dramatic.

"Yes."

Almost exactly three years later, in March 1987, Julia admitted she had not left Ben just because of the restaurant incident but had thrown him out shortly after.

When we got married, he moved into the house I had been renting. I had my son's cat. The bathtub in that bathroom had claws; it didn't go to the floor. He used to take this umbrella and drive the cat under this bathtub and poke at it.

I went in the bathroom and told him, "Let the cat alone." I said, "Don't you ever dare frighten that cat again or chase it under the bathtub." So he grabbed hold of me and threw me down and beat me up. I think he would have killed me if I hadn't had the sense to pretend I was dead.

I was still lying on the floor when he went out the front door. Ben's mother and stepfather lived about three or four doors down. I called up his mother and told her I was going to throw all of his stuff out in the street and she'd better come over and get it. And I threw his stuff out. I moved out of that house into another house in a different part of town.

He was determined that I wasn't going to divorce him. He used to follow me and sometimes I had to climb out a kitchen window and go through my neighbors' backyard to get the bus I took to work. I got a separate maintenance order ordering him to stay away from my house. He broke into the house and he raped me. So I had an abortion.

I called up Dr. Equi and she sent me to a man that did abortions here in Portland. It was still illegal. He had not only an office, but he had a regular little hospital there with nurses. He gave an anesthetic; they put you to sleep. He knew what he was doing. He kept people that had abortions there overnight to be sure there was no difficulty. So that experience was very different from the first one.

It was after Dr. Equi had quit, but when I explained to her all the trouble I had had, she sent me to this place.

Dr. Equi ceased her active practice in 1931.[4] In trying to determine where Equi sent Julia and who the abortionist was, I consulted Rickie Solinger, author of a book about abortion in Portland before Roe v. Wade.

"I don't think the reference could have been to [Dr.] Watts since he left Portland in the late thirties," Solinger wrote me, "but it certainly sounds as if it could have been him, otherwise. Are you sure of the dating?" she asked.[5]

When Julia first admitted she'd had abortions, she told me she'd had three. But when and who were the men involved? Solinger's response added weight to my suspicion that Julia was not being completely honest, that she'd had an abortion in Portland in the 1930s. When I questioned her further, the stories only became more contradictory.

Once she said, "I don't want to discuss my third abortion because it was my fault I got pregnant." She went on to say it was after her divorce from Ben and the man didn't live in this country and when she found out she was pregnant he had already returned home. Later she told me she'd gotten pregnant during her marriage to Ben, he hadn't wanted a child, and she'd had her second abortion then. She said the third was when Ben raped her. I reminded her of the story she'd told me of the foreigner. She said, "I must have made all that up. I don't remember telling you that."

Then immediately she said, "Well, now, I'll tell you the truth. The third abortion, I wasn't sure who was the father because I had a brief love affair with a member of the woodworkers' union who was a Canadian, and he had spent the early part of the evening with me, and later the same evening Ben came and broke into the house and raped me. So that was it." And she said the good abortionist had gone to California and Equi referred her to another doctor.

If her second abortion took place at Dr. Watts' clinic, it was before she married Ben. As part of the discussion of leaving her husband Butch, Julia had said, "Well, I had become quite interested in another man that I'd met in the union world. That's an episode in my life I don't really regret either. I learned a great deal from him about unions. He belonged to a different union, an AFL union, and he was interested in the Centralia case. I knew it was a dead end when I embarked on it. I did learn a lot from him about how unions function that weren't mass-production unions."

I believe Julia is describing S. P. Stevens, the president of the firefighters' union, an AFL union that wasn't a mass-production union. He was, with Julia, coleader of the FRBC in the late 30s before Dr. Watts left town. Both Julia and Stevens were married, i.e., a dead end. Julia was very secretive concerning this affair and when I pressed for more, she said, "Subject's off limits." I believe her second abortion was then, when she was married to Butch and having an affair with Stevens. Her third abortion still confuses me—Ben or the Canadian? There is no way to know.

I didn't intend to get a divorce. Divorces are costly and I didn't have the money. I've always been dreadfully poor. How I happened to divorce him is because I was in the hospital when I had a lump cut out of my breast which was benign.

A number of people came to see me and brought flowers and candy and that sort of stuff. Irvin Goodman came to see me and appeared to be very embarrassed that he hadn't brought me anything. He said, "Well, I'll get you a divorce and it won't cost you a penny, for a get-well present."

When Irv asked me if I wanted alimony, I said, "Hell no, I can support myself. I don't want anything at all from that man except to be rid of him." So that's how come I got a divorce in 1946.[6]

Chapter 8

THEY WERE PARANOID IN THOSE DAYS

In the late thirties, Julia's attention turned to issues of peace and war. Following World War I, many Americans took a dim view of war. That war had promised to "make the world safe for democracy" and to be "the war to end all wars," but public opinion grew to view the war as a gory and senseless slaughter. Religious leaders, women and students, and both the American Socialist and Communist Parties came out strongly against war. A number of large and influential peace organizations were formed, including the American League Against War and Fascism, which ended up under Communist Party control.

But the peace movement began to wane as the rise of fascism in Europe entered the American consciousness. Pacifist groups realized war could not be prevented and focused on keeping America out. Other more conservative organizations shifted to the idea of collective security. The Spanish Civil War ended the Communist Party's pacifism and the Party changed the name of the American League Against War and Fascism to the American League for Peace and Democracy.[1]

The war in Spain was precipitated by the election victory of the Popular Front, an alliance of working-class political parties and left republicans, in February 1936. The new government promised land reform. Landowners were joined by industrialists, the military, and the powerful Catholic church in opposition.

In July, General Francisco Franco led an army revolt against the young Spanish republican government in Spanish Morocco, then invaded Spain itself. Franco's forces received aid in the form of modern arms and soldiers from Fascist Italy and Nazi Germany. President Franklin Delano Roosevelt, bowing to pressure from Catholic voters, said he wanted to de-escalate the war and embargoed aid to Spain, leaving the republicans (or Loyalists) with only the Soviet Union and Mexico to help. The United States was officially noninvolved but "permitted large quantities of oil (a 'non-war' material under the Neutrality Act) to reach the insurgents."[2]

In the United States, support for the Loyalists was centered in the left: liberals, Communists, Socialists, anarchists. Two thousand eight hundred Americans volunteered to go to Spain and fight to defend the elected government. Their unit was called the Abraham Lincoln Brigade. They joined over 30,000 others from 52 countries. One hundred twenty-five American men and women also served with the American Medical Bureau in Spain as nurses, doctors, and ambulance drivers. The North American Committee to Aid Spanish Democracy raised over one million dollars and sent aid in the form of food, clothing, and medical supplies, including 175 ambulances and motor vehicles to aid the Loyalists.[3]

Despite wide international support, the republican forces were badly outnumbered and underequipped. The Spanish republic fell in March 1939. Franco headed a repressive fascist dictatorship until his death in 1975.

The Spanish Civil War, well, that was the big cause célèbre back in the late thirties. It brought people together. There were a great many writers and artists and musicians that were interested in it. I don't think they were all left wing, but they seemed to be interested in the human aspects. Also there were many artists and writers and poets and people of that kind involved in the republican government. I suppose that attracted their fantasy.

I knew a number of people that enlisted in the Abraham Lincoln Brigade and went over there to fight. A member of the IWA died over there in Spain.

I belonged to a committee that was raising money to send an ambulance to Republican Spain [Oregon Committee to Aid Spanish Democracy]. It was a very large committee. I went to the meetings, tried to raise money, harangued my friends, and went to all of the deals where we had speakers that came from Europe. I remember the different ineffectual attempts that several of us made to get the Portland Woodworkers' local to support it. They finally sent someone to a meeting but all they did when he went back was a lot of redbaiting.

There were many speakers that came here. Some had to speak through interpreters. I remember hearing Jay Allen, the internationally known war correspondent. He was born in Oregon and most of Portland turned out to hear him at the Civic Auditorium. At the end of his talk there was questions and answers. Someone asked if the republicans weren't reds and he said, "In the yellow dust of Spain, their blood is red, their blood is red." I'll never forget that.[4]

I remember going to a huge hall with my first husband and we had to sit in different places because it was so crowded. When we took up the collection— he hardly ever was carried away by anything except gambling and drink—he emptied his pockets in the hat and, as I didn't expect him to do that, I emptied my purse. So we had to walk home. We lived in St. Johns; it was quite a long walk from downtown Portland, six or seven miles.

One speaker that we had here was a priest from Spain. Some of the bishops and people like that were with Franco but the priests were with the people.[5] The speakers talked about why the people had gotten tired of things the way they were and why they wished to change. And they talked about the efforts of Mussolini and Franco and Hitler to interfere with what they were doing. They talked about the policies of our government, which were very bad.

The shocking thing about it was that our government refused all of the efforts that were made to stop shipping arms to Franco. So some of the work of the committees was to get the Roosevelt government to stop that stuff. Now, Russia, of course, sent arms to the republicans, but a great many of us felt that Russia should have done more. But I think Russia's position at the time, listening to the hard-liners, was that she couldn't antagonize the West by sending more.

I had no idea that the republicans would lose; it was one of the great shocks of my life. I think a lot of people were more realistic about it than I was. Nevertheless, there's no getting around the fact that that was a prelude to World War II, which I didn't realize at the time.

The left warned that Spain was a trial run by the fascists for World War II. Not only were they ignored, but those who fought for Spain were later called premature antifascists by the red hunters of McCarthyism. It was a code term for Communist.

Once the USSR signed a nonaggression pact with Germany in 1939, the American Communist Party followed the lead of the Soviet Union and launched a peace campaign with the slogan "The Yanks Are Not Coming." Part of the campaign was the founding of the American Peace Mobilization at a mass meeting in Chicago on September 2, 1940, which Julia attended. (After Germany invaded the Soviet Union on June 22, 1941, the Party changed the name of the American Peace Mobilization to American People's Mobilization and began a campaign to support both the Soviet Union and Britain in their struggle against Germany.)[6]

Before we entered into World War II, the left and the more militant unions in this country took a dim view of the war. All of us felt that it was just going to be a way for the armaments makers to make money and to kill off young men. I went to a huge convention-type of meeting in Chicago to protest our entry. Unions all across the country sent enormous delegations to this meeting in Chicago.

It was really a tremendous meeting and it really showed the power labor and the left wing could be if they got it all together. 'Course, it turned out wasn't too long after that that the left and labor became quite involved in World War II.

I remember having an argument with a Jewish attorney here before I went back to that meeting, because he told me that we were crazy. He said he'd spent a great deal of money getting relatives out of Germany that were going to be exterminated. Of course, he was right. You know sometimes it takes a long time to seep into your consciousness what's going on.

Julia had already experienced the red scare in the IWA and CIO, but anticommunism was not confined to unions. In 1938, the House Committee on Un-American Activities was formed to investigate un-American propaganda. In 1939, the FBI began a list of those who were alleged security risks. During World War II, the FBI worked with the military to check out both defense plant workers and federal employees who had been named by informants as disloyal. Thousands were investigated. In December 1942 it was Julia's turn.[7]

I had gone to work out at the civilian depot out at the Army air base testing gyroscopes and other instruments on planes in the Western Air Command in the first part of World War II. I was very poor at the work I did, so poor that the foreman in the instrument shop moved me up to his desk to do the paperwork. He said, "God help the aviator on any plane you'd worked on the instruments." He was quite right too.

The employers have an espionage system. That is why the FBI got the idea, I assume, that I must be a CP member. The foreman of the instrument shop said the FBI had come to see him about me and they wanted me to come down to the FBI office in the Pioneer Post Office Building.

I went down there to see what this was all about. I was quite afraid of the FBI because I thought they might throw me in jail incommunicado. I took the precautions of taking a couple of hefty loggers and even an AFL official that I knew, who had been in the IWW as a young man, with me. They stood outside the door in the hallway. They said if I didn't come out in a certain length of time they'd break the door down and they'd get an attorney.

So I went in there, and God the FBI is stupid! Well, they are. I'm not kidding you. They grilled me about why I was working for the government in that position and about my views and so forth. And they started asking me questions about did I know this person, did I know that person. They had a big stack of documents and anything I ever said or did was in there. They accused me of donating money to the Harry Bridges Defense. I remember saying, "That's a lie. I donated twice that much. Your records are wrong!"

Mostly they were trying to find out about different people. Do I know this person or do I know that person? The person they seemed the most afraid of was Martina Gangle Curl. She's an artist, you know. I said, "Yes, I know her, know her quite well. She's a close friend of mine."

"Did you know that she was a Communist?"

So I said, "Well, judging by the trend of your remarks, that's a serious question and since I have no knowledge of the subject, I'd be doing her and the U.S. government a great disservice to answer at all."

"Well," they said, "would you hazard a guess?"

I said, "No. I don't believe in guessing in serious matters."

They had taken down the stuff I'd said and then they presented this to me and wanted me to sign it and I said, "No, I didn't say some of this stuff," so I wouldn't sign it. In fact I think I managed to grab it and tear part of it up. Eventually the men that was out there started kicking the door, so they let me go.

The FBI was interested in ascertaining Julia's loyalty and her positions on the war and peace. Not surprisingly, they asked her about known and suspected Communists and about her connections with organizations known to be part of or influenced by the Communist Party. The transcript of the interview reveals that Julia's responses during the interview were less heroic than her recollection. Her account is part of the creation of the heroic myth of Julia standing up against the authorities. In reality, it is an interview with a woman who hopes to keep her job.

The transcript, like the rest of Julia's files and all files released by the FBI under the Freedom of Information/Privacy Acts (FOIPA), has deletions—black slashes that do not yield to an eraser. The most commonly cited reason for censorship in Julia's file is that the release of the information "could reasonably be expected to constitute an unwarranted invasion of personal privacy."

Q: Are you a member of the American Peace Mobilization?
B: I am not now a member of the American Peace Mobilization.
Q: Were you at one time?
B: I went to their peace conference at Chicago. At this time I believed that peace could be maintained and that the United States could be kept out of war. I am not a pacifist, but I do not like war, but sometimes war is inevitable and then we have to fight. . . . I am not at all ashamed of having been for peace. . . .
Q: . . . When did you become for war and cease to be for peace?

B: Well, it was a sort of gradual growth of things going on all over the world. My ancestors were Irish, and it didn't seem to me like we should pull the British chestnuts out of the fire, if you understand what I mean. It seemed to me that this country suffered enough in the last war and our boys were killed, and the oceans seemed wide, but they are not really wide any more, and Hitler got worse and worse, and since England and France didn't stop him it seemed to me we could. But things just kept building up and getting worse and Hitler kept getting further. . . . I began to see that the war was getting closer to us. Then Russia was invaded and I always thought that Germany was afraid of Russia. . . . and then there was Pearl Harbor. You just can't sit back and not fight then. By that time the accumulation of all these things, and it seemed to me that the man England now has was different, and after Pearl Harbor the war was here. When you are attacked you fight back. . . .

Q: When did you change your mind? . . . There must have been a date. . . .

B: . . . I suppose you might say that December 7 was when my last ideas that peace could be maintained were destroyed. But actually before that I had begun to doubt that wisdom of our not having anything to do with it. We couldn't stay out. . . .

The FBI devoted much of the interview to Julia's associations with the Communist Party and Communists. Did she know Martina Curl and did she know she was a Communist? Julia admitted knowing her casually and said she didn't know if she was Communist and it would not be fair to guess. Did she subscribe to the People's World? *No, not any more. And finally, "Are you a member of the Communist Party?" Julia denied having ever been, though she acknowledged attending public meetings. At the end she was asked if there was anything she wanted to add to the interview and, according to the transcript, Julia said, "I would like to add this. I have told you as closely as I could all of my activities in behalf of peace. I think every one is interested in peace and wished that war could be outlawed. I have spoken quite freely and answered any questions you asked me about my work for the working class of papers, and I am glad to go on record too that I think my patriotism is unquestioned. . . . That is why I am working at the Portland sub-depot, and I hope that I can stay there. I believe in the people of this country and it is my country, and it is important to me." And she signed the transcript.[8]*

The first time I asked Julia if she had ever been in the Communist Party she told me that was a red-baiting question and she wouldn't, on principal, answer it. But, as we got to know each other better, she volunteered the information that she wasn't in the Party, that her father had raised her to think for herself and she couldn't submit to its discipline. I believed her.

The FBI, on the other hand, despite her denial during her interview, remained convinced Julia was a member of the Party. In 1946 they designated her a "key figure," citing both her employment (presumably her journalism) and her activity in the Communist Party. They watched her, stood across the street from her house at least once a year to make sure the photo they had on file still looked like her, and recorded her new address whenever she moved. Her file is full of memorandums and routine checks.[9]

I really had hoped by going down there I could save my job at the Army, but it wasn't too long after that they told me they were going to transfer me to Montana. It was a polite way of firing me. So I quit and went to work at the Oregon Shipyard. As I had been so badly beaten up on the picket line in 1935, I couldn't work in any of the shops out there where you got decent money. I had to go out there and work in the marine pipe control office writing up requisitions.

The AFL office workers had jurisdiction over office workers working inside the yards, so after I was there for awhile, I sent in my first month's dues and my initiation fee. For four or five months I heard nothing from them. Then I got a letter from the office workers' union asking me to come before their executive board and when I got there they accused me of being a CIO spy trying to worm into the AFL. I got fired. The office workers' union got me fired.

They were paranoid in those days. The breach between the AFL and CIO was very deep. You have no idea what it was like. People didn't speak to one another, close friends. It was frightful.

Then Mike, my son—by that time I think he had become fourteen years old—went to work in the shipyards to support us. Quit school and went to work. He looked so pitifully young. Then he got sick. All this time I was a delegate to the Portland CIO Industrial Union Council. One of the officials I met there went up to the hospital and said to him, "Kid, as soon as you get out of the hospital, I'm gonna try and get you into the school they've got in Southern California so you can go on the Merchant Marine."

So Mike went to this school. He went in the Merchant Marine. He was in what they call the black gang. Oh they work on the engines, below deck. He was out in the South Pacific in the Merchant Marine, and he said it was far more hazardous on their ships than it was when he eventually was in the Marine Corps.

Then Mike came home over Christmas and didn't take the next ship out. He was gonna stay over, take the next one out. They had a law in Portland, you had to go to school or be eighteen. And so some of the stool pigeons that lived across the street from me in those days turned him in. So that's when he went down and enlisted in the Marine Corps with the aid of a faked-up baptismal record for which he paid, I think, seventy-five cents. It said he was two years older than he was.[10]

Chapter 9

MY BAD REPUTATION CAUGHT UP WITH ME

Nineteen forty-three was an eventful year for Julia. She divorced Butch, married Ben, worked for a short time at the shipyards, and then got a job that would last a while at State Public Welfare.

In addition to working her nine-to-five job, Julia continued and expanded her work as a freelance journalist, sending stories to the Federated Press news service, the Dispatcher *(the ILWU's paper), and the* People's World *(a Communist paper). She wrote many labor stories, but any injustice was important to write about as well, whether it was families cut off welfare or prisoners being exploited.*

I took this civil service examination, went to work for State Public Welfare Commission and I became the medical division secretary. The only difference between me and the people on the other side of the desk when I was in Public Welfare was the width of the desk and one paycheck.

When I was working for the Public Welfare, I took the pen name of Kathleen Cronin because I knew that my ideas of what was so and Public Welfare's wouldn't coincide, which they didn't. I was spending a vacation in San Francisco. I was at a party and it was decided that they should put some first names in a hat. They drew out the name Kathleen. Then they were thinking what would be my last name. Francis Murnane was at that party and he said, "Cronin would be a good name." It was the maiden name of his mother. So I became Kathleen Cronin.

I used that name until I married Oscar Ruuttila and they changed the name on my press card from the *Dispatcher* to Kathleen Ruuttila. All the longshoremen used to call me Kathleen until their attorney Frank Pozzi got up at a Longshore meeting in Portland and said, "She isn't Kathleen Cronin or Kathleen Ruuttila. She's Julia Ruuttila. Call her Julia Ruuttila."

I worked at Public Welfare for five years. All this time I was working for Federated Press on the side, vacations and weekends. Often I'd stay downtown and get a cup of coffee and a sandwich and go back to the office—as I was the senior girl in the office—and write up the stuff for Federated Press on *their* damn typewriters.

Federated Press was a national news service that labor papers took. AFL *and* CIO. They had some farm papers and a few independent dailies and some *real* left-wing papers like *People's World* in San Francisco and the *Daily Worker*. They used to send me a copy with a list of papers that my stuff had been in. Their editing was very good. I outlived them; they went under in 1957.

Federated Press' correspondence file with Julia shows she became their correspondent early in 1946 at $15 a month plus expenses (which included stamped airmail en-velopes), with an occasional bonus for special stories. Considering that Julia's work for Federated Press was always her "second" job, the quantity of her writing for them, and the correspondence that ensued, is impressive. It was not that Julia didn't want to work for them full time. In 1947 she outlined what she could do if she could devote herself to the job, but Federated Press couldn't afford a full-time salary and she knew it.[1]

The man that headed Federated Press, Carl Haessler, was quite prolabor; I mean *radical* prolabor. Of course, I never denied that I believed in socialism. When he died, I learned to my horror that he had left me some stock in some lumber cor-poration, Northwest Hardwoods. Isn't that funny? Well, he had a son who had become a lawyer and he was practicing law with a very right-wing law firm here in Portland. Apparently he had bought that stock because of his son being the attorney for that company.

I was just simply petrified to get this stock because I'd never believed in owning stock. My father always talked about that as unearned income. I kept thinking to myself, "Wouldn't I be in terrible trouble if the workers in that plant went on strike?" So I thought, "I've got to get rid of this stock."

I was determined not to keep them any longer than it took to get rid of them, so I looked up the office of that company. It was in the First National Bank Tower. They occupied an entire floor at the top of the building. They were very lavish offices. I said to whoever it was that I talked to there, I wanted to sell this stock. He said, "How do we know you're who you say you are? We've never heard of you. You've never been to a stockholders meeting. How did you get these?" In other words, he insinuated I'd stolen them.

I said, "Well I have a little money in another First National Bank branch and I'm sure if we go down to the one that's located in the lower portions of this building they can call up and identify me." So we went down there and he called up the branch where I had this account.

Then this executive said he would buy the stock, so this bank man said, "You know that's illegal." I suppose, for him to buy stock from a stockholder because he was an executive of that company. Isn't that interesting? So he simply said I'd have to go back to his office on the top floor and wait awhile. He said he'd get the money in cash and give it to me. So I said, "Well, I'll go back up there, though I feel very strange and terrified in the office with anyone like you, and a law breaker on top of everything else, and an exploiter of the workers. But if you'll give me some coffee," at that time I was still on my twenty cups a day, I said, "I'll wait for you."

So an hour or so later, he came back and paid me in bills. Then he said to me—oh, he made all manner of fun of me, but I didn't care, I was rid of the stock—he said, "We have a present for you since you didn't come to the last meeting. You missed out on what we gave around, and here it is." See that thing down there, it's a cutting board made out of hardwood. Then I was afraid if I chopped any cabbage or cut a sandwich on it, it would poison me. But I took it. I did take it.

I did one research job that really panned out. That was in 1946 when peonage was going on down on Sauvies Island. Well, it was a very interesting affair. It was Irvin Goodman that first tipped me off to it.[2]

I went down on Sauvies Island with a union official I knew and with Irvin Goodman to see what was going on down there. It was very interesting. There was a conspiracy going on. The Fazio brothers were truck farmers and they had truck gardens all over different parts of Portland, out by the Columbia as well as Sauvies Island. They had got ahold of land down there through the State Land Board.

It was a municipal judge that was working with them. They were trying to get a dormitory erected to house prisoners. They were making a big deal with it that they would put them out there for rehabilitation on the island out in open air, healthful conditions, good farm food, and all that hooey. It *was* hooey. So the judge would sentence them to long sentences, particularly if he found that there were any carpenters, plumbers, electricians, building laborers that he could send out there that would be useful in erecting this barracks and big cookhouse.

At that time—it's before they had the bridge to get to Sauvies Island—you went across on a ferry. On the island end of the ferry there was a guard tower with a thug in it who had a rifle. That was to keep people from walking off the island, escaping. So you see, there were a lot of people involved in this.

Now I went up to the county courthouse. There was a man up there who helped me who was running for city council. He was a county commissioner but he wanted to get on the city council. He sent one of his staff to help me look up the deeds of land out there and different places. So this was quite a proceeding.

Julia discovered that Fazio had bought the land from a city commissioner who later voted for the appointment of the judge in question, and that Fazio had been farming the land at least a year before purchasing it.[3]

We went down on the island and we got into the bunkhouse and the cookhouse where they fed them. There were about twenty people eating around this table and they had about two cucumbers in vinegar in a dish and some stale bread and I forget what else. The food really wasn't fit for pigs. That was their "good, wholesome, country food."

I talked to some of the prisoners. They told me the conditions there were absolutely deplorable. Absolutely deplorable. And if the work they wanted these people to do hadn't been finished yet, the county'd just extend their sentence, claiming they caused a riot or something.

I was interested in talking to the farmers out there, the ordinary, plain farmers, not the Fazio brothers. They bitterly resented what the Fazio brothers were doing. They were extremely helpful in furnishing all kinds of information. They had protested loudly and long to various authorities and so had the AFL, which felt that carpenters should have been building the barracks and cookhouse instead of prisoners. And oh, how those farmers resented that guardhouse and the tower.

I wrote that up and it was printed in the *People's World* (I started writing for the *People's World* in 1938, but I don't remember exactly how, except that it had some connection with my being a delegate to the CIO Industrial Union Council). The county commissioner that was running for the city council, he heard about this article and he ordered two thousand copies of it and distributed it in the district where he was looking for votes. That is the most *People's World*s that were ever sold. It was a good story.

The State Bar Association had come across a copy of these articles and they called me up and asked me if I'd furnish them documentation, which I gladly did. And they put a stop to it. It was ended. Looking back over my misspent life, the only fight I ever won was stopping peonage on Sauvies Island.

Julia's story in the People's World *was published May 7, 1946. On May 19, Melvin McGrann was arrested for absconding from Fazio's farm. He sued for habeas corpus.*

In September, the same week the Oregon Bar Association's Committee on Portland Parole System presented its report calling for a halt to the practice of paroling prisoners to private individuals, circuit court judge Alfred P. Dobson ruled on Mc-Grann's case, finding the paroling of prisoners for work purposes illegal. However, in September 1949, after Frank Pozzi—just out of law school, but later to become the lawyer for the ILWU and a good friend of Julia's—took a job as deputy city attorney, he discovered municipal prisoners were again being released to Fazio. The story appeared in the Oregon Journal *and the practice was stopped again. A formal probation and parole system was instituted in Portland as a result.[4]*

One of the fights Julia lost concerned the city of Vanport. Though second in population only to Portland in Oregon, it wasn't a real city. It had no elected government and didn't even tax its residents. Totally managed by the Housing Authority of Portland, in other respects Vanport—the largest housing project in the United States—felt like a city. Though the Housing Authority did not permit taverns, Vanport did have schools, shopping and recreation centers, a library, theater, fire and police departments, and, in later years, a weekly newspaper.

Built in 1943 on a large tract of floodplain next to the Columbia River between Portland, Oregon, and Vancouver, Washington (hence the name Vanport), Vanport's sole purpose was to house workers (and their families) from across the nation to build ships in the local Kaiser shipyards. Surrounded on all sides by high dikes with only one road out, Vanport was an unappealing place to live. Comprised of ill-heated, thin-walled units in buildings only 20 feet apart, the project was noisy at all hours of the day and night. Twenty-four-hour daycare made it possible for parents to work any shift. Recreation opportunities for children were excellent, but nearly nonexistent for adults.

Oregon had had a little under 2000 African American residents—nearly all living in Portland—when the country entered World War II, but the influx of war workers changed that. By 1945, the black population was estimated at 18,000. With few other local housing choices, a sizable number of them lived in Vanport, where they were, for the most part, segregated from other residents.[5]

In 1945, with shipyard orders declining, white families began to move out. The end of the war that summer accelerated the departures. By October, African Americans constituted 35 percent of Vanport's residents.

Vanport was always meant to be a temporary housing project, and after the war was over there was talk of demolition, but the housing shortage had not abated. Many war workers decided to stay in Oregon, veterans returned, and workers who had jobs elsewhere during the war came back as well. Still, Vanport was not popular. Some units were demolished and others stood empty.

A policy, instituted after the war, of discounted rent for low-income residents and servicemen helped boost the population, as did the founding of a college for veterans wanting to take advantage of the GI Bill. Vanport College held its first classes the summer of 1946. It was very popular and took the pressure off the University of Oregon in Eugene, where housing was difficult to obtain.

On May 30, 1948, after a month of heavy rain, the dike broke and Vanport flooded; it was estimated that 18,500 people were living there at the time (down from a high of about 40,000 in January 1945).[6]

When the war was over, the City of Portland and the City of Vancouver tried to get all the shipyard workers that had come from the South and the East to go home. The mayor of Portland, Earl Riley, had offered money to people to leave, but the blacks that had come here decided they didn't want to go and they stayed on.

I had been working on a feature story about Vanport when the flood came in 1948. I knew there was going to be a flood because the firefighters' union had warned the Housing Authority the dikes were going. They moved out the records from the Housing Authority office and they moved the safes out of the supermarket, but they didn't move the people.

Some people walking on the dikes saw raging floodwaters outside and were frightened. They hired move-yourself trucks and were loading up to move anyplace just to get out of there. The Housing Authority sent around this dreadful notice, "Don't panic. It's perfectly safe. Should there be danger, you will be given ample warning and help in moving out." Therefore, a lot of people unloaded their stuff and moved back in these houses. That was about ten o'clock in the morning that they sent that around. At four o'clock that afternoon the dike broke. A wall of water twenty feet high tore through the dike at the railroad embankment, sweeping the flimsy war housing off its foundations.

I was sitting in a theater on Memorial Day Sunday with Francis J. Murnane when it was flashed on the screen if there's anyone there from the National Guard to report to the Denver Avenue fill. So I knew that meant the dike had gone. I said, "I'm leaving."

He said, "Oh no, you can't. I bought this ticket."

I said, "Oh, to hell with that." I left him holding my jacket, ran out in the street, and took a cab out of there.

I saw a woman and a man struggling up the side of the embankment with a refrigerator. They had to let go of it and it sank back in the water. I saw human chains trying to get up the sides of the dike out of the water. It only took, I think, an hour, hour and a half. The houses were already disintegrating; it was just cheap war housing. I used to say in speeches I made before groups at that time that Vanport was destroyed in less time than it took the bomb to fall on Hiroshima.

The behavior of the unions was great. The bus drivers kept running the buses into Vanport and taking people out until the water got in the engines and they couldn't run anymore. The Firefighters, when they couldn't get to first base with the Housing Authority about the dangers, mobilized all the commercial fishermen that had boats in the Columbia. So within about half an hour after the dike broke, they had these little boats in there taking people off of rooftops and so forth. The firefighters' union and the commercial fishermen and the union that the bus drivers belonged to, they were the heroes of the flood.

The next day they had the National Guard out. By that time some of the houses had toppled over. They had set up a bureau there for people to look for their missing relatives. Because this happened on a Sunday and many people were outside Vanport, they didn't know if their relatives were alive or dead.

I remember one woman who had "the curse" and the only garment she had on was some kind of a cotton dress. The whole back of that was covered with blood and she was trying to get this stupid caseworker to give her a voucher so she could buy some Kotex. The caseworker had some red-tape reason why she couldn't. And then people going around there crying and wringing their hands because they hadn't found out what had happened to their relatives. It was a frightful sight.

Far more people were drowned than they ever admitted. I think they finally admitted to seventeen or eighteen, but I know that there were more.

A Citizen's Committee for Flood Disaster formed quickly. On June 17, 1948, the committee circulated an open letter to the flood victims telling them of the demands they had made to the mayor and city council. These included immediate money grants to the victims, housing for them in auto courts and vacant hotel rooms, and jobs such as repairing flood damage. And the letter reminded them "we are only going to get what we struggle for." The committee also organized meetings of ex-Vanporters and held at least one demonstration before the city council, on June 30, to protest the attitude of the various government agencies toward the plight of the flood victims.[7]

The strongly anticommunist Oregon Labor Press *accused the committee of being Communist led and recommended that the AFL unions refuse to cooperate with them. They cited Julia by name as being on hand to "assist in the direction of the demonstration," though she may have been there only as a journalist, not committee member.[8]*

On July 7, about 100 members of the Citizens Committee went to Salem to meet with the governor, but the charges of Communism had preceded them and Governor John H. Hall refused to talk to them. The group picketed instead.[9]

A lot of people filed against the Housing Authority. The Firefighters also were trying to collect some money; they hired me to get affidavits and stuff about what went on. I remember interviewing several people that said they saw the people in the sheriff's office out there [at Vanport] running like mad and pushing people out of their way to get ahead of the water. They weren't doing a thing to help anybody. I also knew, because of the stuff I'd been collecting for a feature on that place, that they had been warned by the Corps of Army Engineers that it was an area of calculated risk where they *built* Vanport.[10]

What was so awful was that about a fourth of the people down there were on welfare, you know, and they lost all their possessions, everything they had but the clothes they had on. Public Welfare said it was a national disaster. They cut off the welfare grants and said the Red Cross had to feed them. The Red Cross said that they would provide housing and feed those that had *not* been on welfare, but they wouldn't do a thing for those that *had* been on welfare.

While this controversy was going on, I'll say this for the churches, they stepped into the breach and opened the church doors out in North Portland. The schools opened their doors and private individuals out there opened their homes. For once they forgot about being racist and they took in black people too.

Vanport was supposed *not* to be racially segregated. But, as a matter of fact, blacks and whites lived out there but they didn't live in the same housing units. I had established that fact in the investigation I did when I was working on what I thought was going to be a big feature story for Federated Press. I knew that after the war ended the city officials had tried to force all the blacks to go back where they came from. I knew who was on the Housing Authority and that the real estate people and building and loan people that controlled the Housing Authority tried to sell houses at inflated prices to any of the laid-off shipworkers with money.

They finally moved the flood refugees down onto Swan Island. There was war housing there that shipyard workers had lived in. Now half of Swan Island was under water because, of course, the flood had backed up into the Willamette too. So I was down there on the island and there was still only one way there. I had to wade through the water. I talked to a great many black people who were down there and terrified. They thought they'd been put down there to drown. Looked like it all right, because the water wasn't far from the top of the island even on the part that wasn't flooded out. After the disaster, there was no segregation on Swan Island. People were living in the same bunkhouses, whites and blacks.

The day after the flood, I remember calling up the chairman of the Portland Housing Authority. I said, "You know that you'd been warned that the dikes were going. Why didn't you move those people out?"

This man was the head of the apartment owners' association. He said, "We didn't have any place to move them to." He didn't deny that they'd been warned the dikes were going.

I said, "Well there were a lot of hotels and apartment buildings."

He said all the downtown hotels were being reserved for Rose Festival guests. Isn't that dreadful? I remember putting that in one of the stories I wrote for Federated Press. I wrote a series of stories focused on criticisms of the State Public Welfare Commission and the Portland Housing Authority.[11]

Well, then the Public Welfare began to try to find out who wrote these stories because they appeared in newspapers all over the country, not just AFL and CIO papers, but the *People's World* and the *Daily Worker* and some independent daily papers and a lot of farm papers. I wrote them under the name of Kathleen Cronin, but eventually they found out it was me and then I got fired.

When I wrote these articles for the Federated Press I knew I was signing my death warrant, but, you know, when you have a press card like I had, you have to do it. S. Eugene Allen was at that time editor of the *Oregon Labor Press*. And he was one of the most vicious right wing . . . I'm sure he's the one that tipped them off. And I think the caseworkers that I ran into up there were suspicious when they saw me running around with a notebook. Well, you might put it that my bad reputation caught up with me.[12]

I was called into the supervisor's office. She had this other deplorable character in there. She told me I had written these stories and I saw that it was being taken down on tape. She told me I had twenty minutes to clear out my desk and leave. She said that this other woman would go with me to be sure I only took what belonged to me. "If you're accusing me of being a thief," I said, "I'd wish you'd repeat it in front of several other people so I could sue you for slander."

Before this happened, the wages were so deplorable there that I decided we should join a union at Public Welfare. The young women that ran the elevators got a great deal more than we did, than the clerks and stenographers. I don't mean me, but many of us looked down on them because we thought of ourselves as white-collar workers. So I began going around and explaining the wages they got and the reason that they got so much more than we did was because they belonged to a union.

Well now, that union was AFSCME, American Federation of State, County and Municipal Employees, so I joined it and began signing people up. I signed up quite a few people, including my immediate supervisor. So when I got fired, I went to AFSCME for help.

You know what AFSCME did? Now I want to make it perfectly clear that AFSCME today is one of the best unions in the country and is very good in

Portland, but it wasn't in those days. It was dominated by middle-aged male chauvinist pigs that held executive-type positions in other agencies. It really wasn't much of a union.

When I went to them and asked for help, they sent for an international vice president. This man came to Portland to interview me, to see if I was a Communist. When he got through talking to me, he said, "I don't see that there's any difference between your ideas and mine. I'm a kind of a socialist myself." But he couldn't get to first base with AFSCME. He told me that they had got into the FBI to see if I was a Communist. Nice thing for your union officials to do! That is one reason I became a women's libber.[13]

Had AFSCME helped me get my job back, I would doubtless have gone on organizing in my spare time, and AFSCME might not have remained—as it did for some time—a small gutless group dominated by male members more interested in searching for reds under office desks than in acquiring the bargaining strength to lift the salaries of public employees out of the poverty level.

There was a great deal of publicity at the time I got fired from Public Welfare. I had a so-called civil service hearing because I thought I was a permanent employee. The hearing was held in Salem and Irvin Goodman went down there to defend me, free of charge. There was quite a large defense committee that was set up with Francis Murnane and some Longshore officials and S. P. Stevens, and there were blacks on it, including one black man who had lost his home in Vanport, and officers in one of the locals in the woodworkers' union. The Firefighters' international rep came and testified for me. The head of the medical division, a highly paid social worker, testified for me. She later got fired for doing that. She was a woman with guts. Several union officials went down there and also a black man, Estes Curry. He later played quite a role in trying to get the State of Oregon to do something for the flood victims.[14]

The governor of Oregon, John H. Hall, had been an attorney for the dog racing interests and the horse racing people and those types. He said that that was a red mob that came to Salem, that descended upon the state capital. Later he was killed in an airplane accident flying to Klamath Falls. If I believed in God I would have thought it was the vengeance of the almighty.

Julia's defense was that she was fired for political reasons, namely the articles she'd written, her membership in the Progressive Party, and her efforts to organize a union at her workplace. The Welfare Commission said they'd fired her because her "activities and public utterances" had reflected upon and embarrassed them and the government. The welfare administrator testified in detail as to Julia's offensive activities: her attendance at the demonstration seeking city aid for the flood victims, her arti-

cles critical of the Welfare Commission in the People's World, *and her part in a protest at a school board meeting when a Communist was barred from speaking in a school building.*[15]

Her lawyer, Irv Goodman, argued that the commission had failed to follow a civil service regulation requiring ten days dismissal notice. Moreover, he claimed that the commission had not shown Julia was guilty of any of the legally specified reasons for discharge of a civil service employee: "misconduct, inefficiency, incompetency, insubordination, indolence, malfeasance, or other unfitness to render effective service."[16]

Lost the hearing. I once knew who the members of the Civil Service Commission were, and they were questionable people, so I knew I didn't have a chance, but I had to go through the motions. They did say that their firing me on twenty minutes notice was a deplorable thing. And that's what I had was twenty minutes notice.

The year after I got fired from the Public Welfare, Loa Howard, the administrator, got fired. A Democratic governor was elected and he fired her. So things do change sometimes.

Well anyway, I had one dollar in the bank at this time and, let's see, I suppose I had a little coming on my paycheck. Well, I went home and I suppose I wrote a story for Federated Press and one for the *People's World* about it.

I remember that pretty soon my lights and gas were turned off because I couldn't pay the bills. I was living in a little house in North Portland. It was a deplorable little shack when I bought it for twelve hundred dollars—two hundred down, and twenty dollars a month. Different people I knew in different unions came there and put plumbing in because the plumbing had burst in a freeze—no one had lived in it for three or four years—and they put new floors in and built a sidewalk to the little front porch and papered and painted it. They "borrowed" the materials they needed from the outfits they worked for.

The man that owned it lived a block away and he came to the house and said to me, "I'm sorry you got fired and I suppose you won't be able to keep up the payments." So he said, "When you get another job you can pay me then."

But after the hearing, Irvin Goodman said to me, "You go and collect what you have coming in your retirement fund. You bring it to me, because there's something you've got to do with that." So I did as he said and when I got back with the money—and I think the red tape held that up a month or two—he said, "I want you to use this to pay off the mortgage on your house."

I said, "Well what am I going to eat on?"

He said, "We'll worry about that later, but at least you'll have a roof over yourself and your typewriter."

Oh, one other thing I should say, after all this publicity about me being fired, a man came to Portland who was an official in the U.S. Forest Service. He had an office in Roseburg and he said, "I was very interested in the stories I read about you. If you will give me your word that you won't write for any of these publications again, I will hire you as a secretary and stenographer, because none of the testimony was against your stenographic, your shorthand or your typing. But you have to give me your word."

Well, believe me, it was a temptation. But I told him no, I couldn't make that kind of a promise. But I remember that man. And actually I would have enjoyed working for the Forest Service, one of the less subversive agencies of our government.

Chapter 10

WHITE TRADE ONLY

Racism was as evil as capitalism in Julia's mind. Her commitment to the struggle for racial equality went back at least to the 1930s. She brought her concern to her work in the woodworkers' union auxiliary and later recruited the wife of one of the first African American longshoremen in Portland into the ILWU's ladies' auxiliary. She also joined or worked with a number of civil rights organizations, including the National Association for the Advancement of Colored People (NAACP), the Urban League, and the Japanese American Citizen's League.

Back in the thirties, when I was president of the Woodworkers' auxiliary, I took to inviting guest speakers from other unions to talk so that our members would learn something about the problems of other unions. Of course, the reason I did that is because I wanted to lead up to getting a black speaker there (although the Woodworkers didn't discriminate the way that the Longshoremen did when I first got mixed up with them). So we invited this officer of the NAACP group here. He was a porter at the city jail.

I remember the speech he made because I was so turned off by it. He said, "We don't want to be invited to your homes and we don't want you in ours, but we feel we're entitled to the same wages and the same civil rights as you people have." I guess black people did have the right to vote at this time, but a lot of other rights they didn't have, and they had these Jim Crow signs all over town, you know.

So when I thanked him for coming and talking to us, I said, "I'm very sorry that I'm not welcome in your home because you and your wife are welcome in mine."

A week or so after that, we got an invitation from the Sleeping Car Porters women's auxiliary [Ladies' Auxiliary to the Brotherhood of Sleeping Car Porters] inviting us to send a delegation of three women to their next meeting, and the nice little letter said that they were in the habit of having refreshments afterward, but that if our women didn't feel that they wanted to stay, they needn't feel that they had to.

I was dying to go myself, but I decided better not waste the invitation on somebody who didn't need it. I was very anxious to see everything went alright, so I appointed a delegation. I couldn't leave it up to an election, it was too important. Not very democratic, is it?

So I appointed this woman who'd been a schoolteacher and one of the loggers' wives whose husband had been in the IWW and a woman who'd been brought up in the South and was very racist, but she was basically a very kind, good, sweet person. You know, some of the people that have the worst ideas are the nicest people. She finally agreed to go.

It was a good decision because when they reported on their experiences there, she made the best one of anyone. She said, "I'm so glad I went because they're just folks the same as we are." Then she said, "Refreshments were so delectable. I want you to get out your notebooks and write down the recipe." Well, I thought it was a perfect report. 'Course, the schoolteacher made the kind of report you'd expect a schoolteacher to make.

I really wasn't too interested in the struggle of the blacks in Oregon because they only had nineteen hundred members and they had made themselves a little safe enclave in the white world. They weren't interested in doing anything about anything really. They just wanted to be left alone and not to be disturbed. But after the shipyards came, a great many blacks came to Portland and they were a different type.

What really changed me about working in the black organizations was the black people I met after the Vanport flood. The ones at Vanport understood more. They were more aggressive in getting their rights. When they came to Oregon, they had believed that Oregon was free. It was a fearful shock to them when they found out that it was worse than in the South, because there was physical prejudice against them. It was really dreadful.

I remember getting on the St. John's bus and a black man got on the bus and sat down in this seat where a white man was sitting. This white man got up—he had a southern voice—and he said, "Put this so-and-so off this bus. I won't sit with him and I don't even want to ride in the same bus with him. We don't allow this down South."

Well, you know, I don't usually lose my temper but I completely blew my cool. I stood up in the aisle and made a speech. I said, "You're not down South anymore, you so-and-so and such." Although I don't really use that kind of language, when I get really mad it seems to come out. I said, "You get off the bus. We don't need you in Portland. We don't need you in Oregon and we don't want you on this bus."

It must have been one of my few good speeches because everyone on the bus clapped and the conductor stopped the bus and asked him if he wanted to get off. But he didn't. The black man looked too astonished for words. I thought about that afterwards. I thought, "Well he didn't even say thank you," but I think he was too taken aback, which is understandable.

I joined the NAACP in maybe 1936 or '37 and Irvin Goodman paid up a lifetime membership for me. So I took to going to their meetings. I went regularly until I moved to Astoria. The NAACP worked hard to get a Civil Rights Act and a Fair Employment Practices Act passed at Salem, but I was very disappointed to find out that the Portland NAACP was dominated by its white members.

One of the people I met through the NAACP in Portland told me about a black friend of his. He was a college graduate and he'd come here from one of the New England states. None of the white liberals would invite him to their homes, so I said, "Well, you hand on an invitation to him to come to my house for Sunday dinner." When I told that to Butch, my first husband, he said he'd leave home.

Then I got interested in the Urban League. E. Shelton Hill was labor secretary of the Urban League and he eventually became the president. I learned a great many things from him about black history in Oregon.

The Urban League had more guts than the NAACP in those days, mostly because of E. Shelton Hill, and they weren't dominated by white people the way that the NAACP was. So, I began to go to Urban League meetings. What I did for the Urban League merely amounted to trying to get people to go to some of their fundraisers, things like that. And then I wrote articles for the *People's World*. I used to go to their office a great deal.

When the black troops got back from the beachheads, how many Jim Crow signs they had to pass when they got off at the union station before they could get the city bus to go home! Isn't that dreadful?

Portland's war industries had required more workers than the city could provide. Thousands of people came to Portland from other regions of the country for these jobs. Among the newcomers were many African Americans. Portland did not assimilate them easily or willingly. The Oregonian *newspaper encouraged the new immigrants to "go back to the farm" after the war, but many decided to stay.[1]*

In 1945 Portland's prestigious City Club conducted a study: "The Negro in Portland." They found that most restaurants and downtown hotels refused to serve

Negroes and that Portland was the only city on the coast where restaurants displayed "white trade only" signs. Insurance companies had policies of not insuring Negro lives unless they found the applicant to be an exceptional physical and moral risk, and those accepted paid higher premiums. Blacks could obtain car or liability insurance only through the Oregon Casualty Association for assignment of risk and had to pay a 15 percent premium over standard rates.[2]

I took to going with blacks to restaurants that had these Jim Crow signs. I would sit at a counter pretending I didn't know the two blacks that would be with me and I would order food and they would too, and they didn't get served and I did. So then I would say, "You didn't serve these people." Then they'd say they didn't serve colored people. I'd say, "Well that's illegal under the Constitution, both of the United States and the state of Oregon."

I would get up and leave my half-eaten food and I wouldn't pay for it. The only time that I remember that anything happened was—and I was by myself that time—the restaurant owner ran after me and threatened to have me arrested. I said, "Okay, just you do that and I'll have you arrested. You're breaking the laws of our Constitution. I'll have you arrested."

One time a president of one of the AFL locals was trying to say thank you for some typing I'd done for him, so he took me to a fancy restaurant. They had a committee in Salem to get some kind of a state civil rights commission. He should never have been on it, but he was. Well anyway, during the conversation over dinner, he said he thought that they deserved equal rights and that's why he had volunteered to serve on that commission, but he said he had once been approached at a party to dance with a black woman and he refused. He came from Minnesota. In fact northerners were worse really than southerners, because southerners were used to the proximity of black people.

There was a "white trade only" sign in that place and he was perfectly willing to leave and not pay for the food. I was telling Irvin Goodman about it the next day and he said, "Why don't you call him up and tell him that those people have traced his license plate and they're going to have him arrested. Have some fun with him." Irvin Goodman had quite a sense of humor.

So I called him up and I said, "You better watch, you know that restaurant we left, they have got your license number. They came after me, but I said 'I don't own the car.' They are going to have you arrested. You better go and get a lawyer right away or else leave this state." Oh, he was scared stiff. I was in Irv's office when this happened, and he was with me on the extension phone and, oh, how we enjoyed that.

After I left my second husband, my son and I bought a little shack in the Portsmouth area of North Portland. Before we bought that house, we decided we'd move down in the ghetto, down around Williams Avenue, but the real estate people had put up the prices so high—they'd profiteered on the black discrimination by charging high rents and high prices for houses—we couldn't afford to live in the ghetto. So we had to live in the Portsmouth area, which was pretty much white.

Well then, I'll tell you the experience I had with my third and final husband. One time we had come to Portland and we went to eat in North Portland. I took him there on purpose because at that time the NAACP and the Urban League were still trying to get rid of those "white trade only" signs. It was a place that had a sign, and I went there because I intended to do what I had done for many years, which was to go in there, order some food, and leave without paying for it. When I called his attention to the "white trade only" sign, he was perfectly willing to leave, but he thought we should pay for the food. I said, "Now that's carrying honesty too far." So he left with me without paying.

When we were trying to get rid of the Jim Crow signs in the restaurants, the Unitarian church embarked on a crusade to help. My mother at that time was secretary of the women's alliance of that church. Every member of the alliance was asked to ask a black woman to lunch and see what would happen. So this black woman met my mother and she begged my mother not to subject her to that. She said she had brought some sandwiches and a thermos in her handbag. "Let's go to the park and eat," she said.

My mother said, "Well, I'd be happy to eat with you any place but that's not the point. We'll have to go to a restaurant." So she took her there.

I went to interview this man for a story I was writing for the *People's World* who was brought in by the Portland Council of Churches. He's the one that told me how many people had come here during the shipyard days to pass for white, and they passed right into the white world. I've often wondered if any of them married into the bigoted white families. The subject's of considerable interest to me.

The waterfront was lily-white. The railroad brotherhoods were lily-white.[3] The brick masons were lily-white. They were lily-white practically all of them. Even during the shipyard days, the unions that took blacks in and received their dues had Jim Crow auxiliaries for them to belong to. And it continued after the war. The Building Laborers, I think, was one of the first unions that took blacks in. A great many black teachers were hired to teach at Vanport College. I used to spend a great deal of time doing research on those subjects and writing articles for Federated Press and the *People's World* and I used to go to different trials and things.

Out at Guild's Lake—that's where they moved some of the refugees from Vanport, some of the black refugees—the Portland police went out there on a raid and broke into this apartment and shot a black man. They were looking for someone else. I went to the inquest. Irvin Goodman represented the family.

The Portland Police Department was terribly racist and it was really a shocking inquest. It was an all-white jury. I had a photographer and he took a picture of that jury. A great many of them were elderly women, and as they were looking over at the family members, they had such looks of hatred and contempt on their faces. And yet they were good Christian white women. Shocking! And that police lieutenant that committed this murder, he went on to high office in the police department.

I used to go to Salem [to lobby] when we were trying to get the civil rights bill passed. I could go into restaurants and bring coffee and sandwiches out because the blacks couldn't go in and eat. That was the bill that said you couldn't discriminate in places of public accommodation against people because of the color of their skin.

We first got an ordinance in the city of Portland through the city council and then the people got an initiative petition to have that taken off the statutes. So it went to an election and the working people in North Portland voted to have it taken off the books and the rich people up on the hills, in the Heights, they voted to keep it on the books; however, they got outvoted because there's more working people than rich people. Oh, that was a fearful shock to me, one of the biggest shocks of my life, that the poor people and the working-class people would vote to take that off the books.

The public accommodations ordinance, passed unanimously by the Portland city council in February 1950, was immediately challenged by an initiative petition organized by restaurant and hotel owners. In November 1950 the ordinance was defeated 77,084 to 60,964. Some precincts in Portland Heights and other affluent neighborhoods voted to keep the ordinance, as did precincts in the area most blacks lived in and scattered precincts in middle-and working-class neighborhoods around the city. However, in working-class North Portland, where Julia lived, the measure was indeed solidly defeated.[4]

Then we went to get it through the state legislature and it was easier. It was easy to do because Multnomah County [which includes Portland] was the only county that had any numbers of blacks in the state and this wasn't much of an issue in other places. So it passed there. Getting a fair employment practice through the legislature was much harder to do.[5]

Here's another great shock of my life. I decided to write a leaflet with the help of E. Shelton Hill of the Urban League—he was great on research. In order to get it printed—I hate to say this, it sounds like I'm red baiting, I'm really not—I approached some members of the CP, because they don't discriminate, you know. They're opposed to that type of thing. They said they would raise money to have it printed and help to distribute it. So I was researching material for this leaflet on the struggle for black rights in Oregon. One of the people that helped me get the material together was a black former shipyard worker from Vancouver. It really was pretty good.

When I took the draft copy to the members of the CP—I think there were three of them that were supposed to okay it and raise the funding—they disagreed with it. The part of it that referred to the city council meeting where we had got the civil rights ordinance forbidding Jim Crow passed, I didn't mention that there was a member of the Communist Party there.

I have always attempted to write as factually and as truthfully as possible. I said, "No, I didn't say that because there wasn't one there. You people knew about it because I called you up, but you didn't send anyone. So I couldn't say that you were there." This one man was indignant and so they cut off the funding. It didn't get published. I had promised Shelton Hill that before it got printed, I would show it to him and he thought it was great!

Chapter 11

IT'S WORK THAT INTERESTS ME

In 1948, Julia was on her own—Mike was grown and gone and she wasn't mar-
ried—and her prospects for a new job didn't seem good after her very public politi-
cal firing. Fortunately, she still had her typewriter, her writing skills, and friends in
the labor movement. The ILWU was involved in a bitter strike over control of their
hiring halls. The employers association was refusing to negotiate because ILWU pres-
ident Harry Bridges would not sign a non-Communist affidavit. It turned out to be
good timing for Julia. She was drawn into their struggle and the union and stayed
on for nearly 40 years.[1]

The ILWU was born in 1937 when the Pacific Coast District of the Inter-
national Longshoremen's Association, under the leadership of Harry Bridges,
voted to affiliate with the CIO. From the beginning the ILWU was committed to
internal democracy and took active stands for peace and justice. Because its con-
stitution prohibited discrimination based on political beliefs, Communists held
key positions.

There was no chance of getting work, as my firing and hearing was in the newspapers on the front page. The 1948 Longshore strike broke out and they had a
big soup kitchen. Some of the ILWU officials called me up and told me to come
down there and work on the publicity committee. They said I could eat in the
soup kitchen and the cooks from the Marine Cooks and Stewards (it was a joint
maritime strike; the other maritime unions were involved in it also, the offshore
unions) would make me up food to take home.

My end of the publicity was to get pictures into other labor papers, like the
different maritime union papers, *Voice of the Federation,* and the *International
Woodworker,* the Woodworkers' paper. We had a longshoreman who had worked

as a photographer and I used to go on the picket line with him. He'd take these pictures and I'd write up the captions to go with them.

When the strike was over, the Longshoremen came and told me I had better come to work for them, for their paper, the *Dispatcher,* and to be secretary to Matt Meehan, who was the international representative in that area. I went to work for the Longshoremen and continued to work for them until I was almost eighty.

When I got fired from Public Welfare I made up my mind I was never going to work eight hours again as long as I lived because there were other more important things to do. When I went to work for Matt Meehan, I worked half time. I thought, I'll just work and see if it interests me. 'Course, sometimes I think I put in more than eight hours a day on the *Dispatcher,* but at least it's work that interests me. The best thing that ever happened to me was my getting fired.

A great many of the old-time longshoremen came out of the IWW. Matt Meehan did, too. He had belonged to the Seamen's Division of the IWW. And for that matter, so did Harry Bridges. There wasn't much the conservatives in the local could do about Matt because he was appointed by Bridges. And when I was his secretary there was no way they could get at me. Anyway he was so smart and so good on the floor and he had a lot of support among the rank and file. The phonies were not nearly as smart and they couldn't maneuver as well. He was one of the smartest people I've ever met and he had only gone through the eighth grade.

As Meehan's secretary, Julia could be open about her political beliefs and activities. And she respected her boss.

Matt Meehan was one of the original organizers of the ILWU and its first secretary-treasurer. It was Matt who suggested the Longshoremen adopt the motto "An injury to one is an injury to all." In 1948, when he hired Julia, he had just become a full-time ILWU union representative.[2]

Though they were in the ILWU, Hawaiian longshoremen were paid 32 cents an hour less than their counterparts on the West Coast. In 1949, they went out on strike for parity.[3] During the strike, a ship loaded with Hawaiian pineapple was turned away from Seattle and Tacoma when longshoremen there called it "hot cargo" and refused to unload it. The ship then came to the Columbia River port town of The Dalles, where there was no ILWU local, but Local 8 got wind of it and put up a picket to prevent unloading. The ensuing ruckus became known as The Dalles Pineapple Beef.

Frank Pozzi, the Portland ILWU's lawyer, referred to the Pineapple Beef as an alleged riot that wasn't supposed to happen. He said the Longshore pickets had been lectured in Portland before they left: no trouble, no violence. But they couldn't control themselves.[4]

When I worked for Matt there were lots of funny incidents always happening. During the 1949 Longshore strike in the Hawaiian Islands, a barge of scab pineapples was sent across the Pacific and sneaked up the Columbia River in the fog to The Dalles. It was gonna be loaded on trucks and sent down to California to some factory where they made fruit cocktail.

Matt sent a bunch of longshoremen up to The Dalles to picket. He went up and established a headquarters in a hotel at The Dalles. He warned the Longshore pickets that went up there that there was something very funny going on in town, because there were reporters and writers there from all over the United States. He said he was sure that the employers were going to foment some kind of trouble and he urged them to be cool and cautious.

This scab truck charged through the picket lines and almost killed a couple of longshoremen, they jumped out of the way just in time. Somebody said—and that was one of the provocateurs, as we called them—somebody yelled, "Let's get them fellows!" and they charged down. A couple of hundred men charged down after this scab truck and turned it over and took the driver out—I think there were two men in the front seat—took them out and started to beat them up. One of them was about to be killed and would have been if it hadn't been for Toby Christiansen, business agent at Local 8. He knocked the guy out that had this truck driver down. He told me all about it. He said this guy said, "Toby, you're hitting the wrong man, this is me."

That incident gave rise to what they called The Dalles Pineapple Beef, because the Longshoremen were sued by the Hawaiian Pineapple Company for a huge sum of money, I forget how much, an enormous sum of money.

Matt called me up and he said to get hold of Francis Murnane and for us to write up a leaflet about what The Dalles Pineapple Beef was really all about and what the 1949 Longshore strike in Hawaii was. We were to take it down and run it off on the mimeograph machine in the Local 8 office, and we were to get someone with a car—Murnane never did have a car because he always gave all his money away—and we were to take it up to The Dalles so Matt could have the pickets up there distribute that leaflet to everybody.

So at the crack of dawn I went down to the Longshore hall and there was a White Finn (that's a right-wing Finn; there were the Red Finns and the White

Finns) who was the secretary of the local at that time named Mackie. He wouldn't let me go back in the room where the mimeograph machine was.

Now Mackie was an ex-boxer and he was a very powerful guy, but I was so angry and I was determined to get this leaflet run off so it could be picked up and get it to The Dalles.

I said, "Get out of my way, Mackie," and without thinking how idiotic it was, I rammed him in the stomach and he slipped on something and fell back into this big wastepaper basket. He had quite a rump on him and he stuck in there and he couldn't get out of it.

I rushed back in the room where the mimeograph machine was and while I was starting to run off this stencil I heard these longshoremen who'd come in to pay their dues laughing their heads off. They said, "How'd you get in that contraption, Mackie?"

He was cursing like anything. Then I heard him say, "That little so-and-so knocked me down," and then how they laughed!

Well, I never stopped to think, I just rammed him in the stomach without thinking. If you stopped and thought too much you never did it, you could always figure out reasons why you shouldn't.

Here's something else funny. Pretty soon here comes Murnane. He had had a couple of hours sleep, I hadn't had any, and he'd also had some tea—he was a tea drinker, being an Irishman—and he had located someone to drive us to The Dalles. So we loaded the leaflets in this guy's car and started for The Dalles.

We got partway up there and this guy says, "Open the glove compartment and see what I've got in there." He had a stash full of pistols. Murnane made him drive up a side road and bury this stuff under a log in some little wooded area. We couldn't have that with us in The Dalles. This guy meant well, but that was the worst thing he could have done. We met Matt at the hotel and he had lined up all these pickets to go out and distribute the leaflets.

I was up there another time for something in connection with The Dalles Pineapple Beef, and Matt said the National Guard was all over the docks and he told me to go down there and try to find out what's going on, because, after all, I had a press card.

When I got down there they had all their bayonets on their guns and they wouldn't let me go through onto the dock area; they didn't pay any attention to my press card. I saw this *Oregonian* reporter in there and I yelled to him to come over and identify me as a reporter so I could get in and he wouldn't do it. I got the best of him later—a year or so later—I was at some sort of Longshore meeting here in Portland, and this same reporter was trying to get into that and I said, "You can't get in."

He said, "How did you get in?"

I said, "On my press card, but your press card isn't any good here." And he couldn't get in.

Julia being led away after trying to get through the line of state police at the Dalles Pineapple Beef, 1949.

Anyway, the *Oregonian* or *Journal* photographer, I forget which—they were still all down there waiting for something more to happen—took a picture of me standing, it was really hysterical. You know that's one clipping I wish I'd kept. I believe it was on the front page and it showed all these National Guardsmen with their bayonets and their rifles all lined up. The photographer was a good one. It must have struck him as very funny because I was even smaller then than I am now, because I was very thin, and there I am against all those armed men.

They threw the pineapple in the river. And that is not all that went in the river. They threw the cameras of the photographers in because they were sympathetic to the Pineapple people, the employers. But later they were sorry they did it and they bought cameras for them, to replace them. Probably Matt told them to. One of them turned out to be a great friend of ours in the Portland newspaper strike and he used to laugh about it.

You know how those things drag on. I was living in Astoria and married to Oscar by the time it came to trial in federal court in Portland. I flew from Astoria to Portland to cover that trial for the *Dispatcher*.

They lost the court case but they never had to pay the fine, because they had me come to Portland and do some research in *Moody's Industrial* on all the companies that were involved with the pineapple company that had shipped that over. They had slowdowns at all those companies. So finally the pineapple company called it off. They wanted the slowdowns ended and the union didn't have to pay. When they use the power properly, it's very strong and powerful.

On June 8, 1956, the Supreme Court refused to hear the ILWU's appeal of the judgment against Local 8 awarding the Hawaiian Pineapple Company $278,000. A month later, on July 6, 1956, during Longshore Hawaii negotiations, the parties announced they had reached a settlement for $100,000. If there was a slowdown it was not reported in the newspaper accounts.[5]

The United States had tried to legally oust ILWU president Harry Bridges for years (there were also conservative elements in Local 8, the Portland local, who opposed him). The first warrant for Bridges' arrest and deportation to his native Australia, on the grounds that he was a Communist, was served March 5, 1938. Bridges won dismissal on December 30, 1939. He was rearrested in February 1941 after the Alien Registration Act (commonly called the Smith Act) was enacted in June 1940, but again won dismissal, this time by the Supreme Court, on June 18, 1945. Three months later he was sworn in as a U.S. citizen, only to be indicted in May 1949 for perjury for denying he was a Communist at his citizenship proceedings. He was found guilty, along with the two men who testified on his behalf, in April 1950.

Two months later the Korean War began. The officers of the San Francisco ILWU local introduced a resolution at a union meeting endorsing President Truman's decision to send troops to Korea and pledging that shipping would not be disrupted for the duration of the war. Bridges, who was out on bail, introduced an amendment stating that the union should support the United Nations' order for a cease-fire and negotiations.

The local did not adopt Bridges' amendment, but the public outcry over his stand resulted in his bail being revoked. In August 1950, he spent nearly three weeks in jail before bail was reinstated. The Supreme Court reversed his perjury conviction on June 15, 1953, and in June 1955 Bridges won the civil suit to rescind his naturalization and kept his U.S. citizenship.[6]

Another funny thing was the time that Bridges was in jail during the Korean War which he opposed. There was a Coastwise Caucus meeting in North Bend in the Longshore hall. I went down there to cover the meeting. The right-wing elements on the waterfront thought this was a good time to get rid of Bridges. The Portland local was an anti-Bridges local. The leader of the right wing was this Finn, Mackie. He was down there and they had determined that they were going to pass a motion at the caucus to get rid of Bridges. They had notified the reporters and people and they were all outside trying to get in to see what's going on, but, of course, they didn't let them in because it was a closed meeting. Some of them had gotten a ladder and had scrambled up so they could peek through a transom.

A friend of mine that belonged to the local that they had at Rainier, he said to me, "You'll have to go out on the street too, with the other reporters, you can't be in here." He thought I was the reporter for the *People's World*.

Just then Matt came in. "What's this commotion all about?" he said to this guy.

He said, "Well, she can't be in here."

Matt said, "Oh yes, she can. She's my secretary. Now you shut up, you so-and-so." That guy was very embarrassed.

Oh, it was a very heated meeting, because a resolution was introduced against Harry Bridges. What kept that motion from passing was a speech that Matt made. It was one of the best speeches I ever heard in support of Bridges. He talked about the Centralia case, about the stuff that labor had gone through in its efforts to organize and that Bridges had followed because he started out in life as an IWW on the ships. It was a very moving speech in the kind of language that longshoremen understand. A lot of other people made speeches too and the motion was shouted down, absolutely shouted down. It was delightful.

They ended up by sending a telegram of greeting and support to Bridges. Every-one in that hall except three people signed it.

The reporters were just simply flabbergasted and furious. Their trip was for nothing and I was trying to explain it to one of them. I said, "You know, their motto is 'an injury to one is an injury to all,' and for once, they used it."

Matt's parents were Irish immigrants and he had quite a brogue, and the Immigration and Naturalization Service thought that he was a foreign-born Irishman. Matt and Bridges fell out once over something and Immigration and Naturalization kept track of all the stuff like that, so they thought, here's their opportunity to get Matt to testify against Bridges.

So they went to his house one evening, rang the doorbell, the Immigration. They said they had some very private business to discuss with him and they ap-proached him on the subject of Bridges. Then he said, "No." He wouldn't co-operate. He disagreed with Bridges, but he wouldn't cooperate because Bridges was a first-class union man and a member of his union and so he wouldn't help them.

So they said, "Well, promise us that you won't tell Bridges that we talked to you."

He said, "I give you my solemn word, I won't tell Harry until I can get to the telephone in the kitchen." I'll never forget Matt saying that.

What they had disagreed about was over World War II. Bridges took an ex-tremely patriotic stand and felt that there shouldn't be any labor disputes while the war was going on, but Matt felt that there were some labor disputes that couldn't be put on ice. I think Matt was right, but they had a valid disagreement. One of the few times that I disagreed with Bridges.

We disagreed about the draft during Vietnam. And also over the Ray Becker case. I've never understood why he did everything possible to keep that from being brought before the longshore union. He was annoyed at everyone that was involved in it. I've often tried to figure that out and the only thing that I can think of is that Bridges was still in great danger of being deported. I think he thought it detracted attention away from the efforts to defend him, or maybe he thought that it was prejudicial to his case. Ray Becker didn't represent a major up-to-date struggle on the labor front, which Bridges' case did. [Ray Becker was released a year and a half after the attempts to deport Bridges began.]

Sometimes there's a conflict between the needs of the whole and what an in-dividual needs. I didn't used to have enough intellectual muscle to grasp that, but I can grasp it now; though I'm sure I would never have changed my posi-tion on any of these matters. But I can see now how some people I was very an-noyed with at the time, why they took a different position.

Congress adopted the Smith Act in 1940, making it a crime to teach, advocate, or encourage the overthrow of the U.S. government or to organize or be a member of any group or society devoted to such advocacy. The first to be tried under the act were members of the Socialist Workers Party in Minnesota in 1943. A trial in New York of the top leadership of the Communist Party followed in 1949. After their conviction was upheld by the Supreme Court in 1951, other Communist leaders were also arrested, tried, and imprisoned. Julia got involved when the trial touched the ILWU.

When the top hierarchy in the Communist Party was on trial in New York, one of the voluntary attorneys was the Longshore attorney from San Francisco [Richard Gladstein]. The judge sentenced all of those attorneys to jail for contempt of court on some trumped-up charge.[7]

You couldn't very well call up people and say, "What do you think of the Smith Act trial?" because people were so petrified over the Smith Act trials they couldn't think straight, so I started calling up ministers and asking them what they thought about the conviction of attorneys defending the damned. One minister, who said he thought that every person, irregardless of who they were, had a right to be defended in court, volunteered to write a statement. It was very good. In fact, it was excellent. I got three other of the top-line ministers to sign it.

The minister of the First Unitarian Church wouldn't sign it, Dr. [Richard M.] Steiner. Well, my mother was quite active in that church, so I was stunned, absolutely stunned. In fact, we got into quite an argument and he hung up on me. The head of the Congregational Church and First Christian and Presbyterian Church did sign it. But Dr. Steiner wouldn't.

I got to thinking what I could do next, so I started calling up other people and I called up the man, I can't think of his name, but he was the board chairman at the First National Bank. I read this statement to him and he endorsed it.

He was the leading layperson at the Unitarian church and a heavy contributor, so then I got my mother to get Dr. Steiner on the phone 'cause I didn't think he'd speak to me. Then she gave me the phone and I said, "Maybe you'd be interested to know what so-and-so said." He hung up on me again.

I wrote some stories for the *People's World* and for the Federated Press and I sent a copy of the letter with the signatures. I sent a copy of it to the ILWU attorney who had been thrown in the clink.

During the many years Julia was associated with the ILWU, she was loyal but not uncritical. She was particularly troubled by racial discrimination within Local 8.

There are three classifications of workers on the waterfront: Class A longshore-
men are fully registered and are the only workers eligible to be members of the union.
Class B longshoremen are partially registered and are called to work after all the class
A men have been placed. Their position is somewhat analogous to an apprentice. Ca-
suals, or "white cards," have no official standing. Technically a "white card" is issued
to any man asking for one on a day when there are no available A or B men when
more workers are needed.

During World War II there was plenty of work on the waterfront and many ca-
suals were hired, including blacks, but when it came time to register the blacks, the
vast majority of Local 8 members objected. Still, there was a minority of Portland
longshoremen determined to integrate the local who tried to recruit volunteers and
worked with the NAACP and the Urban League to that end.

The Urban League had recruited two men in November 1961. In December,
after the league negotiated with the union, the men got their "white cards" allowing
them to work as casuals. The league publicized the victory in its newsletter and urged
other men to show up at the hiring hall.[8]

But when it came time for advancement into B status, the door was still closed.

I remember going in the office of Local 8 one day [in 1943] to pick up some
pictures. The *Dispatcher*s had just been delivered to the Longshore hall, so, as I
came up to the dues window, papers were all lying on the counter. This dreadful walking boss [longshore gang foreman] said to the secretary, "Don't give her
any news whatever. She's a so-and-so and such-and-such," and he slapped me in
the face as hard as he could with this folded-up paper. It really hurt. He said,
"Look what you so-and-so's have done now. You nigger lovers," and a few other
epithets.[9]

I found out afterwards the paper had a picture of Paul Robeson on the front
page. He had been made an honorary member of Local 10 in San Francisco,
which has always had blacks, and they've got, I think, 60 percent black membership today.[10]

I had learned, when I got so badly beaten up in the Woodworkers' strike in
'35, that it's pretty stupid to fight with someone that's two or three times your
size, but I lost my temper completely and I decided to hit him where it would
hurt the most. I drew up my foot. I was going to kick him in the balls. That's
when the secretary of the local came out from behind the dues window and took
me by the arm and pulled me into his office. He said, "Now you see what I have
to put up with all the time."

Once I asked Matt Meehan why there were no blacks in the Portland local
when there were so many in San Francisco and some in Seattle and all the other

ports. He said during the '34 strike that the shipowners imported blacks to San Francisco to scab on the docks and when they found out the score they went over to the strikers. And after it was over they were taken into the union. But they didn't have to do that in Portland, there were so many scabby whites willing to scab.[11]

In the ILWU, if someone traveled from one port to another, take for instance if someone had relatives that were ill or in the hospital or some reason they wanted to go there and work, the port that took that man in they also had the right to travel someone back. So the first time that Portland wanted to travel someone to San Francisco, Bridges said, okay, and then he traveled a black up to Portland to work. He did it on purpose. But the longshoremen in Local 8 threw that black man into the Willamette River. He went back to San Francisco. He couldn't stay here.

Things got so bad that Lou Goldblatt, secretary-treasurer of the international union, came to Portland. He was Jewish and he was really a great guy, one of the best people the union had. That was a time [1964] when work was booming on the waterfront and they were going to take in four hundred new B men, and Harry Bridges had said that every one of the four hundred should be black to make up for the years of discrimination. Lou Goldblatt came to Portland and he said, "Things can't go on like this," and he said, "There's got to be a compromise. You've got to take in forty blacks."[12]

Francis Murnane was the hero of the waterfront. He was able to get up before a meeting and make everything sound like something that you'd want to do even in that right-wing local. He is the one that told them, "We can't get away with what we've been doing for years anymore. We've absolutely got to take in blacks," and there were enough decent people in the local so the compromise was accepted.

When they finally did take those forty B men in, it was still difficult for the blacks because there was a ruling on the waterfront if you were in a fight—you know it's so dangerous working on the waterfront—that the people in the fight would both be fired; but it worked out, in those early days, the only ones that got fired were the blacks. So some of the real racists down there would provoke fights and they got rid of a great many of them.

In February 1964, 46 of 299 new B men registered in Portland were black. The Coast Labor Relations Committee (CLRC) approved the addition of more B men to the Portland list, but, in 1967, the minutes reported that "Local 8 is still resisting the addition of 100 new Class B longshoremen in Portland as agreed to by this Committee." This was because there would have to be blacks among the new B men.[13]

The CLRC retaliated by refusing to advance B men to A. Local 8 responded by dispatching B men as if they were A, a practice declared in violation of the coast agreement. In May of 1968, the coast committee ordered Portland to cease and desist such dispatching and to select at least 50 blacks for the new B list. The Portland employers agreed to follow the coast directives, but the local continued to resist.[14]

Finally in August an agreement was reached, but while it did proclaim that approximately one-half of the new B men beyond the present 247 would come from minority and underprivileged groups, it went on to state that only a minimum of eight were required to be Negroes.[15]

Earlier in 1968, some of the blacks had filed a complaint against Local 8 and the Pacific Maritime Association, the employers, with the Equal Employment Opportunity Commission (EEOC), under the 1964 Civil Rights Act. They alleged that the joint committee intentionally engaged in unlawful practices.

In June 1968, the EEOC "found that reasonable cause existed to believe defendants . . . were in violation of Title VII," the section making discrimination in employment illegal. In late October, when conciliation efforts to achieve voluntary compliance proved unsuccessful, 23 black longshoremen, along with two men denied white cards, filed suit in U.S. District Court. By this time the August agreement was in effect and at least ten black B men had been advanced to A status; however, nine of the plaintiffs in the suit were new A men who had been refused union membership. The suit also cited a point system for promotion instituted after the black B men were registered in 1964 that was used to discriminate against blacks.[16]

In early December, representatives of all the parties met in Judge Gus Solomon's chambers to work out a settlement. The consent agreement provided that the approximately 65 men with complaints would have their status reviewed immediately and their places fixed, that 12 men would be advanced to A each month until the B list was exhausted, and that by August they would be proposed for membership.[17]

When Julia's grandson Shane went to work on the waterfront, he found it very difficult to tolerate the way some white workers tried to pick fights with black workers. He said, "Anytime a black would run the winch, the white guys down in the hole would yell at him and say he was doing a bad job, even if he was a much better winch driver than a white guy that had been on previously."[18]

In 1984, Julia acknowledged, "There still is discrimination and racism on the Portland waterfront but nothing like it was." And again, despite the continued racial tension on the waterfront, in 1991, Julia reflected, "Today I think it's better, quite a bit better. There are women on the waterfront now too. Things have greatly changed since I went to work first for Matt Meehan."

Chapter 12

YOU FIND FRIENDS IN IMPROBABLE PLACES

Multiple fractures of the left upper arm resulted when Julia E. Eaton, 44, . . . shot herself with a .25 calibre automatic pistol Sunday afternoon. The bullet entered the left upper chest but apparently ricocheted off a bone, lodging in the arm. She was admitted at Emanuel hospital. . . . Officer Robert Thompson said a note had been written. A charge of disorderly conduct by attempting suicide was made, with bail at $50. The wound was not considered critical but would require several days hospitalization.[1]

The first question after a suicide, or an attempt, is nearly always "Why?" Julia was a fighter. Why would she suddenly give up?

Nineteen fifty was not a happy year for her politically: American soldiers were fighting socialist North Korea in an undeclared war; members of the left were in prison, convicted of violating the Smith Act; the CIO had completed its purge of 11 so-called Communist-dominated unions, thereby losing nearly one million members; Julius and Ethel Rosenberg were awaiting trial for espionage; Senator Joseph McCarthy had begun his anticommunist crusade; and foreign-born union activists were being threatened with deportation under the new Internal Security Act.

Julia's personal life at the end of 1950 wasn't ideal either. She had only part-time work. She had had two failed marriages, and was probably lonely living by herself. She'd never done so before. And now her son Mike, who had married in 1948, was getting divorced, causing her to feel guilty for putting her political work before caring for him when he was young.

Julia was depressed. Her friend Helmi told me it was romantic troubles. Julia said she was overwrought from living on coffee. Moreover, she believed her father, whom she'd always admired and identified with, had taken his own life. Suicide had a certain appeal.

My father had committed suicide and my son committed suicide. I really think it's possible that there is a tendency in some families. Well, my father was a melancholic depressive. I'm more or less a recovered melancholic depressive. We're really not very much attached to life and if we have any disappointments or things don't pan out as we think they should, we go into fits of depression. Sometimes we go into them for no reason at all.

I drank a bottle of iodine once when I lived at West Oregon. I was so frustrated and bored at West Oregon and there was no way at all you could get anything through Butch's head. We had a terrible quarrel over the fifty cents a month I was spending on an educational insurance policy, so-called, for my son Mike. Butch thought that was ridiculous and we had a violent argument. We were very poor. This was before the union. So I ran in the bathroom and drank a bottle of iodine.

If you ever decide to commit suicide, don't do it that way. It scorches your throat. The minute I did it, I knew what a terrible thing I had done. Stupid. I thought, "What's going to happen to Mike, my boy?" So I screamed to Butch to go and get Dr. Brous, the company doctor.

Butch just stood there screaming, "What'd you do it for? What'd you do it for?"

Fortunately, at that moment one of my neighbors came to the door. She was a woman that could act quickly and actively. She went and got the doctor.

You know, you find friends in improbable places. The company doctor at West Oregon was a close friend of mine, and yet he was a company doctor. He was very understanding. He said he had thought about committing suicide himself at one time. He said he had had a rich patient who had died. The patient had no family and left him a little money. Patients of his started the rumor that he had killed this man. He said it was such an agony of thought that he thought about killing himself. He talked to me for almost two days, off and on, about the subject of suicide.

For many years suicide appealed to me as a way out of any difficulty. One day [in 1950] I got fed up with the world. 'Course it's not the first nor the last time. I remember sitting down and thinking about all the awful things that were happening around me and the awful things I feared would happen. It just seemed to me it was like a swirling flood and you couldn't keep your head up. It was a period in which there were a great many people out of work; there was a great deal of misery around.

And then I got these bills. Actually, compared to bills I've owed at other times, they were really insignificant. I've never been too concerned about my creditors really, unless it was some friend I had borrowed five bucks from. That always worried me.

Usually the final thing that triggers you off is not the real reason, it's just the last straw, as you might say. It was a telephone bill that I got. There were a great many long-distance charges on it and I didn't see any possible way I could pay that bill. And if I couldn't pay the bill, I didn't see how I could continue to write for Federated Press or other of the labor papers I sent news copy to.

Also, I got down to the point where I was living mostly on black coffee. I had gotten a part-time job on the waterfront working as secretary to Matt Meehan, but it was just a part-time job. Then my son and his wife separated and she took Shane—he was just a baby—and went back to Canada. That's where, as I recall, the long-distance calls came from. I just decided, "To hell with it." I decided the best thing to do was to commit suicide.

It was just pure accident that I didn't succeed. I had a pistol that had belonged to my father and I decided I'd shoot myself. I went to see a doctor I knew and told him I was writing a "true story" about a woman who committed suicide by shooting herself. I said, "Where should I say she pointed the gun?" So he showed me.

What happened is that I'm sitting on this hassock and the stand I kept the telephone on was near the hassock. In order to nerve myself up to do this I had made myself some coffee and poured some whiskey in it. I'd drunk a couple of drinks and then I pointed the gun at the place where this doctor told me to point it. Just as I pulled the trigger, the phone rang.

You know, it's surprising what your reflex actions are. I presume what happened is, as I reached out to pick up the phone, I shot myself through the side of my chest. It came out through my arm, smashing my arm and shoulder. It's a wonder the doctors were ever able to patch it up. I've still got the scars. It knocked me back off the hassock onto the floor.

I must have been out because this Filipino friend of mine, Ramon Tancioco, came by and when I didn't answer the bell, he looked in the window and saw me lying on the floor. He called an ambulance and the ambulance driver alerted the police, customary in such cases.

When I came to, I was still lying on the floor, and Ramon was there, and the ambulance driver was there and his assistant and this dreadful captain of police stationed in North Portland, with whom I'd had all sorts of encounters. He was really a dreadful person, this police captain.

Those dreadful cops in St. Johns had been after me for some years because of some of the exposé articles I had written on their activities. He said to me, "Now I've got you where I want you. It's illegal to try to commit suicide. I'm gonna put you in jail and keep you there."

So I said, "You goddamn son-of-a-bitch, I'll be dead before you get me there." That's what Ramon said I said.

I passed out again and when I came to I was in Emanuel Hospital back of a picket line. The hospital was being picketed by one of the hospital employees' unions. Well, I was unconscious so I didn't know, but I'm sure I would have jumped out of the ambulance.[2]

The first thing I asked when I came to in the hospital was what hospital I'm in because I had an awful fear it was Emanuel. Imagine my shock. It's a wonder that didn't kill me! I also was shocked that I wasn't dead.

They first had me in a room on the third floor with bars on the window because they thought I'd jump out, finish the job, and, of course, I meant to, but at that point I was too feeble to get out of bed. They also had cops stationed outside my door all the time because as soon as I could leave the hospital they were going to arrest me.

It upset some of my Filipino friends in the Longshore union so much that they persuaded the hospital to let them "stand guard" outside my door and replace the police. Irvin Goodman informed the police department he was my attorney and, if they arrested me, he would file a lawsuit. They did not arrest me! He had a lot on the police department.

Eventually, as I was there a long time [three weeks], I was taken down on another floor and put into a room without bars and I decided to finish the job. When I was being brought on one of those gurneys from the elevator, the gurney was stopped outside this door and I looked in there and I saw this cabinet where they kept instruments.

So one night I went in that room and I was gonna get one of those deals out and slit my wrists or maybe my throat, don't remember, it's too long ago, and then all at once (I suppose, if I were religious, I would think it was divine intervention) it struck me how much trouble the nurses would get into. You know, some of them might even be fired. And they weren't exactly scabs because this picket line was an informational picket line. I thought, "Well how can I ever justify getting some people fired off jobs that they probably desperately need."

Then it seemed more important to do something about the picket line; the nurses had told me about it and so had Matt Meehan. Matt came through the picket line to see me. He said, "Well, I told them my secretary was in here and I absolutely had to see her, so they okayed my coming through the picket line."

I called the union headquarters and arranged for leaflets to be brought to a side door; when I was a bit stronger I put them under my bathrobe and I went all over the hospital and distributed them on every floor, what it was about.

Then I began to think about the whole deal. I had caused a great deal of trouble to a great many people and it hadn't worked anyway because I was still alive with all my old troubles, complicated by the fact that the doctor didn't think I'd ever be able to use my arm properly. So I thought, "Well, that's the end of that, it's too risky. If it doesn't succeed, look at all the trouble you caused to other people."

The doctor I had was a very conservative doctor as far as a national health care plan went or anything like that, but he was a very decent individual. He also fought for me. When they objected to me having a typewriter, he said he had recommended it as part of my therapy. You know, doctors are bosses, so he got his way and I got the typewriter.

Someone asked me why I didn't let my mother visit me when I was in the hospital. They said that was very cruel of me. So I got to thinking, why did I leave word she couldn't get in to see me? And I thought, I must have realized that it was gonna be a difficult pull and that if I was going to use all of my powers to get on top of my problems, magnified by my new ones, that I couldn't listen to any of that stuff.

I always found it pretty difficult tousling with my mother. Although my mother was really quite a pioneer in her way—she really could think—yet still she couldn't get it out of her head that the thing that counts most is being, they now call it, upwardly mobile. Oh, I hate those two words.

"You should be a successful person in some kind of a career or profession"— she was always jawing at me about that, particularly after my brother began to be so startlingly successful in his hateful career with the War Department.

She would always come to my shack wherever I was living and start out being very nice, bringing cookies and things for my son. She dearly loved him. Then she'd take out some letters she'd got from my brother and she'd read about his latest successes. And then she'd tell me I should go back to school and get my degree, which never interested me in the least.

I remember when she came to see me at the hospital. She stood in the doorway and she said, "How could you do this to your mother?" I thought to myself, "I didn't do it to you, mother, I did it to myself."

I had already started reading books on psychology to figure out why some of the men I married behaved the way they behaved, and then I began to read books to find out why I behaved the way I behaved. I concluded I was a melancholic depressive. I read one book by Karen Horney that was very good and then

I read one by Karl Menninger, *Man Against Himself.* It was a very good book, too.

You can get onto yourself. Of course, I've always had a sense of humor, that's a big help. Anyway, I'm now a "recovered" melancholic depressive. But it took other books and a lot of effort to achieve that status. Anyway, I was in good company. The Menninger book described Abraham Lincoln as a melancholic depressive!

The chaplain of that hospital gave me this wonderful book to read. It was written by this rabbi. His name was Joshua Loth Liebman. It was called *Peace of Mind.*

You know, one thing that used to depress me was thinking about all the things I had done wrong in bringing up my son, because I'd put all the movements that I was involved in and all the books and poetry I was trying to write ahead of things that I should have been doing for him. I used to beat myself over the head thinking about these things. Liebman said that you shouldn't beat yourself over the head. The past is the past. You have to go on.

It was funny about that chaplain. He spent a good deal of time talking to me, but then he tried to convert me. One day he wanted me to get out of bed and kneel down on the floor and pray with him. And you know, that wasn't my idea of salvation.

Do I believe in a heaven and a hell? I don't believe in hell. There's no need for one, we've got one on earth. I will admit that there's something more than we know. Sometimes you look all around at all the things in the world, the different sorts of trees and flowers, the mountains, the rivers, and you think about the other planets in the universe, and you think there must be more to it than meets the eye. On the other hand, I think sometimes that if there is a superior being, how could he or she let some of the terrible things happen that happen?

But you know, even in all of the things that went on when I was in Emanuel, many of the things that happened over there were very funny. These union officials standing in the door that were afraid to come in because they thought I must be insane and maybe I'd kill them, thinking that I had tried to kill myself over them. You know the egotism of some men is really horrendous.

The funniest thing of all was that one of my ex-husbands [Ben] thought I had shot myself over him. Before this all happened I had got to the point where I was living on coffee mostly and where it was very difficult for me to do my writing for the different outfits that I wrote for. So I thought what I really need is to rest. I thought about a place that my second husband owned that had a creek on it and a shack and I thought if I could go up there and stay two or three weeks, I'd be a new person. So I sent him a note and I asked him if I could go up there and he said no. That really wasn't the reason I tried to kill myself, but he thought so. He must have felt some stricture of conscience because he came to the hospital and left an envelope with a hundred dollars in it with the nurse.

You know what I did with the hundred dollars? Well, when I got out of the hospital, I sent a longshoreman friend of mine to the store to buy presents for all of the nurses who'd taken care of me in the hospital. I spent the whole hundred on that.

And then Francis Murnane, when he came to see me he brought me a pint bottle of whiskey (in those days, I used to take a drink occasionally). Struck me as very hilarious, because he was very opposed to drinking and tried unsuccessfully to stop the drinking on the waterfront. I had him hide it under the mattress and I gave it to a black nurse who was on duty at the hospital. He brought a bowl of goldfish. Of course, it was very annoying to the nurses because they had to feed the fish.

When I was taken off the third floor where the bars were I was put in a two-bed ward and there was a young prostitute in the other bed. She'd been in a car wreck and her face was smashed. She said she wouldn't be able to go her trade until she got her face fixed. She'd have to have plastic surgery. After I got out of the hospital, my arm was in a sling. I couldn't use it. So Francis Murnane got the idea, I should take her home with me. Murnane said she could live there for her room and board as long as she did the cooking.

However, it didn't work out. There was a bedroom in the shack and then I had a couch in the living room. I slept on that and she slept on the bed. I woke up one night and she had a customer she was entertaining in the bedroom. And then she took off every afternoon. She would go down to the tavern where she had fished for customers and wouldn't come back till the middle of the night.

So one night when she was gone, I called Matt up and told him he better come out there and bring another lock for the door, because he had to put a stop to that. She'd evidently been taking some sort of drugs because I found a needle in her paraphernalia. Matt dropped that off the Broadway Bridge and put new locks on the door.

Several months later, I got a letter from her. She was in San Francisco. It's very strange about her. She was very fond of poetry and she made off with some of my poetry and sent it back. She also made off with a few pieces of jewelry that I had, which I didn't miss as I've never cared for jewelry anyway, but she thought that I did. She said she'd pawned it and she was very sorry. So I answered her letter and thanked her for returning the poetry and I said, "Don't worry about the jewelry. I don't like it anyway."

The reason Francis Murnane had this idea to take this prostitute is because he had the romantic notion that many working men of that period had about prostitutes. In the '34 strike the prostitutes were very sympathetic to the strikers. They always had a room that they lived in, but they had another room someplace else where they practiced their profession. So they allowed the single longshoremen and the seamen, that had joined the strike when their ships came to Portland, to sleep in those rooms. So the longshoremen were very sentimentally attached to the prostitutes. But there had been a change since the 1934 strike and these times, because pimps had taken over the oldest profession. It had been taken over by the syndicate.

You know when you do something like try to commit suicide, something happens to you afterwards. I once read a story about broken bones. It said in many cases that that bone, after it heals, is stronger than it was before. Well, in looking back on what I did, it always seemed to me afterwards that something like that happened, that you're tougher afterwards. I like to think I was.

I learned a great deal out of that episode. I learned that when you get absolutely exhausted, you've absolutely got to stop. You've got to stop everything you're doing and get a good night's sleep and play some soothing music. That was a good lesson to learn.

But, you know, I think suicide runs in my family.

The Morning Light

They rise to haunt me, ghosts I cannot slay
Out of the jungle of some yesterday—
My hydra-headed demons of the night.
Reach for a pill, a book, turn on the light!
Awareness of some labor left undone,
Some wrong to union brother, lover, son
Leaps the stockade from the Freudian past
To stalk the dark until I sleep at last
And wake, from the long duel in the night
To count my grievous wounds in morning light.[3]

          —Julia Ruuttila, n.d.

I MEAN TO BE YOUR FRIEND

In 1951, when Julia was forty-three, she finally married a man who suited her. Oscar Ruuttila was a Communist and shared Julia's anticapitalist views. He worked as a warehouseman and was active in his union, the ILWU; Julia had met him at meetings of the Columbia River District Council. Though he had been born in California, he was raised in Finland and was very much a part of the large Finnish community in Astoria, Oregon. Oscar was a year older than Julia, but this was his first marriage. In 1953, they took in her grandson Shane, and after Julia's mother suffered a stroke, she too came to live in the Ruuttila household.

Oscar came to the hospital from Astoria to see me. I think that was when he decided he was going to marry me.

I had a number of visitors, but Oscar was not that aggressive, so, when they told him I couldn't have visitors, he simply sat down in the hospital office and wrote me a letter. I remember he had a postscript on it that said, "Do not despair, I mean to be your friend."

I've thought a lot about Oscar; he was always the man, in the days when he sailed on ships, that took care of the ship's cat and saw the cat its milk and water. So that's probably how he thought of me.

I'd known Oscar for a long time. I used to see him at District Council meetings—he was usually a delegate from his local and I was always at those meetings to write them up for the union newspaper. But I'd never paid any attention to him and he'd never paid any to me because he was an orthodox CP member and I was only an unaffiliated red.

How we began to get really on more intimate terms, he wrote me a letter and bitterly criticized an article I had written about a council meeting. He said

Oscar (with his lunchpail), 1959.

I had misspelled Matt's name and that the man that I had listed in the story as secretary of the council was not the secretary.

I was simply furious and I wrote him a letter in reply and I said, "Well, Matt was very interested to know that all these years he's been misspelling his name." And I said, "Don't you realize that a month ago, if you'd kept up on what's going on, the secretary was voted out and another one was voted in."

He wrote to apologize. We began to write to each other and Oscar's letters were quite interesting. He had a way with words. We used to argue in the letters, because, you see, I am not an orthodox red. I admit I'm a red, but I'm not an orthodox red.

Of course, he knew I shared the same ideas that he had about social change and about the unions. I could never have gotten along with anyone that didn't have the same sort of views that you had to get rid of the capitalist class and make a better life for all of the people. Of course, I don't understand how anybody could not be for social change and the end of capitalism and a different social and economic system.

When I got out of the hospital, my arm was still in a sling. Matt Meehan told me I had to go to Longview and cover a caucus the union was having. I said, "Well I don't see how I can write this story up, I can only use one hand."[1]

He said, "Oh you'll find a way."

So I took my typewriter to Longview and I forgot that I couldn't use the other arm and I used it. Oscar was there and he suggested that I come down to Astoria to recuperate.

In the early 1870s, journalist Charles Nordhoff arrived in sixty-year-old Astoria by steamer from San Francisco. He was unimpressed. "When you have seen it, you will wish you had passed it by unseen," he wrote. "Astoria, in truth consists of a very narrow strip of hill-side, backed by a hill so steep that they can shoot timber down it, and inclosed on every side by dense forests, high steep hills, and mud flats."[2]

The high steep hills and mud flats were still there in 1951, but the forests had been cut; only the hilltops remained wooded. The resulting lumber had been turned into piers, canneries, streets of boxy houses, and a few mansions. The lumber industry had given way to the fishing industry.[3]

Earlier in the century, Astoria boasted the largest Finnish community west of the Mississippi. In 1950, Astoria had a population of 12,331; of these, 935 were born in Finland. Most Finns lived in Uniontown, on the west end of Astoria, facing the Columbia River. The hill rises abruptly from the river, and Uniontown's main residential street, Alameda Avenue, runs one block above Marine Drive, affording a view across the river to the hills of Washington State four miles away. In 1951, the riverfront was a busy hub, with fish canneries, a large boat basin, the Pillsbury flour mill (where Oscar worked), the Oregon Fur Producers Association, oil wharfs, a box factory, a dairy cooperative, lumberyards, and the dock where ferries departed for the Washington side of the river several times a day.[4]

Early Finnish immigrants to this country were mainly politically conservative, but those arriving after 1898 were deeply influenced by the struggle for nationhood and reform in Finland, and most were radicals. Many immigrants were political refugees. Of the more than 300,000 Finns who came to North America between 1869 and 1914, over 215,000 arrived after the turn of the century. Finns contributed proportionately more radicals to the United States than any other immigrant group, and the Finnish American Socialist Federation was at one time the largest of all foreign-language groups affiliated with the Socialist Party.[5]

The Astoria Finnish Socialist Club (Astorian Suomalainen Sosialisti Klubi [ASSK]) was founded in 1904. It began publishing its daily newspaper, the Toveri, *in 1907. In 1911, a weekly Finnish-language women's paper, the* Toveritar, *was added. Also in 1911, the club dedicated its five-story Finnish Socialist Hall. The ASSK became not only the center of the socialist Finns' political life but of their cultural and social life as well.[6]*

The hall boasted a theater, ballroom, gym, and library, and supported classes, lectures, dances, and performances. The club had its own orchestra, choir, and brass band, with a salaried music director; athletic clubs for men, women, and children; a sewing club and reading circle; committee for entertainment; and an agitation committee, whose job was "arranging speeches and more serious entertainment." And every week the drama club, with the aid of the hired drama director, produced a play.[7]

Despite the vitality of left-wing Finnish life in Astoria, the Finnish community was not politically homogeneous. Political bitterness dominated relations between the Red Finns (radicals) and the White Finns (conservatives), mirroring the split that had ripped apart their native country in civil war in 1918. The membership of the ASSK was never above 10 percent of Astoria's Finnish community, but membership among the Whites was even less. Most Finns were what Julia called "the dancing Finns," those who were not committed to either faction.[8]

When Julia visited in 1951, Astoria was still split along these lines, although the Reds had lost much of their influence. Their five-story hall had burned down in 1923, the next generation was more "American," and the ASSK was no longer the force it had once been in local life.[9] The red scare was in full force and the Communists were no longer running candidates for public office. Nevertheless, the Red Finns were still a presence in Astoria and Oscar was a leader of that community.

So I went down on a short visit and I thought Astoria was a fascinating place and I thought the Finns were crazy and fascinating people, which they were. Somewhat to my amazement, Oscar suggested that instead of going back to Portland on the day I had planned to return, that I remain and we get married.[10]

I was willing to go down there and live, but I didn't want to get married. I was absolutely stunned when he insisted. I tried to get him to realize there was no reason why we should go through a marriage ceremony. I'd really had it with that stuff, too hard to get divorced. But he maintained that he couldn't afford to live in sin in a small town like Astoria. The only difference that he could afford was his political differences.

He was quite right about that. It was a very rigid, respectable community. In fact, after he married me, he became a much more plausible figure to the people in Astoria because before that he had no money troubles. But after he acquired me and we acquired Shane [after Mike's marriage broke up], he had the type of money trouble as the other working-class heads of families had, and the people in the place where he worked began to listen to him more. He said it was amazing the change.

Well, of course, you never could quite figure Oscar out. He had been brought up in a rigid Lutheran family in Finland so he may also have had some feelings from his Lutheran childhood, which, of course, he would never admit. He had become an agnostic because of these three-hour sermons they had on Sunday, when the minister would see some poor helpless child nodding off and start ranting and raving that that infant was going to hell.

Astoria native Betty Wollam recalled seeing Julia with Oscar at an outing in 1950. "The memory that I have of first realizing that they were going to be a couple was at a picnic out along one of the lakes. He was sculling a scow or rowboat, and she was sitting facing him and she had put her arm up around the back of her head and was looking at him very roguishly and coquettishly, and he was being very Astoria Finn and not making any motion at all except that, if you looked for it, there was a twinkle. Within six months they were married, and she had moved to Astoria."[11]

As I recall, we got married at 11:30 in the morning [on January 3, 1951] and at 1 something I took the bus back to Portland because I was Matt Meehan's secretary.

The only man I have ever been involved with, he was basically honest, who had courage, imagination, and warmth, was Oscar, the Finn. I wasn't in love with him when I married him, but I liked him and I grew to love him. I married him to get the hell out of Portland and away from racism on the Portland waterfront.[12]

When my mother found out I was going to marry Oscar, she had an absolute fit. We were already married as a matter of fact. I remember what she said: "The Finnish men hook their wives up to plows." And I said, "Well, he doesn't have a farm and he has no plow and he has no horse." But she became very fond of him after she had a stroke and had to come and live with us.

I stayed in Portland for two or three months after I married Oscar because Matt wanted me to find a replacement, but everyone I sent to interview didn't suit him, so at the end of three months I told him I was moving down anyway. He had two locals in Astoria at that time and he had to go down to service them from time to time, so he said he'd bring all his letters and reports down there for me to do. Which he did even after I went to work for the fishermen's union. The gillnetters came after me. They came and asked me to come down and work there, which I agreed to do if they would let Matt bring his work to the office.

The fishermen's union had this terrible strike while I was there [1952] and they lost an entire fishing season—the Columbia River Fishermen's Protective Union, the gillnetters. I thought they were very foolish to go on strike because they had no affiliation. They were an independent union. They had no money in their treasury. The cannery women, who once belonged to their union, had been raided away by another union. But they went on strike anyway.

The amount of money the packers wanted to pay for the fish was the problem. The Columbia River Packers Association are a terrible outfit. Later it became Bumble Bee. The strike lasted quite a long time and it was a very bitter strike.

During the strike I worked ten and twelve hours a day. What we did was we put out leaflets to the membership. There were different locals up and down the river that belonged to the Columbia River Fishermen's Protective Union. The union members of Greek extraction lived in the small fishing port of Clifton. I wrote a daily bulletin for distribution, and I remember asking one of the Greeks from Clifton the Greek word for scab. He replied, "There is no word for scab in the Greek language because no Greek ever scabbed!"[13]

The supervisory employees and the packers themselves that lived there attempted to go and can the fish. A lot of it rotted on the cannery floor and they slipped around in the slime. It was really hilarious in a way. Well, the strike ended in a draw. Neither side won, but at least the gillnetters didn't lose.[14]

Because of the strike, all their money was gone—they didn't have any anyway—so they couldn't afford to have me anymore. I continued to write for the *Dispatcher* and the Federated Press because they couldn't find anyone else to do it. And I continued to do work for Matt Meehan and took care of Shane.

At the time I went down there to live, almost all the people in Astoria belonged to one union or another, but the town was run by Republican hard-liners and most of the union people weren't registered to vote. Astoria was controlled by absentee owners. I was so shocked at the political situation, so I did two things.

I felt it was necessary to get all the union people to register to vote so we could drive the Republicans out of local office, off the city council, and off of the county commission. So the union sponsored this registration campaign and everybody registered to vote. And then, you know what happened? It's almost incredible. All of the officeholders—naturally this was no secret we were doing this—they changed their registration to Democrat and they all got back in again.[15]

The other thing that I thought was important was to get the unions down there to buy some books on labor for the library. I took that up in a District Council meeting in Coos Bay and they thought it was a great idea. The District Council passed a resolution, which went to all of its affiliates, that they buy books on labor for the libraries in the different cities where longshoremen lived in Oregon and southern Washington.

I was instructed to call up the ILWU locals, the two locals in Astoria and also other unions, and see what they'd like to see there. I well remember what the man in Local 50 said, "The only thing we read are the labels on whiskey bottles." I wrote for the *Dispatcher* about this project and, of course, some of the locals had sent in very excellent lists, so I put that in, but I also put his quote in too.

Later the town's leading businessmen, members of the Elks Club and of the Legion, went to the public library and intimidated the librarian and they had a book burning. Isn't that dreadful? They went there openly. They told the librarian they had a list of books. Anything that they found subversive. Of course, it was their ideas of subversion. They'd evidently been snooping around before that.

Among the things that they got rid of was that little magazine *Mainstream*. Oscar, very unwisely I thought, had given the previous librarian—who was a very liberal woman that subscribed to the Library Bill of Rights—he had persuaded her to accept a gift subscription to the *People's World*. So they took all of those papers out and burned them.

Well, the daughter-in-law of a close Finnish friend of mine in Astoria worked in the library and she sent word. I rushed down there to protest. They were coming out with what they had out of the library, with what they decided to destroy. I was the only spectator, if you want to call me a spectator.

Someone pushed me, I forget who it was. So I decided—although I've got a very good sense of balance and scarcely ever fall—I decided to fall down. The librarian became quite frightened and he picked me up and carried me into his office. He said the push was purely accidental and I said, "Oh, no it wasn't."

I should have kicked him instead of letting him carry me into his office because when I came out everyone was gone and so were the books and papers. If it hadn't been for this woman who worked there I wouldn't have known anything about it.

During her IWA days, Julia had seen how powerful the wives could be in a union's struggles if they were organized into a ladies' auxiliary. There was no ILWU ladies' auxiliary in Astoria when she moved there, so she set out to remedy that deficiency.

I decided to organize the women's auxiliary down there, but there was a right-wing Finn who was president of the Longshore local and he would have nothing to do with it, so the members of this auxiliary in Astoria—and it lasted four or five years—were the wives of the Warehouse local down there. Local 18 it was called. Their husbands worked in the flour mill where Oscar worked. [The longshoremen had their own local separate from the warehousemen.] We used to hold meetings and sponsored a Christmas party and passed resolutions on various political subjects.

Even though Oscar and Julia's political beliefs were compatible, Julia didn't join the Communist Party. Oscar's party activity was not a problem in their marriage, except for one time when the Oregon Party brought charges against friends of hers in Portland, including Martina Curl and her husband, Hank. As a nonmember, Julia didn't know any details, but she was sure the Party was wrong. She referred to the incident as a witch-hunt and fought Oscar over it.

We had a good life. Oscar was someone that was not a rigid left winger. I've often wondered if the European reds are more liberal than those in this country or if it was just that Oscar was more liberal. He was not a hard-liner except on that one occasion when I would not speak to him for three days.

When I married Oscar we promised not to interfere with each other's opinions or views. I knew he was a hard-liner and he knew that, although I definitely believed that our political and economic system doesn't work for the benefit of the people and you might say I'm a communist—if you look at the definition in the old dictionaries—I'm not and never could be a hard-liner. We only had two arguments during the years we spent together. One of them was quite serious.

The CP had a witch-hunt in Portland, so they had people come from all over the state to participate in the witch-hunt trial. Well, it didn't take me long to find out that Oscar was one of those that had been told to come to Portland and participate. You know, in a small house, if they hold meetings there, because that's the only house that is not afraid to have a meeting—and one thing Oscar was *not* was a coward, he had a lot of guts—so meetings were held there and *I* had to cook the coffee. Well, how could I not know what was going on?

When Oscar came back, he told me that they had expelled four people. There was a stool pigeon in Portland then and I had a pretty good idea who it was. I told him they had picked on the wrong people, that three of the people were close friends of mine, and none of them could possibly have been involved in whatever it was they were supposed to have done. I knew they were not class enemies of ours, far from it. And he didn't know them.

Each affiliate group had to pass on the judgment of the witch committee, as I called it. So a meeting was set up in Astoria to rubber-stamp the decision. That's when we had the big quarrel. We just stopped speaking.

I would have left if we hadn't taken Shane to bring up. That shows you how much I had grown up, because I realized I couldn't leave him because Shane definitely needed a father and a father just like Oscar. So I didn't speak for three days.

Then one day I thought to myself, "Well this really can't go on. It's got to end." We were drinking coffee. I was seated at a little table by the door and he was seated at the kitchen table. He'd made the coffee. He made good coffee.

So I got up and I said, "Well, how's the old super-duper left winger this morning?" So, he got up. I could see he was about ready to weaken, and I said, "I'll walk halfway across the floor to you, if you'll walk the other half." But he was a tall man—he was six feet two inches or six feet one or something—and so he got to me before I got to him. And that was the end of that.

After we started speaking again, I began talking to him about these three people. So, he finally decided that they were not going to hold any meeting because I said, "If you do, I shall come out of the kitchen, where I am cooking the coffee, and speak up in their defense. And that'll be the end of the charges against them. I'll just blow them sky high."

Each morning I'd say, "So how's the old witch-hunter this morning?" Well, I guess I convinced him I was right and the witch-hunters were wrong and that they were after the wrong person. You could get along with Finnish people if you will let them have their way in everything unless it was extremely important.

Oscar canceled the meeting and he went around and told everyone that he had received more information and he considered the whole thing and decided it was a mistake to have a meeting and to go along with that verdict and that he had received information that there was a stool pigeon. It later did come out there was one that was going around and starting stuff to split up the left-wing group up here.

And then Bulldog [Julia's nickname for Bert Nelson, the Washington State Communist Party chairman] came down from Seattle and gave Oscar hell because they hadn't held the meeting and they hadn't gone along with the verdict. So I sat in the living room listening to Bulldog and finally I told Bulldog to get the hell out of our house. He said to Oscar, "Are you going to sit there and let that irresponsible so-on and so-forth woman order me out of your house?"

Oscar said, "Well, it's her house too. You better leave."

They must have thought I was a bad influence on Oscar.

I believe in practically everything that group [CP] stands for and I'm a no-torious non–stool pigeon. I have been to a great many CP meetings that were open to the public and several that weren't, but it is impossible for me to sub-scribe to any hard and fast doctrine because I was brought up on two volumes that my father possessed that tell about the struggles of the working class before the time of Christ, *The Ancient Lowly.* If you read the history of the proletariat back over several thousand years, it's very interesting to see what happens to the struggle for people and to left-wing groups. It gives you a sort of perspective so that you don't ever get the idea that any one group is perfect and everything they say is so, because people are human beings. And then of course, I was brought up in the IWW, not the CP.[16]

If you have read as much as I have read about the struggle for the have-nots and the haves, conditions and things change in this world. If you have been brought up or learned through adversity to do your own thinking, that's some-thing you've got to hang on to. But I've met some very wonderful people that I think were Communists.

Of course, let the party be publicly attacked by the newspapers or by the ac-quaintances of friends of mine, and I always rise up to refute the charges, be-cause I definitely do believe in communism. I think the definition in my oldest dictionary is pretty good: "A system of social organization in which the goods are held in common, involving common ownership of the means of production and some approach to equal distribution of the products of industry." Now what's wrong with that? I've never objected to the owners of factories being op-posed to Communism or being opposed to trade unions. What I can't under-stand is why the slaves in the factories fall for all that stuff about "watch out 'cause Russians are coming."

Politics were important to Julia in a man, but she cared about other things as well. She genuinely liked Oscar and they both enjoyed the outdoors. And Julia had always been attracted to tall, good-looking men.

Oscar was an intellectual. He was quite well educated, though he was mostly self-educated. He read books in two languages. When he came to this country he couldn't speak a word of English, but he learned and he wrote articles for dif-ferent labor papers and articles that were published in Finland in Finnish and in this country in English. He liked some of the same books that I liked. He had a terrific sense of humor, which is why he could be talked out of some of these, to me, depressing hard-liner attitudes.

He was tall and what hair he had was blonde. He had blue eyes. And he was extremely fond of many things that interested me like swimming and walking in the woods and along the seashore. There's many things that you can do down there: fishing and clamming and watching the ocean and there are many places to go on hikes and picnics. He got extremely interested in gardening, which has always been one of my major interests. And Oscar was interested in art. He was fairly good at sketching. He got Shane interested in drawing.

It was a wonderful life except for these intervals when awful things were happening, but looking back, you know, they sort of fade into the background and I just see the overall picture.

We had this little house built in a part of Astoria that Oscar said he would never live in because he didn't want to move off Alameda Avenue where all the Finns lived. That was in Uniontown and the Finns were so crazy about that area that they were living three deep. They would build apartments in basements and attics rather than move off of Alameda Avenue. To move away from there on the other side of the hill to him was unthinkable.

I said to Oscar, "I don't want to live on this side of the hill because the soil isn't any good." I said, "I want to move on the Bayside." So we argued to some degree about that but finally he agreed to go and look at it and we bought three small lots over there and built a very tiny house in the middle of the three lots.

We didn't have any money so I said to Oscar, "You can apply for a GI state loan," and he said he didn't think they'd give it to him. So I put in the application and I also drew the plans for the house, and somewhat to my surprise they were accepted by the loan people. I drew the elevations as well as the floor plan.

Well, my father could do all kinds of things. At one time he quit working in the logging camps and started building houses in Eugene and I always went around on the job with him. I simply bought a drawing board and a T square and a straight edge and drew these plans.

Oscar hired a Finn—naturally a Finn—that he'd once been shacked up with during the Depression. He and three other men cooked mulligan stew in this little shack down on the waterfront. After the Depression was over, he'd become a sort of a contractor. So he built the house. Then it turned out, since this was done on a state GI loan, the man down there, I forget if he was a banker, he had to put in the final say on the money being released. He refused to do so, so Oscar was simply petrified because none of these people had been paid and we owed for paint and we owed for linoleum and lumber and roofing and you name it.

So I said, "Well, Oscar, for once the business people in Astoria are going to have to join us in getting that money released because they want their money."

Oscar said, "I don't think it'll work." He said, "We'll have to let them take the house and sell it."

So I called up some of these people that were involved, that needed the money, and invited them to come to the house and asked them to join us in putting pressure on the authorities to release this money so they'd get their money. And believe me, they did.

Well then, what was so funny, the man called me to come down to his office and the money was all there, but there was something that Oscar and I had to sign. Oscar was so anxious to get his hands on the money that he didn't notice. He didn't sign it.

So the next day, early in the morning, he called up and he said, "I have to send the papers back to Salem. You and your husband just came in here and argued with me about how I'd held up that check and you didn't sign the papers. Come down," he said, "I'll be in a lot of trouble."

I said, "Well isn't that just too bad. We're going out of town and we won't be back for a week or two and when we get back we'll try to come down at our convenience." So we let him stew for a few days; served him right.

Betty Wollam recalls the house Julia and Oscar built:

> The outside was very pleasant, but the inside showed that she could have done anything. She had designed every inch of it to use small space, so that around under the windows were all the bookcases, and then she had made cushions to cover them, so there were also places to sit when there were meetings at her house, which was fairly common, strategy meetings for the fishermen's union and the longshore union. You were amazed how many people could sit comfortably in that little tiny house. She would have twenty-five people sitting, cheek by jowl, but all with a place to sit.
>
> The cupboards in the kitchen, the one right over the sink was narrow so that you could stand there and it didn't come out and hit you in the face, and then the next one was a little wider and as it got up over her head, they were full-width shelves.
>
> Every detail was planned, it was like a ship. Craft that the same way she did a story.[17]

When Julia married Oscar she gained more than a husband; she became part of the tight-knit Finnish community.

So I met the Finns. I had only known one Finnish person before in addition to Oscar. I had the idea that Finns didn't drink because Oscar didn't drink. In fact, I used to accuse him of being the founder of the Women's Christian Temperance Union. And the woman I knew who was Finnish drank nothing but coffee.

The first time I went for a walk with Oscar, we went past the tavern in Uppertown and just then the door opened and the bouncer threw some very drunk

Finn into the street. So then I learned there were the coffee-drinking Finns and the whiskey-drinking Finns.[18]

I've always liked the foreign-born people that I lived around. First I lived in an Italian neighborhood in St. Johns and they were my favorite foreign-born people. Then when I went to work for the longshoremen's union, I met the Filipinos that belonged to our Alaska cannery workers local. They had a sublocal here in Portland and they became my favorite foreign-born people. But when I went to Astoria, I concluded the Finns were the best of all.

'Course they had this frightful hang-up on cleanliness and order. They were paranoid on the subject. After I went down there to live, I hadn't been there more than two or three days when Oscar informed me he was going to put me back on the bus to Portland. He couldn't stand the disorder. He said, "When you're through reading the newspaper, you should pick it up, fold it up neatly, and put it on the coffee table."

I said to him, "I can't stand all this carping about order and disorder. If you don't cut it out you won't have to put me on the bus, I'll put myself on it."

So we decided to negotiate a settlement and he would be less paranoid on the subject and I would try to be more orderly. I looked around our apartment and I saw it with new eyes. I saw he had some right to be critical. 'Course I've always blamed my lack of order on my mother. She had never done any housekeeping whatsoever and she was quite disorderly too. She never dusted the baseboards or anything like that. She spent all the time with books.

I thought when I went down there that I'd have a great deal of time to write books and poetry, so I started to write the life of Maria Raunio. She was head of communications and transport in the strike in Finland in 1905 and she was also a member of the Finnish Diet [the legislative assembly in Russian-controlled Finland]. She was going to be deported to Siberia for her activities—you know Russia owned Finland at this time—so she came to the United States.

She was used to being around intellectuals and there were a few intellectuals in Astoria, but not too many, and she was extremely unhappy there. She'd had to leave two children behind her in Finland. So she committed suicide. That was another way in which I got into difficulty with some of the super-duper left-wing Finns, because they denied she'd committed suicide. They said to do such a thing was very "un-Communist."[19]

I became interested in her because they would go out to the graveyard, Greenwood, to decorate graves before Decoration Day so that when the people came out on Decoration Day they'd see that the left-wing Finns were not forgotten. So they told me they were assigning me to decorate her grave because I also was a scribbler and she had been one. I was very annoyed because I felt it was very silly to decorate graves or visit graveyards, but as Oscar was unhappy with my refusal to have anything to do with it, I said I would and went along.

Then I became intrigued because there was a hammer and sickle on her tombstone, and at the time that she came to Astoria in 1910 or thereabouts, that was before the Russian Revolution. What she was, of course, was a Social Democrat. So I was intrigued at this discrepancy and I began to ask questions about her and I became enormously interested in everything I heard about her and about her life. So I thought I would write a biography of her, which I began. Then I realized that to finish it I would really have to go to Finland and do research. And, you know, you get caught up in a lot of other things, day-by-day activities and so forth, so I never went to Finland. But I did interview a lot of people who knew her.

At one time all of the street signs in Astoria were printed in both Finnish and English. I used to know a few phrases and I intended to study Finnish because they had night classes where you could learn it, but soon after I got down there I went to work for the gillnetters' union and they went on strike and I didn't have time to go to night school. So I never really did learn Finnish.

There were two halls there. Columbia Hall was the left-wing hall. At the time I lived there, the life of the Finnish community centered around Columbia Hall. When various causes came up that interested the left-wing Finns, they held meetings and passed resolutions and made motions on those causes. As there were dances held, the dancing Finns went to both halls. But the Finns were pretty much divided. We called the right-wing Finns, the Mannerheim Finns. General Baron Carl Gustav Mannerheim ruled Finland one time.

One time Oscar had a fight with another Finn in the steambath. That happened before I went down there to live. This other man also was a veteran of World War II and he was a right-wing Finn and they were arguing about Russia's invading Finland in the so-called Winter War [1939–40].

They got into a fight and banged each other with those wooden buckets and then everyone in the public steambath got involved in the fight. They burst out into the lobby—nude, of course—swinging at one another and then out onto the street and someone called the police. Oscar slithered up the path that went past the fire station to Alameda Avenue, and he was taken in and provided with clothes, but Kankkonen, the right-wing Finn, was hauled off to jail in a paddy wagon. Uniontown was still laughing about this when I moved to Astoria.

Fortunately Oscar was born here or he would certainly have been deported. He was born in Lompoc, California [in 1906], but his mother was dying and when he was about eighteen months old she wanted to see her family again and see the town where she grew up in Finland, so they went back there. She lived three or four days after the ship landed. His father came back to this country and left Oscar behind. He was brought up by his grandparents and his aunt. So he was like an old-country Finn.

When his father sent money for him to come to this country, I think he was seventeen. His father and stepmother were living in Gobel, that's a little town down the Columbia River. And they were having a very hard struggle. His father couldn't get work as a carpenter, which was his trade, and they were struggling on this little tiny farm, so Oscar started shipping out on ships.

Oscar never wanted to go back to Finland because when he was growing up in Finland in World War I the Finns were starving. His aunt was the public health nurse in Raahe, which is just this side of Lapland, and so he could go to the hospital and get one meal a day there. Nevertheless, he remembers how desolate and dismal it was and how much hunger there was in Finland.[20]

When Oscar was in his teens, why he must have been younger than that, he'd been with other boys out in the country to beg bread from the peasants. He was coming back past the stockade where some of the Red Finns were imprisoned (because, you know, they had a civil war in Finland—the Reds and the Whites—and he lived in a White Guard stronghold) and he saw this man looking at him between the bars and his eyes were glazed with hunger. He was looking at this bread Oscar was eating. So Oscar broke the loaf in two and gave the largest portion to this man. He said to Oscar, "Thank you, tovarish." That's the Russian word for comrade. I think he began to think about things that were going on. And then he began to think about there has got to be some kind of a world in which there would be food for all people. So he began to look for answers and solutions.[21]

He was coming along the street one time, and that was before 1917 when Russia still owned Finland, and the Cossacks were coming along the street on horseback and ran someone down that didn't get out of the way in time. Well, it made it an impression upon him. He couldn't endure suffering when it was other people who were suffering.

I was amazed when I was going through his papers. I found, I think it was, five stories he had written. Most of them were based on his experiences when he'd been a seaman, but one of them was an experience that he'd had in Finland. It was amazing when you consider what his political views were. He had told me about it once so I knew about it.

It was during the period when the Finnish people were starving. His aunt and several other women had gone to the woods to pick some kind of berries, but Oscar was so feeble from not really getting enough food that they left him sitting on a log. When they came back, he said, "Do you see that little house over there?" There was no little house, and he said, "There are men there and they came out and spoke to me." It was the place where some of the Red Guards had been murdered by the White Guards and there had been a little house there at one time.

He believed that, you know, and he was an agnostic. I told that to one of the hard-liners once and he said, "Oh well, he never had enough to eat so that he was having delusions from hunger." I don't think he was. But, you know, unless you have been extremely hungry yourself and gone through a great deal of stress and struggle, there are a great many things that you don't understand.

Come to think about it, the hard-liners that I've never been able to get along with are those that never went through that kind of stress and struggle. I lived in Chicago once for three weeks on a sack of rice. And then when I was growing up there were many times that we didn't have any food.

Chapter 14

THE LIVES OF WORKING PEOPLE ARE FULL OF DESPERATION

Julia's son Mike was born in June 1928, and while he was always a part of her story, he was often in the background. Only later, after he left home during World War II, did Mike take a central role in Julia's narrative, and it was generally when he ran into trouble with physical injuries, alcohol, and a disastrous marriage.[1]

Mike quit high school in 1942 to work in the shipyards. He trained for the Merchant Marine and was issued his seaman's papers about a week after World War II ended in August 1945. He was seventeen. He joined the Marines the next year, shortly after he turned 18. By November 1946 he was serving in the Philippines as a brigade guard. The next month he dislocated his shoulder playing football, a recurrence of a problem troubling him at least since boot camp. In the following months, his shoulder dislocated frequently and the Navy doctors wanted to operate but Mike refused because of fears of incompetent orthopedic surgeons and the experimental nature of the surgery. By this time, he had also developed a problem with alcohol.

In 1948, when Mike got out of the Marines, he married Doreen. Their son Shane was born in May 1949. The marriage did not last long. In 1951, after Julia married Oscar, she introduced him to Shane. Mike and Doreen were temporarily reconciled. Shane was twenty months old.

Oscar and I had been married one week and I was still living in my little house in Portland. Oscar had come from Astoria to spend the weekend with me. Mike and Doreen brought Shane to meet his new grandfather. Oscar had never been around any small children. I was worried he would not know how to make friends with Shane, and that he might even be annoyed by a small child's noise.

Shane could not take his eyes off of Oscar. Finally he said, "Where is Occer's hair?" He was always to love Oscar in a special way because he had no hair. When he was five or six, he took the scissors and surreptitiously cut off all his hair on top and over his forehead, and when I tried to find out what had made him do such a thing, he told us he "wanted a bald-headed haircut like Oscar's."

On Oscar's second visit to my Portland home we were fast asleep when there came a terrible pounding at the door. It was the police. Doreen was with them. Mike, she said, had "stolen Shane" and she had brought the police to find out if I was "hiding" Shane.

So Oscar did not see Shane again until after I moved to Astoria two months later. We had barely settled into our apartment before Doreen descended on us with Shane, bag and baggage. She had found Shane, taken him from Mike, and hidden him. Mike had learned that she was seeing Bill Martinez, a sailor on leave from the Navy base at Astoria. Mike had shipped out on a freighter. Doreen wanted me to help her find an apartment and get her on ADC (Aid to Dependent Children).

Then Bill Martinez was demobilized from the Navy. So Doreen took off with him for California and left Shane with Oscar and me. They went to West Sacramento, I think it was, where his mother lived. They were afraid that his mother would find out that they were not married and that she wasn't divorced from Mike, so she told his mother they had to borrow money to come back to Portland to settle the custody about Shane. Doreen appeared suddenly in Astoria and wanted Shane, because she said they'd have to take Shane back to add validity to this story.

We didn't want to give her Shane back. Neither one of us did. We called up an attorney in Portland and he said there was nothing we could do. Doreen took off with Shane. She didn't know where Mike was either. Soon after that she got the divorce.

Shane remembers Bill Martinez with fondness, but not his mother. His memories of his time in Sacramento are bad: "Being tied to the couch in real hot weather without water was one memory I had. I don't ever remember anything good prior to moving with Oscar and Julia." He talks of his life in Astoria with them with gratitude: "It was nice living with Julia and Oscar 'cause for the first time I had enough to eat. Clothes to wear. They took a real interest in my education. Made sure that I saw the doctor and the dentist and provided me a good home. I remember thinking how lucky I was to have Julia and Oscar instead of being with my mother."[2]

Then in 1953 Doreen called me up—and in the meantime she's pregnant and she said they couldn't keep Shane. If we still wanted him we had the first chance;

he was up for grabs. So Oscar told her on the phone that we would come and get Shane. We still wanted him, but she'd have to sign papers. She said she would. So Oscar laid off work and we drove to California.

I'll never forget when we got to the little house where she was living, Shane ran up to Oscar and got him around the knees and he said, "Oh Occer, Occer!"

She had his things all packed, if you want to say his things, his little worn-out clothes. He had virtually no toys. She had him about a year. She didn't shed a tear when we left, but Bill Martinez came outside the house and kissed Shane goodbye and gave us a baseball glove that he had used when he was in school.

I said, "You may need this for your son because she's going to have a baby."

He said, "No, this was for Shane."

The last sight I saw of him, he was standing on the little porch, leaning against the wall, and he was leaning against his arm and you could tell he was sobbing.

We went into a restaurant to get something to eat and Shane said, "Look at all the food." We stopped in some town and bought a whole bunch of clothes for Shane and also some toys. All at once Shane said, "I want to go and show all my new clothes and all these toys to Bill."

We're in a motel the next night and Shane started to scream and to pound his head. I was going to go over and pick him up when Oscar motioned me not to and dragged me into the kitchenette. Pretty soon Shane quit. We went back in there and he said to us, "Didn't you hear me pounding my head and screaming? I was real bad. Are you going to put me in the corner?"

Oscar said, "Was that the noise that we heard?"

He said, "Yes. Aren't you going to put me in the corner now, or whip me?"

Oscar said, "No."

Shane said, "Well, I was a bad boy."

He never did that again.

Then when we got back to Astoria, he couldn't seem to realize there was always going to be food to eat. We got a cot from our landlady and put it in our bedroom. He used to get up in the night and go to the garbage can in the kitchen and get apple and potato peelings and—you'd see a trail of them to his bed—he'd put them under his pillow. We thought that he had muscular dystrophy or something because he could hardly walk, but it was nothing but malnutrition. I think it took about five months before he was the size and weight that he should have been, maybe longer than that.

I was in my forties and Oscar was eleven months older than me. He had never had children before. But it wasn't hard to bring up a little kid at my age, because that's the first time I'd ever had a husband that behaved like a husband. I had real help from him.

My father gave a great deal of lip service to women's rights, but the first man I met that really seemed to understand women's rights was Oscar, the Finn. He was on shift work, you know, and if he was home and I was working, he would have dinner ready for me when I got home. He would wash dishes. He would even iron. He was one of the few people I thought that was really suited to live under socialism.

Well, a great many of the radicals I've known were chauvinist, the men, and when their wives worked, they didn't share the chores at home. Some of the Red Finns were real chauvinist male pigs! I remember one man whose wife worked in the cannery, and he worked in the flour mill in Astoria. He was one of the leading Red Finns. I remember seeing them walking up the hill from the shopping center in Astoria to their home, and he was walking ahead carrying nothing but himself and she was struggling behind him with the groceries.

After Mike broke up with Doreen, he disappeared. I didn't know where he was. I tried to find him, without success. Everyone kept telling me he was dead, but I had the absolute feeling if he was dead I'd know it.

One day in Denver, something told Mike to go to the newsstand where they sold Oregon newspapers, and there was a story on the front page about me being witched by HUAC, so he called up Irvin Goodman to get my telephone number and address. Called me up in Astoria. He was afraid I was in jail or something.[3]

Then, in about 1957, Mike came on a visit from Denver with his second wife and her two girls that he was very fond of. He had first taken to her because she was working in a boarding house so that she could have her two little girls with her; one of them was hardly more than a baby when Mike married her.

One day when Roz, his second wife, and the girls and Shane went someplace and there was just Oscar, Mike, and me there, he said, "I guess you know one of the reasons why we came is I want to take Shane back with me. I have a wife who's fond of children now and a home and I can take care of him. And I have a good job." Which was true, he was doing layout in sheet metal.

I said, "I think Oscar and I will have to do some talking."

So Oscar and I went to a restaurant, had coffee, and Oscar said, "I have no intention of letting him have Shane. We saved Shane and he's ours."

Mike and I went for a drive and he said, "I guess you know that I could get Shane now because my life is stable."

I said, "Well, since you're my son, I could turn myself back into his grand-mother if I tried, but Oscar refuses to give him up and I am going to stand with Oscar. I don't think you are going to take it to court."

He said, "No, I won't."

Shane, who was about eight years old at the time, remembers this incident somewhat differently.

> Mike came out a couple of times. The second time he decided that he wanted to take me back to Denver with him.
>
> I was down in the basement with my two stepsisters, and I could hear them talking upstairs about it. Oscar, I could tell, was just panicky. He was really worried that I wanted to leave because, you know, I got along with Mike. He was more athletic than Oscar was and younger and stuff.
>
> I think Oscar misunderstood my curiosity about Mike. Julia said she was really mad at Mike for wanting to take me back there. Finally they agreed to let me make the decision. I had gotten kind of close to Mike and I didn't want to hurt his feelings, but I just told him I'd been there so long, and that that was my home.[4]

That was the last time I ever saw Mike, but at least we used to talk to each other on the phone and we wrote back and forth. And I sent him snapshots of Shane. It was only a year and a half later, his ailment from the South Pacific having caught up with him, that he found out that he wouldn't be able to work any-more, and he started drinking again.

In October 1958, Rozalyn, Mike's wife, called Julia from Denver to let her know Mike was in jail pending a sanity hearing. Rozalyn had signed a complaint, in part because he had attempted suicide. Julia wrote letters to the U.S. Veterans Service in Denver and to Colorado's senator trying to get Mike transferred to the veterans' hos-pital, but when he was released from jail, less than a week later, there was no room at the hospital. Julia's account implies that Mike then killed himself, but in fact his suicide was a year later in November 1959. Shane thinks he did it because Rozalyn was having an affair.[5]

Mike committed suicide in a very civilized manner. He moved into a cheap hotel, so as not to do it at home where he had a wife and his two little step-daughters, and hung himself. I don't know if it was so much the fact that he had found out he couldn't work anymore and that he couldn't get in the veterans' hospital—and I presume what he was after was counseling—or whether it was because after he couldn't get into the VA that he had taken a few drinks and that he thought, "Oh, is that gonna start over again?"

You know, the lives of working people are full of desperation. I don't think that's very well understood. But, you know, especially if they have any sensitivity or imagination, and they can look around and see all of the violence in the world and the inequities and unfairness. It's very difficult. Unless you're a tough person like my mother always was. She never would've given up or done anything like that.

If they'd let Mike into the hospital, he'd probably be alive today. They called up when I was back helping to arrange his funeral and said they now had a bed. He was dead. So that was that. Oh I suppose he was maybe thirty-two years old.

I had a gold chain that Ray Becker made for me. I was wearing the chain around my wrist. I took a pair of scissors and cut the chain in half and buried half of it in the casket with Mike.

So we brought Shane up as our son. He still thinks he's part Finnish. He must know different, but he maintains, he always says, he's Finnish. Shane learned to think. I'm often surprised when he writes to me about some world affairs, that that's exactly what I have figured out myself.

We had been unable to adopt him because the county judge down there, who was an ex–sewing machine salesman without legal training, had had stock in the Columbia River Packers and during the strike I was working in the strike office for the gillnetters' union. A lot of fish rotted and he lost a few profits. Oscar wrote a petition, very nicely worded, about why it was in the child's best interest for us to be permitted to adopt him. He got three hundred fifty signatures, including some from the business people, and a lot of union people, and just ordinary people.

I took it down to my favorite local of the fishermen's union, which was in Clifton. All the fishermen that lived down there were Yugoslavs, Greeks, or Finns. It wasn't during one of their fishing seasons so they were all gathered in the place where they played cards, and there was a whole lot of them in there. One of them got up and said, "When we were on strike, she helped us. She worked hours and hours of overtime in our office and wrote all those bulletins that we took around. Now we have to help her," and then he broke into Greek and then into Finnish, and then he says, "I hope there isn't anyone in here," and he used some swear words, "that's so low down that they won't sign this petition." They all signed it. The person that delivered that petition to the judge down there was the rector of the Episcopal church. [But the petition was unsuccessful.]

After Oscar's death I tried to get veterans' benefits for Shane and was turned down. I wrote to Senator Morse and he told me to try again to adopt him. In the meantime, the county judge had been removed from his post. The new judge ruled in our favor, possibly because he was a fair-minded man, possibly because he was a member of the Episcopal church I had sent Shane to, and possibly because when the case was called in court it was announced as the case of Shane Arthur McDonald. Shane stood up—he was about thirteen—and said in a clear, loud voice, "Your Honor, my name is Shane Arthur RUUTTILA."[6]

Harry Bridges (left) and Matt Meehan.

Chapter 15

YOU SURE MET SOME WONDERFUL PEOPLE

Anticommunism in the United States abated somewhat during World War II, when the Soviet Union was an American ally, but quickly resurfaced at war's end when the World War was replaced with the Cold War.

When Republicans accused Democratic president Harry S. Truman's administration of being soft on Communism, of having allowed Communists to infiltrate the government, Truman—on the defensive—instituted loyalty oaths, thereby initiating the second red scare. Soon defense-related work required a security clearance, and both houses of Congress had high-profile committees investigating subversion and un-American activities. Progressive union activists and other left wingers and liberals found themselves subpoenaed by these committees, asked to name names of "dangerous subversives" (i.e., Communists and Communist sympathizers) and to disavow their own political pasts. Some refused to answer questions, claiming the Fifth Amendment to the Constitution. This saved them from being jailed for contempt of Congress, but not from losing their jobs, or from being blacklisted and shunned by their communities.

Less visible to the general public was the Coast Guard's security program instituted shortly after the Korean War began in the summer of 1950. All longshoremen were required to apply to the Coast Guard for a "port security card," which supposedly certified that one was not a security risk. Seamen needed "validated papers" from the Navy. Denial of card or papers meant denial of work.[1]

Another aspect of this red scare—which became known as McCarthyism, after one of its most visible practitioners, Senator Joseph McCarthy (R-WI)—was the deportation and attempted deportation of "subversive" immigrants, many of them union activists. While the Walter-McCarran Immigration Act of 1952, passed over President Truman's veto, contained some reforms—it provided that the "right of a person to become a naturalized citizen of the United States shall not be denied or abridged because of race or sex," for example—it was also firmly grounded in the Cold War atmosphere of the 1950s and extended the class of deportable aliens to include anyone who had been, since entry, a Communist. Naturalized citizens shown to have engaged in "subversive activity" could lose their citizenship and be deported as well.

The Walter-McCarran Act targeted immigrants. When President Truman signed executive order 9835 on March 21, 1947, the target was government employees. The order instigated loyalty oaths, created the infamous attorney general's list of organizations "designated by the Attorney General as totalitarian, fascist, communist, or subversive . . . or as seeking to alter the form of government of the United States by unconstitutional means," and truly opening the anticommunist crusades. A wide range of liberal and radical groups, including the American Committee for Protection of Foreign Born, appeared on the list.

Executive order 9835 was superseded by executive order 10450, signed by President Dwight D. Eisenhower on April 28, 1953. It removed the words "designated by the Attorney General," though the list continued to be known as the attorney general's.

An atmosphere of fear and desperation permeated Cold War America. A few Communist leaders were arrested, while others went underground. Blacklisted writers were forced to write under assumed names to sell their work. Others fled the country. Friends avoided friends. Disgraced and broke, some committed suicide.

Julia's community—steeped in left-wing beliefs and activity—was profoundly affected by the red hunts. While her everyday life continued—living with Oscar, raising Shane, working for Matt Meehan, writing stories, cooking dinner, digging in her garden—she could not ignore the red scare.

Well, the big witch-hunt started in the ILWU and a lot of people were subpoenaed to come to these awful hearings, charged with being reds. 'Course what the Un-American Activities Committee was after, they were after the union—they didn't give a damn if they were red, yellow, or purple. But the ILWU is a left-led union.

First they had the Coast Guard Screen down there. Well that was something that Senator [Warren G.] Magnuson [D-WA] dreamed up, in which you had to have a pass from the Coast Guard or the Army in order to work on the waterfront or in any facility that was connected with the waterfront, such as fishermen on the river. It was known by us as the Coast Guard Screen. What it was was a fancy name for the blacklist.

Well, this went on for some time. I went to some of these Coast Guard hearings. They usually depended on the unsupported word of individuals. I don't think Magnuson really realized what he was getting into because in many ways he was a very good senator, but he sure stepped off the dock on the Coast Guard Screen.

Quite a lot of people in Astoria were screened. Even my late husband Oscar Ruuttila got screened, but they never tried to enforce that at the flour mill—he worked at the flour mill pulling sacks off the chute—so he continued to work.

Nevertheless, Oscar fought for his port security card for years. The file on his screening is thick with letters and legal papers. The ILWU's attorney, Frank Pozzi, represented Oscar. Pozzi kept filing requests for a bill of particulars—a list of the reasons his card was denied—which court precedent required the government to provide.[2]

It took three years, but finally, in the spring of 1954, Oscar obtained the bill of particulars. It said:

> *(1) That in 1932, you were on the Communist Party ticket for the Elective [sic] of William Z. Foster. (2) That in 1934, you were registered as a Communist. (3) That in 1940, 1941 and 1942, you were a leader in Communist Party affairs in the State of Oregon and you attended Communist Party meetings. (4) That upon your discharge from the U.S. Navy, you once more became active in Communist Party affairs. (5) That in 1948, 1949 and 1950, you attended numerous Communist Party meetings in the State of Oregon. (6) That in 1948, you wrote a letter to the Daily People's World in support of that publication. (7) That in 1949, you helped organize a meeting of the Civil Rights Congress in Astoria, Oregon. (8) That in 1950, you attended a People's World Conference. (9) That you have subscribed to the Daily People's World for many years.[3]*

This Finn wrote a bunch of letters, which I typed for him, that were really hilarious, in which he thanked them for screening him. He was glad he got screened because he hadn't had sense enough to realize how old he was and that he was entitled to quit working.

They screened one Finn in Astoria, Sam Wuolle, as safe to work on ammo at the warehouse in Beaver, Oregon, and too subversive to load flour at the Pillsbury Elevator dock in Astoria. That showed how idiotic it was.

There was something else that was extremely funny that went on. The one stool pigeon that they had down there was so stupid he also screened a leading right-wing Finn in Astoria, whose name was Kankkonen. I think this stupid jerk actually thought that an anti-Communist was some kind of a variety of Communist. That was such an embarrassment to this poor man. It was so delightful.

They made a mistake by screening Francis Murnane, the hero of the waterfront. That was a riot, too. At that time he was an officer in Longshoremen's

Local 8. Murnane had kept anything he'd ever done or signed or said, he'd kept a record of it. So he appeared at his Coast Guard hearing with a big stack of documents about that high and he got cleared and he was awarded his Coast Guard pass. He called me up and he said, "For God's sakes don't ever put a word of that in the *Dispatcher*. I don't want anyone ever to find out I was cleared." He was ashamed of it!

Well then, of course, Matt Meehan got screened, he was denied his Coast Guard pass. So then the employers at Beaver called him up to come down and settle a beef that'd broken out down there. Matt had the pleasure of telling them, "I can't set foot on the dock at Beaver, you screened me, remember?" So they sent a special car to take Matt down there and through the gates and past the screen. Now isn't that hysterical? Then he appealed the screen.

I went to Matt's hearing. He was the first person that had the guts to call in the press. So the people administering the Coast Guard Screen were forced to cough up the names of those who had testified against Matt. Matt was able to prove that one of them was dead when they said this man had made these statements. Another man was so furious when it came out in the *Dispatcher* what he was supposed to have said that he sent telegrams to the government denying he ever said that. But Matt, in spite of that, never got his Coast Guard clearance.

At that time I used to do a great deal of ghostwriting for union officials. There was a magazine that was being published someplace on the East Coast called *March of Labor*. I ghostwrote a two-part article on the Coast Guard Screen.

In the articles, Julia argued that the process had nothing to do with making the waterfront safe from sabotage or espionage—no activity of that kind had been alleged in any of the approximately 1250 cases of men screened off the waterfront. Rather, the screen was another name for a labor blacklist. She noted that at the hearings she attended, the Coast Guard showed little or no interest in ferreting out acts of sabotage on the waterfront. Instead the Coast Guard asked defendants questions about politics.[4]

I was quite proud of the gillnetters' union at the time that the Coast Guard Screen was on. It really wasn't a very left-wing union but those fishermen are really independent. The gillnetters flatly refused to even apply for passes. They said they had always worked the river and that during World War II they had helped patrol the river and they absolutely refused to have anything to do with it. Also, when I got witched by HUAC, they came to my defense.

Well eventually the longshoremen got rid of the screen, but it worked very terrible damage because the people in the offshore unions got screened too, and some of them couldn't ever work again.

The way the longshoremen got rid of it, they'd get sent down to work by the dispatcher and when they got down there they didn't have their Coast Guard pass, they'd lost it or left it at home or it was in their other pants or their other jacket. And they'd have to send for another crew and it went on and on and it became very costly for the shipowners.

I think the next thing that happened was they started in on the deportation cases to try to deport Red Finns that didn't have their citizenship papers. It didn't make any difference whether they were members of the CP or just spoke to members of the CP. It was that type of thing.

The CP had very few members in Astoria and since I've always been an extremely curious person and since I was married to a Red Finn, I knew a great deal about who was in it and who wasn't. At this time none of the noncitizen Finns were in the Party because the Party had apparently advised them to drop out. But it didn't make any difference. In the union you belonged to, you had been too vocal against the employers, that was really the basis of it.

When they started the deportation cases it was under the Walter-McCarran law. I was quite actively involved in the Oregon Committee for Protection of Foreign Born. The committee was organized after they arrested Hamish MacKay, and that Swedish woman, and the Norwegian, whose name I can't remember, and a blind Filipino who had been a member of the Alaska cannery workers' union, his name was Absolar. Well let's see, that was in the late 40s.

The four were Hamish Scott MacKay, John Stenson, Casimoro Absolar, and Caroline Halverson. A defense organization for them was set up in the fall of 1949 eventually known as the Committee for Protection of Oregon's Foreign Born. The struggle continued for over a decade.[5]

When we were organizing this committee we had a very broad representative group including at least one minister and someone from the boilermakers' union, and we had several people from the ILWU. I think we had someone from the Grange there or the farmers union.[6]

They zeroed in on people in the union that they had found out through their stool pigeons were foreign born, but they only zeroed in on the ones that were extremely active and in official positions. 'Course, that's why they were after Bridges. The reason they were never able to deport Bridges is because the union really gave him full support, even the right-wing Portland local supported him.

Sometime after I went to Astoria they deported Hamish Scott MacKay to Canada, where he was born. He'd come to this country with his parents when he was a year old, I believe, and had lived here all the rest of his life. Before his parents went to Canada and became Canadian citizens, he traced his ancestry to the signing of the Declaration of Independence. They deported a Finn named William Mackie (not the Mackie that I stuffed into the wastepaper basket, but another Mackie) to Finland. They deported them on the same day, Thanksgiving Day, and their relatives were all at the airport when they were taken away weeping and wailing, but they got deported.

The MacKay-Mackie Defense Committee told the sad fate of the men in a pamphlet entitled "The Exile of Hamish MacKay and William Mackie." MacKay, born in Canada and living in the United States since he was twenty, and Mackie, born in Finland but living in the United States since he was eight months old, were now both in their fifties. On November 18, 1960, after their petitions for naturalization were denied on political grounds, they were deported without trial under the Walter-McCarran Act. Deportation is a civil case, and therefore lacks the legal safeguards and due process afforded a criminal case. In a civil case there is no right to a trial by jury or appeal, and no protection from cruel and unusual punishments. The pamphlet clearly placed the cases within the scope of the political witch-hunts of the Cold War.

It was on the basis of his belonging to the Oregon Workers Alliance that they deported Hamish MacKay to Canada. He was no Communist. Hamish MacKay belonged to the carpenters union and, believe it or not, the carpenters union supported him in his fight to escape deportation.[7] So the Portland Committee for Protection of Foreign Born notified the carpenters union in Canada and they met him at the plane and they welcomed him to the city of Vancouver. So he led quite an active and useful life up there. Eventually his wife joined him there and eventually he was allowed to come back here twice a year to visit Portland relatives.

Mackie had been a nonunion painter, but the painters union went to the airport. He was very displeased to see them. It was the most left-wing union at that time in Finland. He took the position that if any liberals or left wingers supported him he'd never have a chance to get back. I heard there was a Jehovah's Witness group in Helsinki and he was hired by them as a caretaker for their hall.

In my opinion, he turned out to be quite a phony, the only Finn I ever knew that was. He was allowed to come back into this country some years after he was deported on condition that he sign a document he wouldn't associate with any reds. And he signed the document.

The Immigration agent here, I think he was insane. He was an absolute nut. I was up at his office with a group of American-born relatives of people they were trying to deport—including Hamish MacKay, who was up there with his wife and son—and we had Reverend Mark Chamberlin with us, a Methodist minister.

The Immigration agent went into a rage first at Chamberlin, and he said, "What's the matter with you Methodists? The Presbyterians never give me a bit of trouble." And then he went into a rage at me and threatened to deport me. I asked him where he planned to deport me to. I explained that my mother's relatives had come here in 1638. It was very funny.

We had the relatives of a Swedish woman with us. She was caretaker at the Swedish Hall. They had gone there and searched her apartment and they found a Bible in Swedish that they were convinced it was some kind of a Communist book. You can't believe how incredibly stupid they were!

In Astoria the Immigration and Naturalization and the FBI called people into their offices—Finns that weren't born in this country—and threatened them. Before the interrogations began, foreign-born left-wing Finns met at our house and Oscar explained the procedure—he was fluent in both Finnish and English. I knew some Finnish words. I'd go along as interpreter and, when a question was asked to which the answer might have been incriminating, I would simply rattle off some Finnish words and that meant not to answer that question.

A young woman who was Finnish asked me to go with her to talk to the Immigration people. She said that she could only talk "kitchen English." I was at that time working part-time for the gillnetters' union. They were against this type of thing too. We had the secretary of the union sitting outside. He tried to come, but they only let me go in.

There was an insurance group that was owned by the people that had insurance in it. They also put on plays and things like that. He was trying to get her to say that that was a branch of the Communist Party, which was absolutely untrue. I remember, she said to him, "Oh, I think that that is a different lodge." She meant the CP, that was how little she knew.

The Immigration official got so angry. There was a big stack of books on his desk. He threw them off on the floor. It made a terrible loud sound. The union official thought we were being beaten up so he broke the door down and came in.

Some of that was pretty hysterical. Did I tell you about the time that I couldn't shut this Finn up they were trying to deport because he had served as a pallbearer for Emanuel Pickmosa who was the head of the Communist Party in Clatsop County? So I said my couple of words in Finnish, and this Finn, he couldn't contain himself. He screamed out. He said, "Well, you know we couldn't let him lie in his room at the Karhuvaara Hotel. He was already beginning to smell. Somebody had to carry him out of there." I'll never forget that. You know, it was pretty rugged at times but you sure met some wonderful people.

Several Finns wanted to travel to Finland to visit relatives and the FBI and the Immigration and Naturalization Service wouldn't let them have their visas and papers. They also started a scheme of canceling citizenships.

Then they started deportation proceedings against Filipino members of the ILWU Alaska Cannery Workers' Union. There were four or five of them here in Portland they were trying to deport and quite a few in Seattle and some in California.

I don't remember all of the Filipinos they tried to deport, but it was all the officials of Local 37 and all of the really active members in Seattle, Portland, and also California.[8] What the packers were trying to do was to deport that entire union out of this country. They didn't succeed.

At one of the hearings where I was, one of the stool pigeons was a Filipino. I'm sitting at the press table and when he looked over and saw me, he thought I was from the Immigration and Naturalization Service. He didn't understand the setup there, and he looked so confused. It was really funny. He said everything they wanted him to say, but they ended up by deporting him. Served him right.

When they had the second wave of arrests among the Filipinos, they accepted my advice and set up a separate defense committee to represent their members. It was possible to get money for their defense by going around to ILWU locals, since they were all ILWU members. Now what do you think the Immigration and Naturalization Service did then? They arrested all of the officers of this defense committee. At the same time they arrested a man up in Seattle who'd been active among the Filipinos here in Portland and was active up there. His case went to the Supreme Court. They ruled the Filipinos could not be deported because they'd come in when we owned the Philippines. They'd come in as nationals. So that was the end of those cases.

I had been quite active in the Oregon Committee for Protection of Foreign Born before I went to live in Astoria. Then at the time they started the deportation drive down there, I organized the Clatsop County Committee for Protection of Foreign Born. I was the secretary.

The Episcopal rector was one of the members or advisers of our committee and he advised me not to keep any minutes of meetings. I was very glad because the time I was witched by HUAC, in 1956, they tried to subpoena the minutes of the Clatsop County Committee for Protection of Foreign Born and there weren't any to subpoena. I had never been very good at keeping records, let's put it that way, and I became less good when this stuff started. The other people that were witched to that hearing in Seattle had kept files and the files were all subpoenaed.

The reason they held the witch-hunts into the Foreign Born committees all across the country was because the House Un-American Activities Committee was very anxious to destroy the Committee for Protection of Foreign Born and to stop the drive to repeal the Walter-McCarran Act, under which these immigration cases were all brought. They wanted to kill off that drive and they did— we weren't able to get it repealed.

But I'd never really thought *I* was witched because of my connection with those two committees because these other people got subpoenaed a couple of weeks before I did. I thought it was because Matt had decided that he was going to defeat the congressman from the First District, Walter Norblad. He had me do some research on Norblad and I wrote a leaflet called "Norblad's Life and Times."

Norblad's record in Congress was dreadful. He voted to keep taxi drivers and loggers off unemployment compensation. He voted against funds to clean the pollution out of the Columbia River, although fishing was at that time the main industry in Astoria.

As one of its strategies in its attempt to repeal Taft-Hartley, labor targeted the bill's supporters, such as Norblad, for defeat.[9]

A product of the Cold War, the Taft-Hartley Act was enacted in 1947, in part as a response to a rash of strikes following World War II. The act required union officials to file non-Communist affidavits in order for their unions to use the NLRB. It also permitted injunctions against strikes deemed threatening to the national health or safety, allowed states to ban closed shops, outlawed boycotts, and permitted employers to file damage suits against unions.[10]

Julia attacked Norblad, a Republican, in the Dispatcher *and* People's World. *She quoted Matt Meehan as saying that instead of schools, housing, or tax reductions, Norblad had given his constituents the Taft-Hartley Act. What's more, he was on an overseas junket when Congress voted on raising unemployment benefits, but was there to vote against other bills that would have helped working people.[11]*

Though Norbald won reelection, the Democrats' strong showing locally was front-page news in Astoria. The newspaper seemed surprised. Maybe they should have been paying better attention; Julia had been living there nearly six years and had encouraged many Astorians to register as Democrats.[12]

After I got it all researched and wrote this up, and Matt got "Norblad's Life and Times" distributed around in all the counties where ILWU had locals, Norblad got defeated in the election in those counties. Of course, he had ten counties in his district, so he was reelected by a small margin. That had just happened at the time when I got subpoenaed and Walter Norblad was on the House Un-American Activities Committee.

Julia's subpoena is dated November 8, 1956, two days after the election. She was one of nine Oregonians called to the December 1956 HUAC hearings in Seattle to investigate "Communist Political Subversion," more particularly the Committees for Protection of Foreign Born in the Northwest.[13]

The hearings were all so ridiculous really. Part of the time you'd want to laugh—they were so hysterical, and meaningless, and senseless—and part of the time you'd want to swear and curse. And then, you know, they always bring out this array of stool pigeons. They are the dumbest people you've ever heard in your life. It wasn't the entire committee that was there, it was just part of the committee and one of the men was so old, he kept falling asleep up there. There was a picket line around the building.

I used to call those people in the CP the super-dupers. They had a very poor opinion of my intelligence and thought I wasted too much time on poetry and other things that really wouldn't contribute much to the class struggle. They thought I always laughed in the wrong places because I could always see the humor in situations which to them were very serious. But, you know, you can't help it. I don't know how you'd get through the world without a sense of humor. I really do not!

I had a big argument with all these super-dupers in the area about what I should do, because what I would have liked to have done was to have ignored the subpoena and told them to go to hell, to just not go at all and show utter contempt for them. I was told by the super-dupers, my husband was one, that that was an old IWW attitude. It wouldn't work and if you're going to get subpoenaed, you might as well make it count for something. Matt Meehan thought it was the wrong attitude too—which I thought was very peculiar because he was an ex-IWW.

So this witch-hunt in Seattle in 1956 was a witch-hunt of those who had been active in the committees defending the foreign born. The other ILWU people who were witched in Portland had also been active in the Oregon Committee for Protection of Foreign Born. A lot of people in Seattle who had been active were witched, including one attorney who was there defending a client—they served a subpoena on him right there at the witch-hunt.

So those of us connected with ILWU went to Seattle with two union attorneys. That's why the longshore union is a strong union. It's got guts. They stick together; they defend their members who are under attack. That's why they defended Harry [Bridges] when they tried to deport him because they knew they really weren't trying to deport Harry, they were trying to gut the union.

There were four of us ILWU people who were subpoenaed. One was from Coos Bay, Valerie Taylor. She was the president of the Federated Auxiliaries of the longshoremen's union. It seems to me Mary Jane Brewster got subpoenaed too and a longshoreman who was on the committee in Portland to get rid of HUAC. A Portland longshoreman was subpoenaed. They were also looking for an Astoria man named Roland Petersen who worked in the flour mill, but that's quite a common name down there and they never did catch up with him to serve a subpoena on him.

This man, I think his name was Bert Nelson, I forget if he was in the longshore union or the woodworkers' union, but he also had been a member of the CP, and he was treated very badly. They took a picture of him which appeared in one of the papers in Seattle. He was glaring at the photographer and he looked just like a bulldog. After that I always called him the Bulldog.[14]

They were very educational, those hearings. Francis Murnane came up and sat with us. He was president of Longshore Local 8 then. And Matt Meehan and his wife Juanita, they came up and they sat with us. But I went over and sat at the press table because I had a press card.

I was sitting by an *Oregonian* reporter and beside a man there for the *Oregon Journal,* Jim Running, who was a friend of mine. When I thought it was about time they'd be calling me, I slipped him a note with a statement I had written. I told him I was going to be called to the stand very soon and if he wanted to use this statement, he could have it. He used every bit of it.

The portion of Running's story with Julia's statement:

Reporters' eyebrows went up when Mrs. Ruuttila, who had been sitting at the press table for a day and a half taking notes, was called as a witness.

As the dark-haired woman advanced to the witness chair, she asked that no newspaper pictures, television or movie film be made of her.[15]

Turning to the newsmen and cameramen, she said pleasantly:

"Please accept my apologies as a fellow reporter for asking for no pictures. . . ."

After being excused as a witness, Mrs. Ruuttila handed a prepared statement to the press:

"I REFUSED to answer questions for fear that I, as a reporter, who in her working lifetime has interviewed, talked to and 'associated' with hundreds of people of varying views, might be placed in the position of betraying news sources—in the language of logging camps where I grew up, becoming a stool pigeon.

"As for the Walter-McCarran (immigration) law, it is a cruel and unjust law, as I, who have lived most of my life among the foreign born, know from first hand.

"I shall continue to cover deportation hearings and witch-hunt hearings, just as I covered this one until I was snatched from this table to answer the subpena served on me."[16]

I was on the stand for a day and a half. They asked all sorts of questions. Your attorneys aren't able to act as attorneys—regular trial procedures don't hold. They can only whisper to you to take the Fifth Amendment or whatever other amendment. They can't in any way speak out. When I was on the stand, one sat on one side of me and one on the other.

Well, I wanted to refuse to answer. You can answer a question as to what your name is, but if you answer any other questions you have to answer all questions or be found in contempt. So I wanted to stand on the First Amendment, freedom of the press and so forth, but the attorneys had a whole bunch of amendments, including the Fifth, they wanted us to stand on. I thought that I couldn't refuse to do it because I was worried about what was going to happen to Shane. So I had to take the Fifth Amendment, but I also took the First as well.

Mr. ARENS: What was your maiden name, Mrs. Ruuttila?
(The witness confers with her counsel.)
Mrs. RUUTTILA: I respectfully decline to answer that question, based upon my rights, privileges, and immunities accorded to me by the first, fourth, fifth, ninth, and tenth amendments of the Constitution of the United States.[17]

It may seem silly not to answer such an obvious question, but, as Julia notes, once a witness answers a question, she is no longer free to claim the constitutional privilege of refusing to answer questions that would follow. Also, the fact that Julia had used so many names, pen names as well as her husbands' names, could have appeared incriminating, as if she were hiding something.

Well, I should have been quite flattered because they had a big stack of papers there. Everything I had ever written for any labor paper, they had a copy of it. That's when I found out, to my amazement, that everything I'd ever written for Federated Press had been in the *Daily Worker*. I didn't know before then that they had used so many of my stories about America's stepchildren, the foreign born, who had built up many of the industries in the west and the mountain states and how they were now being harassed and the way they were being treated.

Well, they'd go through this big stack of documents. That's what they asked me about mostly, and my connections and associations. Was I or wasn't I a CP member? I remember Frank Pozzi said to me, "Why don't you say you aren't one?"

I whispered to Frank, "I'm not going to because Oscar wouldn't like it, and anyway I don't think that's a proper answer. None of their business and I will refuse to answer."

This was when the rift was going on about Hungary. They asked me this question, "What did I think about what the Communists had done in Hungary?"

I said, "Which communists?"

The committee was trying to paint Julia as a Communist because she hadn't written any news stories criticizing the USSR for suppressing a popular uprising in Hungary in October 1956, less than two months before the hearings. When the committee asked, "Did you approve the actions of the Communists in Hungary?" Julia's answer was an effort to show that many Hungarian communists were revolting against the Soviets, so in effect, communists were on both sides of the conflict. Pozzi recalled that Julia's interrogator, outsmarted, rose from his seat and shouted at her with his finger pointed.[18]

At one point I had all I could take, so I decided to hell with all this, I am just going to stand up and tell them off. I must have started to get out of my seat because I got yanked down into it so hard by the attorneys I thought my tailbone was cracked.

Well, after they yanked me down in the chair, I got over being scared because I couldn't get away, they hung on to me. I wasn't about to start a fistfight with my attorneys. And the bailiffs would have grabbed me anyway. After a while it struck me so hilarious that the humor of the situation began to intrigue and interest me.

The idiotic things they asked! If they asked you about some strike you'd written about, they wouldn't ask a question that if you had wanted to answer questions—which you couldn't—would be based on what the strike was about, but about what they wanted to impress the reporters that the strike was about. An ordinary strike to those people was a Bolshevik uprising.

One thing I think I shouldn't have listened to our attorneys about. They advised us not to accept the witness fees. I think we were fools not to have taken it. We paid our own train fare and we paid the hotel where we stayed. I wrote articles about it every night at the hotel.

Well, I was anxious to get back to Astoria and see if they had seized Shane. The newspaper there at that time was called the *Astorian-Budget* and it had a very right-wing editor. He was not only a rabid Republican, he was antiunion. The stories in that paper about me were awful. They were dreadful. They had an editorial after me and the headlines were terrible. I thought, "It's going to be interesting to see what our neighbors do."

On December 15, 1956, the Evening Astorian-Budget *titled its front-page editorial "Astorian Refuses Deny She Writes Red Propaganda."[19]*

The papers went on and on about the terrible person that was living in this community. You would have thought I was a very famous person. 'Course infamous is the word. You know they never once called me up and asked for my side of the story. Papers like that are supposed to put on a pretense of being objective. Of course, we know they aren't, but they never put on the slightest pretense.

Julia was not exaggerating. On December 17 the Evening Astorian-Budget *continued its attack with an editorial entitled "Shouldn't Be Surprised," and criticized her for availing herself of her constitutional right to freedom from self-incrimination.*

Finally Matt Meehan got sick of it. He came down there and dictated a letter to the paper, which he signed, telling them off, and for some reason, they printed the letter.

> In regard to your editorial about our Dispatcher correspondent . . . [i]n our country a person is considered innocent until proven guilty. . . .
>
> When the first 10 amendments were offered by the founding fathers, they had in mind just that—to protect the rights of all. . . .
>
> Nearly all of the articles placed before Mrs. Ruuttila and her attorneys were reprints of Federated Press stories. The FP imprint clearly showed through the photostat. Yet Rep. Doyle and the examiner, Mr. Arens, continually referred to them as her "writings in the Communist Daily Worker and Communist Peoples World. . . ."[20]

Arthur Spencer didn't meet Julia until the seventies, when she came to the Oregon Historical Society, where he was a librarian, to do research. They became friends and worked together politically. Julia told him about the ordeal surrounding her sub-

poena. "*She described to me her bus ride back to Astoria from Seattle. It was a multipurpose bus stop, and this Finnish man, who had hardly ever related to her, came running out from around the counter and took both her hands and shook them, and said, 'Welcome home,' embraced her, and she cried when she told me about it. That was harder on her than she always let on.*"[21]

One of our neighbors came out and stared when I got out of the car but she didn't speak. She was scared to death. One of the super-duper Red Finns wanted to come and see us but he was afraid to come up our steps, so he came in the back way. Didn't want to be seen coming in our house. We had a new neighbor who had built a house back of our house and she'd only been there about three weeks when this happened. I had only talked to her once or twice. When I got home, I'm out in the backyard and suddenly her face appeared over the fence and she said, "Well, welcome home." This woman was not in any way a liberal or left winger, she was just a nice person. I was really astounded.

It must have been a day or two later, I went in a grocery store to buy some groceries. I knew that the woman that owned the grocery store was regarded as a friend of left wingers, but she wasn't actually a left winger herself. She came out of her office at the back of the store and invited me to come back in her office and offered me a drink. She said, "I want to congratulate you on the way you conducted yourself at the hearing. We're glad you're back." Now she was one of the dancing Finns, one of the neutral Finns.

Then several days later I went in Hellberg's drugstore to get some medicine and Mr. Hellberg came out from behind the prescription counter. A couple of the really super-duper hard-liner Red Finns had always told me, "Don't ever speak to Mr. Hellberg. He's a man that is not really an enemy, but he doesn't understand anything. So don't be friendly with him." He came out from behind the prescription counter and said, "Welcome back to Astoria."

I think it was two years before one of my neighbors on one side of me spoke and then I think she only spoke by accident. I was picking something in the side yard and I hadn't realized she was right down below this bank. She must have been bending over picking something out of her garden. All at once she reared up and without thinking—since she had stopped speaking to me—I said, "Oh, good morning," you know, automatically. She said, "Yes, it is a nice day isn't it." And after that, she spoke. It's real funny. The neighbor that I thought would stop speaking to me didn't. You never can tell how people will react.

As I recall, the rector of the Episcopal church, the one who was a pacifist, was no longer there; there was another man there whom I had met only once. He came to the house to see if he could do anything to help. After the awful stories in the Astoria paper! The other rector had been an extreme liberal and this man wasn't, but he had a lot of guts. It's strange that sometimes the people that aren't all that liberal have more courage than those who are.

Oscar wasn't fired from his job, although I heard about an argument between a man that demanded of one of the foremen at the plant why Oscar wasn't fired and he said, "What's all that got to do with it? He's a good worker."

The mill may not have minded the Ruuttilas' politics, but Oscar and Julia were under surveillance by the FBI. An FBI memorandum of January 14, 1957, just a month after Julia's questioning before HUAC in Seattle, details a surprise visit to the Ruuttila home to interview Oscar. He declined. Then Julia told them Oscar had broken no laws and ordered them to leave immediately. Another time the FBI came and just spoke to Julia.

God, how I hate the FBI. Did I tell you when they came to our house in Astoria? It was really funny. Oscar had been working on the graveyard shift and he was sleeping, and they wanted to talk to him. They had been all over Astoria talking to Red Finns, and when they came up the stairs, I looked out and recognized, from the descriptions, who they were. So I wouldn't let them in.

They said they wanted to talk to him, and I said he was asleep and I wasn't going to wake him up. One of them pushed at the door. I had hold of our dog and the dog could sense how I hated these men, and he started snarling and growling. I was afraid that he would bite one of them and they'd shoot him, so I grabbed him by the collar. The collar broke and I held him around the neck.

I told them they'd better get the hell off the porch. The dog made a lunge at them. I grabbed him just in time and one of them almost fell down the stairs. The other one ran after him and left in a hurry. But the next place they went, they told some friends of ours that I set our savage dog on them. Oscar didn't even wake up.

It's very strange that at the time all this was going on, Shane never related any of the things that happened to him at school, but years afterwards he told me he was terribly treated by several of the teachers and some of the students. Apparently he felt it would be very disloyal if he complained. He thought we had enough to be worried about without that.

Years later Shane recalled:

She was in all the papers. And that's where it really was bad at school. I think I was in the first, second grade. I'd go out on recess and play, and the older kids would start in on me. I can remember sometimes being circled by a gang of ten or fifteen of them. I just really developed a real bad temper. I popped a few of them, gave them a few bloody noses. They knew if they were going to come in close to me they were going to take some punches before they could get me down. Finally it stopped when I got a little older.

I guess I could sense sometimes when parents were uncomfortable if I came around. I thought that [Julia and Oscar] were the greatest people around, and at that age I didn't understand what they meant in the paper. I really didn't understand any of that then.

You know, you'd hear about all these left wingers that were supposedly trying to overthrow the government with force, and I never met a Communist or a left winger that was really a genuine type person like that that ever even owned a gun. Oscar never had a weapon in the house, ever. All they really believed in was, you know, a little bit better deal for the working stiff.[22]

Chapter 16

I SHALL NOT COME THIS WAY AGAIN

MEMORIAL FOR A WORKER
(for O. A. R.) [1906–1962]

Worker on the flour chute, fisherman,
Boat puller, hay hand, sailor before the mast,
Faller and bucker—nameless and vast
The forests where the logging rivers ran
The trees you cut down to tidewater,
Builder of roads and stone walls that outlast
The hand that held the pike pole and the hammer.

A man may die and the winds may scatter
His chromosomes, his aching, empty dust,
His wife may cease from weeping, sons forget
All that he made with his blood and sweat.

But a man is more than his life, more than his death.
He leaves something of himself in ships and houses,
The dream remembered when the whistle plunges,
The essence of his being and his breath.
And books still read by workers in those places
With his initials still upon the pages.[1]

—Julia Ruuttila, n.d.

Julia's one happy marriage was too short. Oscar's sudden death on December 8, 1962, left her a single parent again, but this time with her mother as a dependent as well. Julia had moved to Astoria to live with Oscar. Despite the political harassment she had felt, she loved the coast, but now that Oscar was gone, there was nothing holding her there. She put the house on the market, and when it sold, in 1965, and the school year was over, she moved back to Portland.

I can look back one time when we came to Portland to march in the Bloody Thursday march [the annual commemoration of the July 5 violence in San Francisco during the 1934 Longshore strike], and Oscar almost fainted as we were turning a corner. I asked him what was the trouble and he said, "I can't get my breath." I think probably that was his heart then because he died quite suddenly one Sunday morning as we were getting ready to come to a District Council meeting of the union.

I was getting dressed in the bathroom and Oscar was getting breakfast. He always made Finnish pancakes on Sunday morning. When I came out from getting dressed, Oscar was sitting in a chair and he was dying. I could tell by his breath, you know, he was strangling for breath.

Shane came out of his little bedroom and said, "What is the matter with Oscar?" Then he ran back in his bedroom and got back in bed and pulled the covers over his head. Oscar died before the doctor got there.

One of Julia's tasks was to inform Oscar's comrades of his death. Within days she wrote a letter to the People's World. *They published it on December 28, 1962.*

> If there is room in the letter column, I would like to say some words of farewell about my husband, Oscar Ruuttila, a friend of The People's World since it was first published and of The Western Worker before that.
>
> Oscar died suddenly last Sunday morning (December 8). He died "with his hammer in his hand." On his desk were copies of the December 7 P.W. The bundle had been coming to our house for many years. In his typewriter were notes for changes in a novel he was writing about the fishing fleet. It was the theme he knew well, who all his life had been a working man. . . .
>
> I have found comfort in writing to you about Oscar. The task has taken my eyes from the chair where he died last Sunday morning, and made me remember—not the silent, sheeted figure which was carried down our steps, but the Oscar who was so tall, so vital, so erect, with the incredibly sea-blue eyes in the kind, brown Finnish face—Oscar in his well worn leather jacket, his head bare to the freshening breeze, a familiar figure in our town on Sunday morning as he moved about the streets of Astoria with his papers and leaflets.

Shane, who was thirteen when Oscar died, recalls:

> Oscar's death was really hard on her. Boy, really hard on her. I know the house was paid for, but they didn't have a whole lot of savings. And I remember she found some savings bonds in a safety deposit box or something that she didn't

know about. She gave one to his stepmother. I always thought that was peculiar. Jeez, I mean, we were tough for money.[2]

*Julia needed the savings bond, but she wasn't the beneficiary. She wrote Oscar's step-
mother and family within two weeks of his death asking, as gently as she could, to
keep it. She didn't get to.*

I was denied anything yesterday at Social security; that is, I cannot get anything until I am sixty-two, and am now only—not quite fifty-six. However, the
mortgage on our house is insured, so Shane and I will have a roof over our
heads, and the house is now clear. But it appears at the moment our only income is the $59.30 a month which Shane received from my dead son's social
security, plus what my mother will pay for her food, etc.—as she has a small,
independent income coming in each month.

If you feel that Oscar would have wanted me to have this bond to help with
the extr[a]'s on his funeral . . . I would use that money to pay these bills. But
I do want you to know that if you feel the bond is yours (as legally, is) then
that will be all right. . . . Because there is no way Oscar could ever have paid
you for the love and welcome you gave him, a lonely, thin, hungry teen age boy
when he came from Finland and you took him into your heart and home. . . .
I owe you much, too. Because Oscar imaged his idea of what a relationship
would be between a man and woman on the relationship between his father
and you. He spoke often of how his father loved you, and by the way he treated
me—never a harsh word in 13 years, never left the house without kissing me
goodby, always made the fire and cooked the morning coffee—and was always
kind and considerate and sweet to me—so I always knew by what he said that
he had formed the idea of how to treat a wife by the way his father treated you,
and you him. . . . Well, I know you once went through what I am going
through, but it is still very hard. Everywhere I turn, I see Oscar—the wood in
the basement he cut all summer on the beach will keep Shane and me warm
all winter. But I would rather have my Oscar back, and freeze.[3]

I think it was about two years before I got a pension. I had so many problems and they sort of kept me alive. My mother had come to live with us. She
lived to be ninety-eight. So I couldn't crack up because I had Shane—he was in
seventh or eighth grade—and my mother. Of course, I still wrote for the *Dispatcher,* even though I lived in Astoria.

While Oscar was alive, we never did tell Shane that Oscar belonged to the
CP because we thought that was something he couldn't handle and wasn't safe,
but about two days after Oscar died, we got this horrible letter from someone
who belonged to the Bible Baptist Church down there. Shane was opening all

the letters—we got a great many because Oscar was quite well known, you know, letters of condolence. So he opened this letter and then he started sobbing and then I said, "What's the matter?" and he showed it to me. The letter said that Oscar was now in hell roasting because of his beliefs and his activities.

As I look back over the men in my life, I realize I only had one husband: Oscar.

Astoria had begun to change after Oscar died. The main reason I decided to leave was because of Shane. As long as Oscar was alive, Shane had a pretty good life there because Astoria is really a wonderful place to grow up in. There's so many lakes and rivers where you can go and swim and fish and so many places you go on trails, and Oscar could take him around in the car. After Oscar's death, everything changed because Shane's friends in school began to learn how to drive. Their parents began buying them their own cars and there was no possible way I could do that.

It seemed to me that I needed to get him into an atmosphere where there would be more poor people like we were. That idea crystallized when he came home from school and said the teacher asked the class—you couldn't ever tell what teachers in Astoria were going to say to their classes—some question in which he said to her, "There are two classes of students here, those whose fathers are fairly well-to-do and those whose parents are on welfare. And then, there's myself. We're not on welfare, but we're paupers."

Before Oscar died, Shane hadn't understood why he was often badly treated at school. By the time he started high school in 1963 he recognized why he was discriminated against by his peers and teachers.

I could really tell which teachers were prejudiced against me because of the politics. Even when I played baseball on the all-star team I had the second highest batting average in the whole league, kids that just didn't have anywhere near the athletic skill I had were put in the game instead of me.

When we left Astoria, at that point I didn't mind leaving. I really enjoyed my childhood up until high school, and then I was very glad to get out of Astoria.

I can remember in Astoria a lot of the kids, some of the Finnish kids that used to give me a bad time—Julia and Oscar had a lot of books and different things that had pictures of some of the people that attended some of the picnics—I never did tell them that some of their grandparents were also reds. There's an awful lot of them down there.

Astoria is where I started to learn about justice is not equal in this country. There's a different justice for rich people than there is for the poor.

This one kid that I went to school with got caught taking some empty pop bottles outside of one grocery store and taking them to another one and cashing them in. So his alternative was either going to reform school or going to Vietnam, enlisting. His name was one of the first names on the wall in Washington, D.C.

But during the same period of time, the mayor's kid and several other sons of prominent business people in Astoria, they were called the "mole gang." What they would do is they would go down under the streets and knock holes into the basements of some of these stores and take out expensive merchandise. Nothing happened to any of those kids. Nothing.[4]

I wanted Shane to grow up with the ideas that Oscar and I had had and I didn't think that was possible in Astoria because the Red Finns hadn't been able to make any impression on their children. I think some of the second-generation Finns were ashamed of the poor English their parents spoke and they were terrified of some of the persecution that went on there.[5]

Anyway, I thought the thing to do is to move to Portland, into a neighborhood that is integrated and also is working class. That was the main reason I wanted to leave. Also, I had to earn more money. Although I still wrote for the *Dispatcher*, one of the locals had folded because the flour mill had closed and moved their export flour manufacture to the Philippines so they could trade with China. Very foxy of the employers. That's when we weren't trading with China; the embargo was on. It's impossible to get a granny sitter, so it was very difficult for me to get away to go anywhere to cover any council meetings or anything else. So I decided the best thing to do was to move us to Portland. I didn't leave for two years because I couldn't get rid of the house I was living in.[6]

In packing up to move, I broke one of my fingers, but I didn't know what was the matter with it. It was very painful and the stupid doctor in Astoria told me I had subcutaneous erysipelas. It's some kind of an infection you can get from being bitten by some kind of an insect. He was having me take these terrible antibiotics. It was called Lyncosene and I got Lyncosene poisoning, but I didn't find out what was the matter until we had moved to Portland and I landed in the hospital. I was there for about two or three weeks recovering.

While I was in the hospital, Shane more or less took care of himself. I put my mother in a nursing home because she couldn't even get something out of the refrigerator without dropping it, though her mind was not affected by the stroke she'd had. Then I realized that I wasn't going to be able to move her in with us for quite awhile, so I got her into Patton Home, which is a very nice place for senior citizens to live in. I was going to have her come live with us as soon as I was able to have her, but by that time she was not interested in leaving Patton Home. She said, "Everything runs on time. The meals are on time. People don't come in to dictate to you while you're in the midst of doing something for me." I think she was there four years. She died there.

Shane was halfway through high school and I wanted him to start to Jefferson, but he had seen some of the kids there that were on the teams and he felt he didn't have a chance if he went to Jefferson. He said he wanted to go to North Catholic High School. It was a small high school and he thought he had a chance to get on their teams. He spent his junior year there. He was on two teams, but the priest who was the head of the school wouldn't let him come back for his senior year. He said his hair was too long. So he had to go to Jefferson.

When he went to Jefferson, I found out they had two high schools [under one roof] there when I got a note that he was failing all his classes. As he was a very bright boy and he'd made excellent grades in Astoria, I went to see about it. I talked to him about it and he said, "Well, I'm not going to read any of those books that they have told me to read because they were assigned to me to read in Astoria in the seventh and eighth grades and when I was a freshman. I told the teacher I'm not gonna waste my time on that stuff."

At the school, I explained all this stuff and put up a pitched battle and that's when I found out, and Shane also had told me, that nearly all of the students in his class were blacks. That's another reason why I had wanted him to go to Jefferson. I wanted him to meet some black people.

But, you know the black students don't get a fair break when they start out in school and the teachers don't say anything that's meaningful to them about any aspect of their lives. They don't talk about reality. Shane said they would appear quite interested when the teacher first came into the room and pretty soon they'd be bored and they'd get out their little makeshift musical instruments made with rubber bands and other things and they'd start playing them and they'd dance in the halls, and then one teacher would start to cry and spend the rest of the class period weeping. That's sad, isn't it?

I went to the PTA meeting once and spoke. I tore into the fact they had two schools there. The school that they had for the whites that had some aptitude was one school. All the best teachers were in that school. They should have been in the other classes because they needed the help so desperately. Then they had the poor underachievers and the poor achievers and the blacks in the other school. They even had to come and go out of that high school by separate doors.

Also, Shane was a week late starting school because he went back to a huge peace demonstration that was held in Washington, D.C. Afterwards they went on to New York and they went to a summer school that apparently was run by members of the CP in upper New York State, because there he met Bettina Aptheker.[7]

She asked him where he got his views and he said from his grandfather. He meant Oscar, though Oscar was only his stepgrandfather.

She said, "What about your mother?"

He said, "Oh, she's only a fellow traveler." When he told me that, I was so amused. I thought, "Well that fits me to a tee," but I was surprised he was astute enough to realize that.

Well, whether or not the powers that be at Jefferson knew that he'd gone to this deal in upper New York State, I don't know. It was a very educational trip.

Of the summer he was seventeen, Shane recalled:

This was '66. I went up to this camp in upstate New York, Camp Webatuck. I remember it was just top secrecy all the way. I was being pretty heavily recruited then by the Communist Party to join.

First we stopped in Washington, D.C., for this big huge demonstration. God, it was big. There was cops just for blocks lined down the street arm to arm. Most of the cops in Washington, D.C., were black. And the black women would go right up to them and just really let them have it. You could tell that they felt ashamed standing there, these cops.

This kid in a workshop I was in—he was a black kid—got up and said that he didn't want to go to Vietnam and shoot at a brown brother when he'd rather see Lyndon Johnson down the end of his gun. Well, the next day they come in and got him. They rode in on horseback, the Washington, D.C., cops, snatched this kid right up out of the group, and rode off with him. It was just like something out of the movies. It was unbelievable. And they held him incommunicado for about three days before anyone knew what had happened to him. They charged him with threatening the life of the president.

Then we were bused up to this camp. It was really neat. Gee, there were kids from all over the country there. Just everywhere. And we'd talk in these groups. They'd all sit there and say, "I come from a very progressive family," and this or that. And we were talking about Watts, what we felt was happening there, and Newark, and all these places.

Then all of a sudden the *Daily News* headline was "Secret Commie Youth Camp Exposed." I can remember going out with a walkie-talkie and a baseball bat at one of the gates of the camp. The *Daily News* had put a map in showing people how to get there and so they were expecting Minutemen and all these right wingers to come popping in. They had some people come up, but when they saw how many of us were there and how well prepared we were, they . . . you know, they saw no weapons other than bats. There was people sneaking in in canoes and coming over in helicopters, so they figured there was an FBI informer inside. Everyone was trying to guess who that was. That was a lot of fun.

I didn't know what to think of some of the kids. They were sure different. You could tell a lot of them came from some real wealthy families and some of the kids came from real poor families out on Coney Island, Spanish Harlem, different places. I found myself being more attracted to some of them than the other ones. They talked a lot about doing stuff instead of talking about who their dad or who their mom was and stuff like that.

I left there thinking that I was more politically like Julia, you know, independent minded. Then another year or two went by and the drug thing kind of took over. I still went to a lot of demonstrations and did that, but more and more drugs just became, you know, the main thing about life.[8]

Julia worked hard to ensure that the racism surrounding Shane did not rub off on him. She knew the schools weren't teaching black history, so she took it upon herself to teach Shane about this topic. He recalls:

She had a lot of books on black history. I can remember her giving me lists of names, with W. E. B. Du Bois, and Frederick Douglass, and Harriet Tubman, and Toussaint L'Ouverture and people like that, and then she'd test me on it. Sometimes that would be a way she'd give me a little extra spending money. At first I didn't understand why I was doing it and then she told me that we had black ancestry.

Even to this day I don't know, you know, if Julia did that just to bring me up not to be racist. I really don't.

When I moved into Portland, my best friend at North Catholic was a six foot seven black kid. He stayed over at our house all the time, and I'd stay over at his house, you know. And I just found myself more and more, as I got older, associating more with blacks and not with whites.[9]

Shane and some of the teachers there went down to a huge peace demonstration in San Francisco against the Vietnam War. One of those teachers took Shane into his class and Shane did quite well there.

When it was time for Shane to graduate, they wouldn't let him come to this graduation ceremony or put his picture in the yearbook. They said his hair was too long. If that was a parochial school, I could see some slight justification for his position, but in a public high school, I could see none.[10]

It was really tragic because I had scraped up money to buy him a suit to wear, and my mother, who had been a teacher, was longing to go to the graduation exercises. She doted on him. They mailed him his diploma.

In the meantime, Julia needed to support herself and her family.

I began working as secretary to the secretary of the District Council and there was a lot more stuff to write up for the *Dispatcher* in Portland. Of course, in between times, whenever money got impossible to find, I wrote a "true story." I had to do a great many things to try and shove Shane in the right direction without obviously doing so. Very difficult. Well, of course, you know, every so often, I wasted a great deal of time writing sonnets and thinking I would resume my career as a writer of proletarian novels.

Julia taking notes for an article as longshoremen gather for the ILWU Bloody Thursday march commemorating the violence of the 1934 strike, Portland, 1972.

Chapter 17

I LOOK AROUND

When Julia was married to Butch she formed a ladies' auxiliary in the IWA. She did the same thing when she married Oscar, organizing an ILWU auxiliary. After Oscar died, she remained in the ILWU auxiliary. When she moved back to Portland, she found the auxiliary there quite conservative and set herself the task of changing it. She recruited new members, including blacks, and became the legislative chair, a position she used to educate the auxiliary members.

With Lois Stranahan, Julia worked to transform the auxiliary from a "ladies" club into a political force. They pushed it to greater involvement with the Columbia River District Council. During a strike, they organized auxiliary members to take part in picket lines and to support strikers and bring coffee and donuts. Julia, Lois, and Lois' husband Jesse, who was a member of the ILWU, would get together and write resolutions that the auxiliary would introduce at auxiliary conventions. Lois said that Julia "was the one that did the typing. She would put the 'whereases' and the 'resolveds' in the proper places." Jesse said Julia wrote a lot of the resolutions but wouldn't take credit for them.[1]

As soon as I recovered from the antibiotic poison and I realized that my mother didn't want to move back, I realized that I could do a great many things, that I would have a lot of extra time. So I looked around for things to do and protests to make against this and that.

Soon after I got back to Portland, I was invited, much to my surprise, to join the Portland Longshore auxiliary. I had organized an auxiliary in Astoria and I organized an auxiliary when I was in the woodworkers' union; I suppose you could say it's my religion.

I was a member-at-large of the Federated Auxiliaries, and so when I came to Portland, I intended to continue as a member-at-large because I was positive—

you know I kept hard-line ideas about what people will and won't do and frequently I'm wrong—the Portland women would not let me into their auxiliary. The leaders of the Portland auxiliary were women that I regarded as extremely conservative. I didn't even try to get in. But soon after I came up here, three of them came to my house and invited me to join. I almost dropped dead of shock! But I readily agreed.

I pursued a policy that I found out was good to follow when you get into a new group: Keep your mouth shut until you have made some friends and found out who the other people in that group might be that possibly could share your views. It didn't take too long, several months. It takes some patience.

I remember going to an auxiliary luncheon and being deeply shocked at the conversation. A very conservative member was there raving because the auxiliary had voted to get some signatures on a petition to nominate Howard Willits—the state representative with the best labor voting record of any down there. She also had a fit because I passed out some grape strike cards for the United Farm Workers boycott. I showed her a one-page clipping about this strike from the *Dispatcher*, and she said, "You never got that out of the *Dispatcher*, it's some other paper."

A gal from the good old days told me a clique ran the auxiliary and they wanted it kept small, that they're antiunion. She said she thought of sounding off at the luncheon, but thought, "Hell, what's the use." I said to her, "Let's not sound off, let's just quietly go ahead and get some of the gals back in that dropped out, let's take in a few new ones," and then it started getting it on its feet, union-wise.

I was put on the legislative committee of the auxiliary. We did different things that the union was interested in in regard to legislation in Salem and in Washington, D.C. We wrote letters; we passed resolutions. Well, also in connection with peace.

I've never been anything except chairman of their legislative committee. I've been to Salem many times when we went down there to lobby for or against measures or bills, but most of it consisted of writing letters to congressmen and senators on different things. Then I was always trying to get them to pass resolutions they didn't much want to pass, but sometimes ended up doing so on various subjects. Well, I remember going to a great many meetings. Seems to me I've spent most of my life in meetings.

Julia was always proud when the auxiliary took a "proper" stand, such as when they moved their convention from the Mayflower Hotel in Seattle in 1969 when negotiations broke down there between the Hotel and Restaurant Workers and an employers association.[2]

Soon after we checked in, word came the talks were breaking down and the hotel might be picketed by breakfast time. Early the next morning, Valerie Taylor, president of the Federated Auxiliaries, called us into emergency session, we passed a resolution supporting the strike, and moved our convention to the Longshore hall, leaving a delegation behind to walk up and down with the pickets. It was a dramatic exodus, nightgowns and notebooks spilling out of suitcases—while the television cameras registered the scene for news viewers.

Of course, the most important job of an auxiliary is to support the union it is attached to. During a strike, as Julia learned in the IWA, the auxiliary's role is crucial. The last ILWU strike Julia experienced was in 1971 through 1972. The issues were wages, pensions, health benefits, and job security in the face of improved efficiency due to container shipping.[3]

The membership in an auxiliary fluctuates and it's never as big as it used to be because so many women today work and have their own organizations they belong to, but let there be a strike like there was in '71 and '72, the membership just zoomed. We got down to one meeting and all the people couldn't get into the room. The men had all told the wives to "go join the Auxiliary. They can probably help us win the strike." And they did.

During the strike, the auxiliary set up what they called a country store co-op. They had a huge clothing depot in the basement of the old Longshore hall and you could go there and get clothing and other necessities. Clara Fambro was in charge of that. And they also had food, they had a leeching committee that went out and leeched food from different stores people had patronized and from the farmers.

Auxiliary members sacked groceries, weighed and wrapped meat, and waited on the long lines of customers. We also kept busy on the telephones enlisting support from other unions against a bill calling for compulsory arbitration which Senator [Bob] Packwood [R-OR] introduced, hoping to break the strike.

But the most interesting thing to me about what they did in that strike was when the employers—they are so foxy—said the grain exports were going to be ruined, which was ridiculous because everybody knows that the wheat elevators get full before they start exporting it and a lot of it lies on the ground and doesn't rot. They went down in the Willamette Valley and got the seed farmers all excited that the seed in the valley was going to get wrecked if it couldn't get shipped.

So then we heard that the seed women were coming up from down the Willamette Valley. They were hiring buses and would be armed with brooms.

They had notified the papers and television stations to come down there and take pictures of them with their brooms and their banners, sweeping the strike into the river.

So *we* made a lot of banners and picket signs and we got our members and a lot of longshoremen's wives who hadn't joined the auxiliary to come down on the waterfront. And there was only one bus that rolled in. The seed women moved up with their signs and we moved up with ours, and we outnumbered them five to one. So we got between them and the reporters and we took over the publicity. Wherever the television people looked to take pictures, there we were in far greater numbers, so we're the ones that got the coverage.

After the television and cameramen had left, we went up to these women— they were kind of scared of us, but as I pointed out to them, "You're the ones that have the brooms. We haven't any weapons."

What was the best part about it, we had a committee going at the Long-shore hall that made coffee, sandwiches, and cookies. We invited the seed women to come to the Longshore hall. We let them tell their side of the story and we told ours. A great many of them said if they had known all about it, they wouldn't have come to Portland.

The strike ended in February 1972 under threat of a congressional compulsory arbitration resolution, when the ILWU accepted a contract giving longshoremen a pay raise, wage guarantees, improved pensions and health coverage. It was essentially the same as what they had earlier turned down, but good nonetheless.[4]

In 1973, 16 Korean and Filipino seamen jumped ship in Portland because of poor conditions and mistreatment. This was the kind of story Julia loved to write, with plenty of horrific details of the workers suffering at the hands of a cruel master, included charges of physical abuse, safety violations, and near starvation. And it was the sort of struggle she thought the auxiliary women should join, because they could raise money and spread the word. Few members, however, were interested.

Down at Schnitzer Steel, the longshoremen found out that a crew was terrified that their boat would sink, it was unseaworthy. They complained to the Long-shoremen and one of them called me up about it. He asked me if I knew any Catholic priests because these men were Catholics. The Catholic priest who taught religion at North Catholic, where my grandson Shane had gone to school, had become a good friend of ours. I called him up and the three of us, the longshoreman, the priest, and me, got the crew off that ship. Then the priest gave them sanctuary in his church.

I learned a long time ago, in spite of the fact that I am not myself religious, that if you find a priest or minister who is really a Christian, in the sense that perhaps Jesus was, that you've found someone that's got a great deal of courage and is willing to do something.

When I went down on the ship to talk to these men and see what they thought we should do to help them, I was the only reporter that got on there. The *Oregonian* and *Journal* reporters weren't allowed aboard the ship. The guard outside Schnitzer's ran after me. Fortunately I was a lot younger and I outran them. They grabbed hold of my raincoat and tore the pocket off, but I got on the ship. I used to have a picture of myself that was taken from a helicopter by the *Journal* reporter they wouldn't let on. I heard he almost got fired over this story. It showed me on the ship talking to these men.

The Immigration and Naturalization Service was going to deport them. It ended up the Immigration had to pay their way back to the Philippines instead of deporting them to the country that this ship had sailed from. It was a Greek ship and the officers on this ship were Greeks. Those were the only Greeks I ever met that weren't any good. I think there was something done about this ship. I remember writing a story about the incident.

Julia's story appeared in the Dispatcher *on October 12, 1973. She misremembered some of the details, for instance, only seven of the seamen who jumped ship were Filipino. Nine were Korean.*[5]

It took Julia ten column inches to detail the "odyssey of horror" these seamen endured crossing the Pacific from Osaka, Japan. The story reports that 12 of the men spent a night at Father Carl Schray's Assumption Parish in St. Johns before leaving for Pusan and Manila, the Longshore auxiliaries providing breakfast and American cigarettes. Julia's story included a long list of those who became involved in the incident: ILWU and other union activists; Philippine Consulate officials; and ministers, lawyers, and politicians including Senator Mark Hatfield, whose father-in-law was a retired longshoreman. And Harry Bridges received a letter from an official of the International Transport Workers Federation in England, who, as a result of reading Julia's story, alerted their unions to be ready for the ship's arrival in the United Kingdom. An official of the Seamen's Union discovered that ten crewmen still working the ship were owed a total of £620 underpayment of wages. He also insisted on a number of improvements on board and demanded that the ship's owners sign an International Transport Workers Federation collective agreement. The letter also reported that the dockers' union refused to work the ship until meaningful negotiations on the agreement were under way.[6]

In 1985 Clara Fambro, who is African American, was elected president of the Federated Auxiliaries, the organization of all the auxiliaries affiliated with the

ILWU. After years of pain around the racist exclusionary policies of Local 8, Julia was delighted to have a black woman, affiliated through Local 8, in this very visible role.

Clara was Julia's friend and her disciple. It was Julia who encouraged Clara to join the auxiliary and Julia who nominated her to all her offices in the local auxiliary that led to her federation presidency. As Clara told me:

> I would not even be in the auxiliary if it hadn't been for Julia. I met Julia on a picket line. Then I went down and I joined the auxiliary and I know that Julia had had to fight and talk a lot; I could just tell from how cool it was when I went. I could tell when she introduced me on the picket line, you know, hey this lady's taking on something maybe she don't know about. But later I found out she knew exactly what she was doing.
>
> When I joined the auxiliary there were no blacks, no blacks at all, and it was not easy. The day I paid my dues, that was fine and they took my name and then they said, "We are gonna practice local autonomy. You have to be in this auxiliary one year before you can make a motion or do anything, you see." No matter what the Federated rules say, they could get around it by saying local autonomy.[7]

The auxiliaries' representatives could attend the District Council meetings, they could speak on issues, but they couldn't make motions or vote (the retired longshoremen, the pensioners, were in the same position). For her first campaign as Federated president, Clara decided to petition the council to give the women a voice and vote. Julia thought it was a great idea. Clara said this was "the last project they had plotted to do":

> We met opposition and so we put it off until March 1986 and she typed up this little thing real quick and immediately the pensioners decided to say, "Well, we'd like to amend that motion" so they could get in. Up until that time there was no support except from Julia. She kept telling me, "Do it, do it!"
>
> The one thing I did not get to do was to write and tell her that we were members with a voice and vote in the council. I had hoped to do that in March, 1991, and they fought me right up until April 21 and she had passed away. But we got it and I'm real proud of it.[8]

As a stringer for the Dispatcher, *Julia needed to get along with the ILWU local as well as the auxiliary. When she returned to Portland in 1965, at first it looked like relations would be as problematic as they had been before she had gone to Astoria.*

It took longer to find a working relationship with the Longshore local here [than with the auxiliary]. The local was anti-Bridges and the bitterness between the local and the International was so deep that the *Dispatcher* would hardly ever print any news from the Portland waterfront. I decided to break that ban down and to get on good terms with Local 8 by putting news in about people whenever they did anything that was newsworthy for the benefit of the union or the membership.

Before I came back to Portland from Astoria, I think you could go through years and years of papers and you wouldn't find any news about the Portland waterfront, but bit by bit that changed. Then it got to the point, a few years after I was back, that a couple of Southern California locals protested that Portland got too much space! So finally, in spite of my views—and I never backed down on a single one—I made good friends on the Portland waterfront.

Julia wrote for the Dispatcher *for about 40 years—first as Kathleen Cronin and then as Kathleen Ruuttila—through several editors. One of them, Sid Roger, praised her skills in 1991 and '92:*

> Because of her, the Northwest, especially the Columbia River area if not also Coos Bay, got more space in the *Dispatcher,* got maybe ten times more space than any other area considering the number of people in the union up there. The Northwest was the only part of the entire union that got absolutely perfect coverage.
>
> She brought a certain political sophistication even to her most simple stories, of say an auxiliary meeting. She was more perceptive than most of the people we could hire who could also write. She put in background from what she herself knew and what she was interested in. She had good information and good sources to say something which she very strongly believed in.
>
> A lot of the meetings that Kathleen wrote about were really not very important, but she managed to find in those meetings an occasional statement about some political situation or some situation dealing with the people on the job, the husbands of the members of the auxiliary, for example. She could dig out of these things something that she could attach to some event or historic event. She had a hell of a lot of knowledge about the history of the union and the history and traditions of Northwest workers and she managed somehow to connect these things without at the same time appearing to be dogmatic or doctrinaire or trying to be didactic.[9]

Chapter 18

VIETNAM

Few Americans knew much about Vietnam in 1964, though small numbers of American soldiers had been there as "advisers" since 1961. Vietnam had been a French colony since the nineteenth century, but was occupied by the Japanese during World War II. Following Japan's withdrawal, the Viet Minh, a coalition of Vietnamese nationalists and Communists, declared an independent republic. The French unsuccessfully fought a war with the Viet Minh to reestablish their control. They admitted defeat and withdrew in 1954.

The 1954 Geneva Conference temporarily divided Vietnam into Communist North Vietnam and Nationalist South Vietnam, pending national elections in 1956. But the government of South Vietnam, fearing a Communist victory, ignored the North's efforts to discuss national elections and declared an independent republic, provoking a civil war between North and South. The United States, also interested in preventing a Communist takeover, secretly provided support to South Vietnam through the CIA.

In the early sixties, the focus of left and liberal activism in the United States was primarily on the civil rights movement, but in August 1964, Vietnam drew America's attention when President Lyndon B. Johnson told Congress U.S. destroyers had been attacked in Vietnam's Gulf of Tonkin by North Vietnamese gunboats. He asked for authority to retaliate. Two days later, the Tonkin Gulf resolution passed unanimously in the House and with only two dissenting votes in the Senate. The resolution was used by the administration as authorization for war in lieu of a formal war declaration. Years later it would be revealed that the attack was a hoax.

Vietnam was the first television war, the first war Americans could watch uncensored every night on the news. The images of American GIs torching bamboo huts and of children burning from napalm challenged the concept the Defense Department

put forth of a just war against evil Communists. Several photographs that became fa-
mous during the war contributed to this "image problem" as well: a Vietnamese monk
committing suicide by fire in 1963 as a war protest; a South Vietnamese police chief
shooting a prisoner point blank in the head; a naked, napalmed girl running down a
road; piles of bodies of women and children in a ditch at My Lai in 1968. These pho-
tographs embedded themselves in the minds of Americans, making it difficult for
many to accept the government's justifications for the war.

At first only leftists and pacifists opposed the war, but as it continued, and espe-
cially as more and more American sons returned from Vietnam in body bags, anti-
war protests grew. In April 1965, 25,000 marched in protest of the war in
Washington, D.C. Before the war was over, millions would march in the streets.
Clergy, students, teachers, intellectuals, mothers, workers, and even veterans would
join the antiwar movement.

In 1964 I went to hear Reed College professor Mason Drukman speak about
Vietnam at some meeting. Although I've always been quite interested in geography, I had to come home and look Vietnam up to be sure exactly where it was.
I knew it was in Southeast Asia. Of course, I knew what the French had done
there when it was French Indochina, as we called it in those times.

So I got more and more interested. Then the next thing I did was to try and
get the Longshoremen and the auxiliary involved because they have more weight
than just one person. There was a Federated Auxiliaries convention in San Francisco. We passed a resolution against the Vietnam War and also another resolution against the draft. It passed with a huge majority vote.

Harry Bridges, who was president of the union then, heard that we had
passed the resolution—which I myself had written—opposing the draft. He had
spoken that morning to the auxiliary convention and got a standing ovation and
was very warmly received, so he came in and asked us to reconsider the resolution. He was against the war and in favor of the draft for some strange reason
whose logic I could never follow.

In fact, that's the speech he made that I couldn't listen to. I was too upset
because I expected to have to get up and rebut his speech. All the time he was
talking, I was planning what I would say. When he got through talking, although I took in the fact he got no applause, except a patter here and there, and
that this black woman who was the vice president of the Federated Auxiliaries
at that time—she was sitting up front where the officers were—when he was
talking she sat like an ebony statue with her arms crossed across her breast. I
took that in, but still I thought I would have to get up and make a speech and
make some effort to save the resolution. But I was sitting by a very smart

woman, a good deal smarter than myself, and she hissed in my ear, "Keep quiet. You don't have to say a word."

She was right because we only lost two votes. Then I looked at Harry and he couldn't understand. I'll never forget that. He looked around the room and he was absolutely stricken. He couldn't realize that to women the thought of drafting their sons was extremely terrifying. He just didn't grasp it at all.

In September 1966, antiwar protesters demonstrated outside the Sheraton Motor Inn in Portland where Vice President Hubert Humphrey was speaking. The FBI estimated the crowd, mostly students, at 200. Julia was among them.[1]

Humphrey had come out to try to raise money to support Democratic Party candidates. He was supporting, or at least not speaking against, the policies of President Johnson in the war, so a lot of people decided to picket him at that hotel over at Lloyd Center. I had Shane with me. I hadn't planned to get arrested. We were just over there with the picket signs walking up and down. There were a lot of people there. There were all kinds of cops and the place was thick and heavy with federal marshals, I suppose because Humphrey was vice president.

There were Secret Service agents there and that is why the police got so wrought up. So when they started beating up the students, it seemed to me the safest thing to do was to sit in the street because then you wouldn't have so darn far to fall. So I sat in the street and then all these other people joined me. And then they started arresting people and dragging them and that's when this cop dragged me and my purse spilled out and all the contents spilled on the street. That's when Shane ran over and hit this cop.

It was a big burly cop and the cop didn't even know he'd been hit, but another cop came and threw Shane into a fence. This student from Reed College, young woman, very slender and small, she came and hit this cop that threw Shane in the back with her picket sign. And then the paddy wagons arrived and the cop that was dragging me in the street tried to throw me into one, but I'm heavier than I look, or was then, so I fell short in the street and I just lay there. He screamed at me to get up, but for a moment I couldn't. I was stunned and then they arrested and threw this student from Reed College, Jon Moscow, in a paddy wagon and they threw Shane in on top of him.

Reverend Mark Chamberlin had come over there to show sympathy for the demonstration, but he hadn't really been a part of it; he was just watching it. Two cops came up and started beating him up and he was unconscious and would have fallen in the street but two students helped him up.

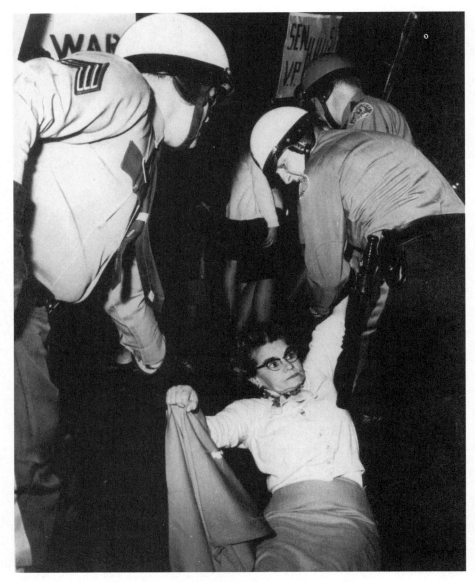

Julia being dragged by police at the Humphrey demonstration, 1966.

The FBI had been monitoring the anti–Vietnam War demonstrations and keeping track of the participants. Julia's file documents her attendance as early as July 1966. Not surprisingly, her FBI file contains a report of the evening's events at the Sheraton.

Subject was among those very actively participating . . . and kept throwing herself on the ground and then apparently feigned a heart attack. When an am-bluance [*sic*] arrived and attendant endeavored to place subject on the stretcher, she jumped up and again participated with the demonstrators. Later she sat down again and when officers removed her, subject again apparently feigned injuries. During this melee, thirty-two of the demonstrators were ar-rested, but subject was not taken into custody or booked.[2]

It was not unprecedented for Julia to purposely fall down or to feign a heart attack; however, the photo that made the newspaper from that evening shows Julia being dragged by police, not being placed on a stretcher. Even if the events described by the FBI are accurate (many people who obtain copies of their FBI files report they are full of errors), the report clearly glosses over the details of what happened "when offi-cers removed her."

Early in the demonstration Shane had left for the shopping center across the street:

Julia forgot to give me her credit card so I went back, and there was a big crowd on the street. I had trouble getting through to her. And when I do get through, who in the hell was being drug down the street but Julia. Her purse was all over the ground, and a cop had each one of her arms dragging her. When I saw that I just went nuts. I tackled the first cop I came to. I just really hit him good, right in the kidneys, and he fell down and broke his finger.

I got some real good punches and kicks in before they finally subdued me. It took about four or five of them to finally handcuff me. I just went berserk. I was calling them names, cussing at them. I don't remember it, but I was look-ing at pictures later, and I could see where some of the picketers were going up when they got a hold of me and they were hitting on them, too. So it kind of erupted into a free-for-all after that. Instead of walking me through this gate, they took me over this fence and knocked me over it. Just completely flattened me over it.

By this time all these people were coming out of the dinner in their tuxes. They drug me over in front of that group just like a trophy. I remember these people yelling, "Kill him! Kill him!" I'll never forget that.

They took me over to this station wagon, and one of the cops slammed my head on top of the car. Then they threw me in and started slamming the door on my legs. They were just going to make sure that I felt some good pain. I'm glad they had me handcuffed, or I'd have gotten in a lot worse trouble.

Then pretty soon here more bodies start coming in. Finally there was five of us in there, and they took us to jail. We were chanting in the car and every-thing, and the cops were yelling at us. We pulled up into the basement of the jail, this one guy gets out—he was plainclothes—he opens the door and backs up, and he pulled his coat open and pulled his gun out.

He said, "Why don't one of you run, so I can make a martyr out of you."

Another thing I'll never forget is when I was in the booking, a cop come up to me and he whispered in my ear, "Some of us here sympathize with you guys," and he loosens my handcuffs. My hands were just purple.

He told the sergeant, "I don't want you to put any of these young kids in the tank here." So they locked me up in a broom closet where they had a bunch of vacuum cleaners. By that time they had taken the handcuffs off.

I remembered that always before one of these things started, they told us never carry anything that could be considered a weapon, even a pencil. Don't do it. Well, I had had metal shop that day and I had a little dinky hammer. I don't think you could hurt anybody with that damn thing, but I took it out of my coat pocket and I was trying to hide it in one of these vacuum cleaner bags and they caught me. So they added that charge on to me: carrying a concealed weapon. They charged me with about five different things. Everyone else was charged with two things. They took me down to the juvenile hall and Pozzi got me out on a writ of habeas corpus.[3]

And what happened next? Oh, I came to and I got up and walked away. I was trying to find where Shane had gotten to and I was looking in the different paddy wagons for him. The paddy wagons were all driven off so then I think the next thing I did was to come back over town to Frank Pozzi's office, you know, the lawyer, so he could try and find out where Shane had been taken.

The next day Julia wrote Valerie:

September 28, 1966

It seems to me we can either put up or shut up. We can crawl into our nice safe "adulthood" forgetting how rough it was in the '30s or we can equate what the kids are doing to right the world with what we tried to do to build the union.

I "put up" last night. I was there as a delegated member from the Col Riv dist council of auxiliaries to the Cit[izen']s Coordinating Committee which, with the student organizations, sponsored the demonstration. I was a non violent demonstrator. And I was manhandled and shoved and knocked into the street and drgged [*sic*] by the arms. I am typing with a sprained wrist, but I'm doing something.[4]

I don't think we were able to get Shane and Jon out until the following day. And there was some kind of a hearing and as soon as I went to the hearing I got subpoenaed. I suppose that some damn cop had recognized me. They subpoenaed me up to testify. I think that's when Pozzi came up and advised me to take the Fifth. They had to let Shane and Jon go. I presume it was some of Pozzi's maneuvering.

Another form of Vietnam War protest Julia participated in was refusal to pay the federal telephone excise tax. This was seen as a war tax because it had been lowered to 3 percent on January 1, 1966—in the process of being phased out—but two weeks later President Johnson asked Congress to restore it to 10 percent to help pay for the war. It was an easy protest that got the government's attention. The telephone company did not penalize the protester, but simply passed on the information to the government, which tried to collect the tax directly from the consumer. Sometimes it did so by garnishment of paychecks or seizure of bank accounts.[5]

I owned this little house in North Portland. One time, because I owed $14 and something in unpaid U.S. telephone tax, they threatened to take my house and sell it at auction. Another time one of those jokers came to the door where I lived and wanted me to sign a paper that I owed this much. I refused to do it and talked to him over the chain on my door and ordered him to leave.

My neighbors across the street heard the commotion and rushed over and told him to get lost. They thought he was an ordinary bill collector. I lived in a poor part of North Portland and they were quite sympathetic. I think they learned quite a bit about what the war was all about during this shouting argument between me and this man. He screamed, "All the people in this neighborhood are nuts," and left.

At one time I had a few dollars in a North Portland branch bank. Then the IRS found out about that and started going to court each month and taking it out of my account. The court procedure, I learned, cost them more than the amount of the tax. The manager of the bank called me up and warned me about it. I told him that if he turned this money over, it was illegal because the war was illegal; it never was declared and was immoral. We had quite a conversation. At least he called me up and warned me.

Even though the war was uppermost on the political agenda, Julia, like everyone else, still had to make a living, still had the worries of parenthood. Her letters to Valerie during this period are about money or politics or Shane or all of the above:

[March 26, 1967]
Had to take on this typing, and stencil cutting assignment—no one else to do it, and I needed the money. Our social security ends May 7 [Shane's eighteenth

birthday], altho [*sic*] Shane's will continue *if* he goes to college. Or rather start
again in September. But mine won't and although I have applied for my "old age
soc. security" there will be a delay, as I'm not sixty yet. Also Shane's VA benefits
stop, and mine are reduced May 7, so I had to do something to get a few bucks
ahead to eat on, when the checks stop. It takes two days a week, and in addition
to the Dispatcher stuff and doing Ray's letters and the peace meetings, and my
mother *and* Shane's difficulties . . . I never seem to get caught up. . . . [6]

Must now tell you what impressed me the most about the peace walk
Saturday. About 1,000 people participated. Many students and teachers.
But the most impressive delegation was the hippies. These are the beatniks
who . . . have withdrawn from our evil society. A few go to art school, or
take music, or other courses at Portland State. Many smoke marajuana
[*sic*]—which is not as bad as it is cracked up to be. They live in pads, five
or six in one or two rooms, boys and girls both, sleeping on the floor. Maybe
one will have a job of some sort. They share what they have in the way of
food. The boys wear their hair very long, some below the shoulders. They
are not activists. But Shane and several others had persuaded them to come
out. . . . Well, anyway, they came, and they had decorated themselves with
flowers! We had a police escort during the march, but the cops disappeared
when we stopped at the Federal building to hear the speakers. A typical cop
tactic, because the [John] Birchers and some teen age hecklers (all with
short hair! I'm against short hair from now on!) tried to provoke a riot. They
hurled dreadful names at the hippies, and these slender, emaciated, ascetic
looking creatures—almost impossible to tell which are girls and which are
boys, in their Easter flowers, and carrying their beautifully made peace signs
looked with sorrowful pity at the hecklers. We have turned some of our children into murderers and sadists; we have helped kill others. We have made
our youth desperate. And we have driven those like the hippies into withdrawal from life.[7]

*Julia's FBI files document her participation in many demonstrations against the war
and some in support of draft resisters. In January 1968, after a demonstration sponsored by the Society for New Action Politics in support of Dr. Benjamin Spock and
others arrested for encouraging draft resistance, "statements of complicity" were presented to the U.S. Attorney claiming equal responsibility with Dr. Spock. Julia was
one of the signers.[8]*

*President Richard Nixon's revelation on April 30, 1970, that U.S. troops were
invading Cambodia set off the largest student uprisings of the era. On May 4, four
protesting students at Kent State University in Ohio were shot and killed by National
Guard troops. In their anger and shock, student protests increased across the country.
On May 6, 1970, Portland State University students set up barricades around the*

university and virtually lived there. On the sixth day of their occupation, the Port-land police stormed the barricades.[9]

The students had this sit-in at Portland State University and Mayor [Francis] Ivancie's Tac squad beat them up. I was waiting for Lois to pick me up at the Public Library downtown where I had been doing some research for the union and we heard this terrible commotion and police sirens. I said to her, "I think they're beating the students up."

So we got in her car and went up there as far as we could drive, and then we walked, and we saw what they were doing. They filled an ambulance with students that had been badly beaten. There was one young man that couldn't get into the ambulance and he had a vein in his leg that had been burst from being beaten. I remember we helped him into the college first-aid room.

Lois recalled:

And of course we got into the middle of it, and once we were *in* there, after we'd parked, we carried these gallons of coffee and cookies in. And more than once did we take people up to the county hospital to have some of their heads treated where they'd been hit by the billy clubs by these, what I call, goose-steppers. I felt like we're taking them into, almost like to a death trap, because as soon as we'd get them up there, they would be treated and picked up by the police and hauled off to jail.[10]

One of the marches, the one in which ten thousand people marched down Broadway, was led by one of our black members of our auxiliary, Dorothy Hames. Her son was drafted.

The march was part of a three-day national protest held November 13–15, 1969, organized by the New Mobilization Committee to End the War in Vietnam. On November 15 it was estimated that a quarter of a million people marched in Washington, D.C. One hundred thousand turned out in San Francisco, the biggest protest ever on the West Coast.[11]

Dorothy Hames' son had a needle broken off in his heel and needed an operation. When he was drafted, she, along with Julia and Lois, enlisted the help of Senator Wayne Morse. Lois explains:

We made every possible effort to try to keep this young fellow in the States if they were going to draft him, and to take him to medical and have this removed from his heel.

They went ahead and they drafted him in spite of this. They took him down to Fort Ord, California, and from there straight over to Vietnam. Three weeks later he came back in a body bag. After that there was a big protest march of about 10,000.

Julia saw to it that [Dorothy Hames] led the parade and spoke. And rightly so, it was very appropriate. That was really a tear-jerking moment for all of us.[12]

I look back on it with embarrassment because I offered to write the speech for her. She said, "Thanks very much. I wouldn't think of letting you write it because I think I could do a better job." And she did. She made a very moving speech. I'll never forget that march.

I think the Vietnam War protests turned this country around because now people that were for that war won't admit that they were. 'Course, I am not opposed to people fighting in defense of their homes if their country is invaded. But when you talk about our interests abroad, it's always tainted by what the multinationals' interests are in those other places.

Chapter 19

TOO OLD TO GET BEAT UP

It was February 1975. The U.S. economy was suffering from both recession and inflation. Julia was sixty-seven years old and Pacific Power & Light Company (PP&L) had applied for a rate increase. She hadn't made the headlines since 1966 when she had been featured on the front page of a local daily being dragged by police from the antiwar demonstration at the Sheraton Motor Inn. Her big media splashes—her firing in 1948 and the subsequent suit, and her appearance before HUAC in 1956— had long been forgotten by most Oregonians. When Julia grabbed the headlines again in 1975, most of the media seemed to have forgotten her history as well. She was just an old woman making too much noise.

Julia's health had slowed her down. She had become frailer, but her ideas weren't tempered. She continued to write for the Dispatcher *and she still walked every picket line she could manage to get to. It had been her policy, at least since her appearance before HUAC, to not put herself forward, to avoid personal publicity, yet in 1975 she ignored that habit and became a celebrity again.*

In 1975 they raised the electric rates. It was a great hardship on the people in the North Portland neighborhood in which I lived, particularly my next-door neighbor. She was a Finnish woman and a widow. Very elderly. She couldn't afford to turn on any of her heat. She used to wrap her legs in old sweaters and old socks and put two or three blankets over herself and sit buried in a chair.

So one day I decided I was going to go down and picket PP&L, but in order to make it count, I thought there'd have to be publicity. I forget who wrote the press releases, but it was Lois who took them around to all the news media, and it was Lois who got the Democratic Party to send the delegation to outside

Julia (left) and Martina Curl sitting in at the Pacific Power and Light Office, 1973.

PP&L. Lois was very good at that type of organizing. So a great many reporters showed up.

The press release, issued by the Committee Against Higher Utility Rates, announced a protest starting at 4 P.M. on Thursday, February 27, at which "[t]wo elderly women will stage a sleep-in in the PP&L office to dramatize what the excessive rates charged by PP&L, PGE and the oil companies are doing to the unemployed and the aged in this bitter winter of 1975." It also explained that the Public Utility Commission had given PP&L a 32.5 percent rate increase in September and now PP&L was asking for more.

Lois said the committee had written slogans and made signs. She picked up Julia, who was carrying a coffee thermos and her asthma medicine, along with her sleeping bag. They got there about 4. Julia and Martina Curl went inside while Lois picketed outside in the cold with the others.[1]

I forget how Martina Gangle Curl found out what I was going to do, but she wanted to go with me. And our next-door neighbor, the elderly Finnish woman, packed up a sack of food so we'd have something to eat in jail, and among them there were three apples. A friend of mine in the Longshore auxiliary lent us two sleeping bags so we'd have something to lie on. So we put them down where people pay their bills.

Before closing time the PP&L offices ordered us out and we refused to go. We said it was the first time we'd been warm in many days. I laid down on my sleeping bag, so they lifted me out like it was a hammock, but Martina sat up, which was a mistake. She had a brand new pair of shoes that she was very proud of and they dragged her out and her shoes were just ruined. One of the cops was starting to be very rough with me, but some people, bystanders, ran up and told him to lay off, so he did.

Martina Curl was no novice. At sixty-eight, she was an experienced political activist, an open member of the Communist Party for many years who knew how to take advantage of publicity, how to embarrass police, how to get the most out the moment.

> Julia started it. It was her idea about sleeping in there, saying that we were cold and we wanted to come down there and get warm in their building. She's good at different ideas, she's very good.
>
> She talked a lot, I talked some, but not very much, and the press asked questions, you know, the ones with the TV. She was, I thought, very eloquent, in her talking. But she exaggerates a little bit, y'know, like the seriousness of it. I think it's a good thing.

We had agreed that we would not go willingly. They took her first. They got a hold of the four edges of the thing, four of 'em, and took her out that way. I can remember her saying, "Don't drop me because I've got [osteoporosis] . . . you're liable to break all my bones." But when they took me—see, I wasn't on the bag, I was in much better shape than she was—so I just went limp, and they had to drag me.

The two officers on each side of me were very embarrassed, they didn't like it shown, them dragging an old woman, so they kept saying, "Well, why don't you get up and walk, look at how this makes us look." I says, "Well, you do your thing and I'll do my thing."[2]

Julia and Martina knew that the protest by two small, older women would put PP&L in a public relations bind. The protest received extensive local news coverage, pictures in the newspaper, and a story on the TV evening news.

When we got to the jail, we were thrown into the dirtiest room I've ever been in in my life. It was a large cell, but it was filthy dirty, and since I have suffered from asthma, I began to cough and sneeze. I thought, I've got to get out of here and get my purse back—which they'd taken away—and get my pills. I had completely forgotten the door was locked, and I tried to open it, and I thought, my God, I'm locked in.

Just about that time, someone began screaming in another cell, I suppose some drunken person. Now this is just between you and me, Martina got very frightened. She thought they were beating that person up and that they would come and beat us up, but I was sure it was a drunk screaming. Soon after that the matron came to the door and let us out, and she gave us back our sack of food, and she gave us a knife to cut and peel the apples with, which is probably the first time anyone in jail ever got a knife.

She took us out into the lobby of the jail. She said that they had sent out for a man that lets you out on your recognizance, but he was having dinner and that we'd have to wait till he got there. She said her light bills were too high also. So Martina cheered up considerably.

Martina tells the story differently:

And of course, when they got down to jail, they took our picture and fingerprinted us, and took everything away. That was the only time I was in jail with her; I think it was the first time she was in jail. I was in jail before during the Depression and for peace demonstrations against Hitler.

She thought I was scared, but I really wasn't. I don't get scared of things. I've been in jail about six, seven, or eight times. I get angry sometimes, but I don't get scared, until afterwards usually. Actually there's nothing to be afraid of, I don't think, in a case like that. They didn't treat us badly.

The reporters asked some questions of her after we got out and I don't remember what she said, but I know it was something that was good, something that fit the thing.[3]

In the meantime, Lois was making the most out of their publicity coup:

Poor Howard Willits [a liberal former state representative and chair of the Committee to Lower Electric Rates]. He immediately wanted me to drive him down to the jail where they had them. He wanted to put up the money and bail them out. Of course, we went down all right, but Julia refused to have any money put up to be bailed out. She was going to stay there. She was going to get out on her own. Which they did.

We got as many people as we could get. At that time we had nice rosters, where you could, you know, call people. I immediately came home and started working on people. There was people down at the jail that you wouldn't believe would ever come to anything. We were down there, you know, screaming and hollering, "Let them out."[4]

After her release from jail, Julia testified at a hearing on the rate hike. A portion of her notes for that testimony reads:

When I wrote to PP&L protesting their excessive rates, they sent a Mr. Cripe to see me. His gripe was that, as a stockholder, he was entitled to clip a hefty coupon. PP&L stock, he said, was a good investment. I said I could see that from looking at my light bill.

He gave me an expensive brochure, ENERGY CONSERVATION ON THE HOME FRONT. "Don't overload your dryer. Limit tub baths to half tub." In spite of the fact I have arthritis, I limited mine to a fourth of a tub for months. And then this goody: "You don't have to hear the bugle to know when it's time for lights out." The one comfort of the elderly poor is to crawl into bed, pile on the quilts and read. But oh no, "Lights out," says Col. Watt!

Many of Julia's friends had tales to tell about the PP&L caper. Democratic Party activist Russ Farrell said Julia took a bunch of PP&L's handbills home and burned them in her fireplace. His wife Lorine started a petition to PP&L with Howard Willits. They found the unemployment office prime territory for signatures. Russ and Lorine's daughter Sharron paid her electric bill in pennies, at Julia's suggestion. Shane said Julia started getting money in the mail after all the publicity and people calling with offers of wood. Julia summarized the experience as "freeing . . . for her, because she realized that she was at an age where she was too old to get beat up, and she could do whatever she wanted."[5]

Chapter 20

THE TRIALS OF PARENTHOOD

In 1991 Shane told me, "I feel real lucky to have been raised in her household. I think it's an experience that's just a real spiritual type thing." Nevertheless, in his late teens and for most of his twenties, Shane caused Julia great pain and worry. Her letters to Valerie Taylor document the change from a proud grandmother to a troubled one. This first letter written just two and half weeks after the demonstration at the Sheraton Motor Inn, when Shane "lost it" and fought the police when he saw Julia being dragged away, is still full of pride.

November 14, 1966
The charges against Shane . . . are trespassing, disorderly conduct, possession of a dangerous weapon and possession of tobacco. He was nominated the best citizen of the year by his English class. . . . He was nominated by a Negro. Half his class are Negroes. The teacher called for additional nominations, and the Negroes began to chant, "Shane Ruuttila, Shane Ruuttila, Shane Ruuttila!" He also won the debate on Vietnam—he took on his entire foreign relations class single handed. He had a stack of material.[1]

Four months later she is drained by what he has put her through, "I hope I never live through anything like the past two months again," she wrote, but she is still sympathetic and drugs aren't mentioned.

Shane's girlfriend, Barbara, had gotten pregnant. Barbara's mother had wanted Julia to pay for half of her abortion. Julia had refused, saying she didn't believe in abortions done outside hospitals (in 1967, a legal abortion could be obtained in Oregon only if two doctors agreed the woman's health appeared in peril because of her pregnancy), but she did offer to borrow on her house so she could put up half the money to help Shane and Barbara set up housekeeping and have the baby.

The class issues between Julia and Barbara's mother are clear and strong in Julia's letter. Julia says that Barbara's mother wants someone with better prospects than Shane for her daughter. When Barbara's mother suggested Julia take the abortion money out of Shane's trust—money Pozzi had won for him after a car accident—Julia said the trust was under court control and she couldn't ask a judge for abortion money because abortion is illegal. Barbara's mother, Julia said, told her to lie to the judge. Julia says she retorted with "maybe on her side of the tracks they went in for perjury, but not on mine!" Shane and Barbara named their expected baby Donovan, but in February 1967 Barbara had an abortion without Julia's cooperation.[2]

And then Barbara got pregnant again. This time there was no abortion. Shane and Barbara married in September 1967; their daughter Rhea was born in December. They separated in 1969. Julia tried to keep in contact with Rhea, but Barbara's family ultimately forbade it.

Meanwhile, Shane turned eighteen in May 1967, making him eligible for the Vietnam War draft. Shane went to his physical high on speed. He had been using drugs for about a year and as a result was given a 4-F (not qualified for any military service) for a year. After the year was up, he started getting letters again from Selective Service. Shane applied for conscientious objector status, but was turned down because he said he wasn't against all wars, just certain wars. When he found himself at the induction center, he drew a peace sign on his papers, snuck out and went to a draft counseling center. By that time, Shane was a morphine addict. The draft counselor had him examined and his 4-F was reinstated.[3]

Julia watched helplessly as drugs got the better of Shane's life. In 1969, in her frustration and inability to help him on her own, she finally appealed to outsiders for help. Shane remembers:

My first wife and I were separated and I was staying at Julia's. I was really getting involved in speed. I had forged one of her checks or something. Instead of calling the police, the store brought it to her attention. So here I am one morning, it was about 7 o'clock, and here's four plainclothes guys busting into the back bedroom in her house. I thought they were narcotics agents at first. I'm going, "Why are they after me?" I stopped dealing two years before then. And J[ulia] was in back of them, and she was apologizing and saying she had to do it for my own good, and so it finally dawned on me. They showed a warrant that they had. They said they were going to hold me at the courthouse for a sanity hearing. They said I had the right to get an attorney, and all this. And I'm saying, "Gee, there's nothing wrong with me. I don't need an attorney." The judge sentenced me for thirty to sixty days out to Dammasch [Oregon State Mental Hospital]. I guess I was out there three times.[4]

In 1970, Shane married Ruth Baker. They had two sons, Jason, born September 5, 1970, and Ryan, eleven months later on August 11. When that marriage ended in 1976, Shane took Jason, and Ruth took Ryan. In 1977, when Shane hit bottom, Julia was close to the end of her patience, but she made one last attempt to save him. With the help of union friends, she sent Shane far from his drug dealers to Chignik, Alaska, a cannery town in the Aleutians where she hoped he could turn his life around.

Shane left Jason with Ruth and accepted Julia's challenge. Alaska was a more successful solution than the commitments and forced drug treatments Julia had tried earlier. In Chignik, he met and married Betty Rose Jerue. He remembered his union background and, when he found a third of the workforce in Chignik had no union representation, he contacted the Alaska Fishermen's Union and helped bring the workers into the union.

I finally reached the bottom back in April of '77. I was tired of going to Julia every now and then, asking her for another twenty-five bucks to help me with my rent down at one of those flophouses downtown. I was just in a real state and really bad on drugs. I'd been living off a prostitute for seven, eight months. So I tried to commit suicide. I must have had a nervous breakdown or something. It was just so weird.

When I called Julia up, it happened to be her birthday. It wasn't intentional. So what a birthday present that was for her to come down to that flophouse in a cab. She called the Longshore hall and no one would help her take me. I guess my reputation had been all through there by then, almost ten years of that crap.

And so I went to Holladay Park [a hospital with an inpatient psychiatric unit]. She said, "I'm going to get you up to Alaska"—you know, through the Longshore local in Seattle—"and if you don't go, don't knock on my door again."

I think as deep as I got into the drug culture, that's the one thing that kept me from really going all the way into it, and crossing the line, and that eventually pulled me out, was to keep thinking, "Gee, how could I do this after the way I was brought up?"[5]

My grandson tried twice to kill himself. He had gotten a job as a maintenance man down at that fancy building that PGE [Portland General Electric] owns. So, 'course, you know, they work after the offices have closed. He's on his way from work and he was set on by three thugs and they were infuriated because he didn't have any bills in his billfold, just some small change. So they knocked him down and kicked him and stepped on his hand, his right hand. It was broken in many, many places and he would have been killed but there're some taverns down there and a big huge Negro ran out from one of these taverns and drove those three thugs off.

And then he called an ambulance and he was taken to the emergency room up here at Good Sam[aritan Hospital] and a woman doctor set his hand. But she didn't even begin to find all the breaks and when he went back to have the cast taken off, his hand was all swollen and there were all those unset bones, his hand was literally smashed to pieces. So he went back to the cheap hotel where he was living and slit his wrists.

Well, a young woman that lived in that hotel, no doubt a prostitute, knocked on his door and she took him to the emergency room at Physicians and Surgeons Hospital and they sewed up his wrists and she took him back to the hotel. It was very kind of her; some of them are kind. And as soon as she left, he filled the bathtub with water, got in the bathtub and slit his wrist again. If you're in water your blood runs out faster, if you slit your wrists.

But someone else found him and they called me. So I took him up to Crisis Care and they got him into Holladay Park. And there he was fortunate enough that the doctor on duty was the best bone doctor in the city of Portland. Many longshoremen that were hideously injured on ships have gone there and he's fixed them up. I suppose that hand was a real challenge to him.

He rebroke the bone that she had set, the only one she had set, the woman doctor, and then he set all the other bones and then he told me that Shane would have to be in that hospital a long time. We had no money to pay the bill so the doctor said "Don't worry, I won't let them put him out until he's ready to go."

I forget how long he was there, but quite a few weeks, and then my two brothers-in-law [Oscar's half brothers] let him come down and live with them at Ilwaco until he was able to use his hand to work. And then I got the Filipino union, the Alaska cannery workers, to dispatch him to Chignik, Alaska. That's where he met Betty Rose. She was working in the cannery too. Well, she's the best thing that ever happened to him.

But you know, a young man, a young working man who has a smashed right hand, what's he got to look forward to? It's the only time I ever asked the union to do anything for me or for him.

Chapter 21

DO NOT LOOK BACKWARD
WHEN YOU LATCH THE GATE

Moving's forever; you must say goodby.
This house was home, and when the movers go
And you are living seven stories high
In one room that you are going to,
Half of a lifetime will be left behind . . .
Beds and dishes, pictures and debris.
Sweep the memories from your heart and mind,
Burn the letters, push the past away.
The very old can learn to live with grace
In a small and very narrow space.

Do not look backward when you latch the gate
At flower faces weeping as you pass,
Someone will run the hose when rains are late
Over the sparkle on the summer grass.
Do not look backward when you latch the gate.[1]

—Julia Ruuttila, n.d.

In 1976, Julia was hospitalized for a severe case of flu. Considering the plethora of ailments she suffered—ulcers, angina, asthma, arthritis—her doctor thought she wasn't strong enough to go back to her little house alone. Under protest, she moved into Marshall Union Manor, a retirement high-rise built by the unions. At first she was angry to be there, turned her nose up at the women who "sit around crocheting," and thought she'd never adjust to a studio apartment. But after a few months she was drinking coffee with the others in the cafeteria and editing the Manorgram, *the*

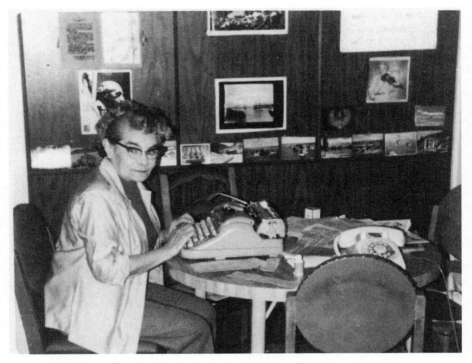

Julia at her typewriter in her apartment at Marshall Union Manor, late 1970s.

building's monthly newsletter, slipping in a suggestion to write your congressman or a few paragraphs on the history of discrimination in Oregon for Black History Month.

There are a few people here that have fairly good incomes, and there are people in here that are very hard up, but no one seems to understand who the street people are or why there are people standing in food lines in Portland, which there are. If they'd only get out and look around they'd see these people. They are so upset because we took in some people here from group homes, young people that are deaf and have other disabilities. There isn't enough awareness of what's going on in our own society, right in our own city. The only thing I can think of is that people are brainwashed, or are they just dumb?

Julia became a Democratic Party precinct committeewoman for her new district. She complained to Roger Auerbach, her district precinct captain, about the conservative residents of the building. He remembers she was concerned the building management might try to stop her from distributing the sample ballot "and, of course, she was not gonna be stopped."[2]

Eight years after Julia moved to the Manor she was interviewed for the neighborhood newspaper. She used it as a platform to complain about the building's administrator. She called the camera in the lobby Big Brother. She said she asked the administrator "if he was going to tap our phones next." She also accused him of trying to stop her from circulating a petition in the building. She said she got to do so only after threatening to sit outside collecting signatures. Remembering her PP&L lesson, she said she asked, "What do you think the press would think of an old lady sitting outside in the rain?"[3]

The executive administrator of the Union Labor Retirement Association, which runs Marshall Union Manor, responded with a letter. He said he realized that "throughout your life you have thrived on and excited controversy in a broad spectrum in all affairs." He went on to remind her that he wanted petitions to be reviewed and voted on by the residents' forum and then be at a sign-up table with an informational sign. What he wouldn't allow, and what Julia surely wanted, was "arm-twisting or form of salesmanship."[4]

When I moved to Marshall Union Manor I transferred my money to a bank in Northwest Portland. Those IRS people are very stupid; it took them ten months to find out that I had moved. They were still after me for the telephone tax. They first found out that my telephone number had been changed. They called up and wanted to know where I lived. I told them that was their business to find out if they were still wasting government money on that type of thing.

One day there was a loud banging on my door. That isn't the way of the sweet religious ladies that live on this floor, so I suspected the worst. I was just getting my coat on to go to the main post office to mail news copy to the *Dispatcher.*

I opened the door a crack and saw this buzzard standing there. He had his IRS credentials in his hand. I banged the door shut. He yelled that I had better come out because he was going to stand there until I did. I said, "Well, I have enough food in here for ten days at least, so you will probably starve to death if you stand there that long."

I had a news story about the Longshoremen that had to make a deadline in San Francisco so I tried to call up my neighbor that was directly under me. I thought that I could lower this envelope to her on a string and tell her to take a cab and I'd reimburse her. She wasn't home. I called up the union hall and thought they would send someone out to get it. After all it was their paper. The person who answered was all by himself and said, "I can't leave."

I was getting desperate when I heard heavy footsteps going down the hall toward the elevator. I went down the hall in the other direction and swung out on the fire escape. I got down to the end of the fire escape and there was still a story drop. I had to swing back in on the second floor, but I found a door to a stairway. I ran through the gardens and through the hospital that used to be here on the corner and to the Longshore hall, which in those days was only ten blocks from Marshall Union Manor. A longshoreman took me to the post office.

In a place like this you have to file a statement of your income. The building administrator told me the IRS agent had gone to his office and demanded information about if I had a bank account where it was. The administrator refused to tell him, saying it was "privileged information." The IRS man threatened to arrest him. The administrator, a former Catholic priest, said he would call his attorney, so the IRS man left. The administrator was on my side.

I learned later that several of the ladies on my floor had heard the commotion and were in sympathy with me. I heard from one of the ladies that the minister in her church didn't pay his tax either, and another lady that her son-in-law didn't pay his telephone tax. So I didn't get in any trouble.

This is the last I had heard of the matter except that when the IRS found out that I was working for the *Dispatcher*. I hate to say this, but the bookkeeper, without informing me—I had money coming for news copy—took that money and turned it over to him. I wrote a letter to the *Dispatcher*. I was furious. I said, "You may think this is a trivial matter and, of course, it is not a world-shaking matter—there are hundreds of people in town that don't pay their U.S. telephone tax—but it is not a small matter to me." So I received an apology from them.

Ruth Ruuttila, Shane's former wife, was in a car accident in March 1983. Her spinal cord was severed and she sustained head injuries. She was left paralyzed and speechless. She spent her remaining days in a hospital and then a nursing home after a failed effort by her family and Julia to obtain in-home care. Jason and Ryan, Ruth and Shane's sons, moved in with Ruth's sister, visited their mother, and saw Julia often. When Ruth died in January 1986, the boys finished the school year and then moved to Anchorage to live with Shane and his wife, Betty Rose.

Julia was terribly lonely without them. Despite her work for the Dispatcher, *her many old friends, and her continued participation at demonstrations and picket lines, Julia missed the boys. She needed family. She felt frail and wanted someone to take care of her.*

Julia had built a strong relationship with the boys. She had watched over them before Shane got his life back together, making sure there was food in the house and

that they received new clothes. "Julia always made sure that they never suffered,"
Shane said. "It's funny, she did that for three generations. She brought up my dad,
me, and then helped with my two boys an awful lot."[5]

In the months leading up to her eightieth birthday on April 26, 1987, Julia
made a decision. She would retire and move to Alaska to live with Shane and his
family. She left for Anchorage on May 15, 1987. On May 2, she was honored at a
luncheon at the Longshore hall during a District Council meeting with speeches and
testimonies. Telegrams were read from the union dignitaries who couldn't make it up
from San Francisco. At the end, small and smiling with her trademark red ribbon
tied in her hair, Julia spoke:

> I used to wonder if any of you read the articles and when someone would
> write a letter to the *Dispatcher* and say I'd misspelled someone's name I was
> happy because I'd know then that someone had read them. I hate to leave
> Portland. I hate to leave this waterfront because this hall has always been my
> second home.
>
> Just now I heard the word "red." Don't be afraid to be called a red. Harry
> Bridges once said, " A red is anyone who wants a nickel more than the boss is
> willing to pay." And another thing I think we can remember is that the pre-
> amble of the IWW, on which I cut my teeth, said: "The working class and the
> employing class have nothing in common."
>
> Now I can't make a speech for two reasons. I'm afraid I might break into
> tears and, two, you have some work to do and one resolution I hope you will
> pass about stopping this dirty little war in Nicaragua. Thanks for these totally
> unnecessary gifts and I'll probably give some of them away.

Julia's life in Alaska was quieter, much of her time spent looking out the window,
watching birds in the backyard. As a result she became more interested in conserva-
tion and began donating to conservation organizations such as Greenpeace. She had
more money to contribute because of Alaska's Longevity Bonus Program—financed
by the windfall from the Alaskan oil pipeline—which provides a monthly check to
Alaskans over sixty-five. Shane thought she probably gave away about 40 percent of
her income.[6]

Julia joined the most left-wing group she could find, Alaskans Concerned about
Latin America, and was active in SANE [National Committee for a Sane Nuclear
Policy]. She argued with the newly formed Alaska Green Party, telling them they
would take votes away from Democratic candidates, who might not be great, but had
a chance to win.[7]

But despite this involvement, she wasn't happy in Alaska. Shane and Betty Rose
moved to a house with a bedroom and bathroom on the first floor for her, but it was

Ruuttila family photo (from left) Shane, Julia, Ryan, Betty, Jason.

far from the city center, and an expensive cab ride to downtown. Julia was disappointed when she discovered Anchorage was not on the ocean. Shane's teenage sons were too much for her all the time. But she said she was too frail to come back; she had barely survived the trip north. She carried on a lively correspondence with her friends back in Portland:

June 14, 1987

Cook Inlet is not the ocean and I now understand why Shane said he misses the Oregon beaches. . . . My great grandsons (the basketball stars) are now through with classes and they listen to comics and soaps all day on TV. Don't know how I will stand it. . . . There are no buses within walking distance; so I shall become a shut-in. Tried to write some poetry to cheer myself up, but seem to have lost the knack (if I ever had one).

Chiseled in stone
The Chugash [*sic*] mountains loom
Over the ice-cold inlet.

Their contours
Cruel and concise

Cut through my dreams
Of spring.[8]

Sept. 9, 1988

The summer's over up here and so is the Autumn. There was frost on the ground this morning and the hours of daylight are greatly reduced. . . . I dread the winter, but in a short walk yesterday for the first time I felt at home up here. One of my favorite walks is on the grounds of Our Lady of Guadelupe Catholic Church (just over our back fence). Suddenly I realized the small trees in several of their plantings are rowan trees. (That's what the Finns called them in Astoria. The non-Finns called them mountain ash.) The berries had turned red, which clued me in on what trees they are. We had a grove of them (7 or 8) only much taller, in our side yard in Astoria.[9]

Nov. 14, 1990

It's very cold up here. Thirty below the other day with the wind chill factor, actually 10 below. I miss Oregon, the politics, the weather, the protests, my friends. But I cannot return.[10]

AFTERWORD

February 5, 1991. Julia is home alone. She feels a pain in her chest and knows it's another heart attack but, not wanting to ruin Shane's vacation (he is in Oregon), she sits and waits as the pain grows more intense. Finally, after several hours, she calls for help.

Julia has been in the hospital for a few days before I hear the news. I call her and she sounds okay—she's coherent. The last mail I had had from her was in December, when I got a holiday card benefiting the Committee in Solidarity with El Salvador. Inside the card, following the multilingual "Happy Holidays," she had typed "AND OUT OF THE GULF!"

Enclosed was a clipping: "Anchorage gulf forum reaches fever pitch." The photo was of Julia with the caption: "Eighty-three-year-old Anchorage resident Julia Ruuttila speaks her mind during a town meeting on the Persian Gulf crisis held Saturday at the University of Alaska Anchorage." Her hair was whiter than the last time I had seen her over three and a half years before, but she looked her usual feisty self. I had been relieved; she'd reported too many angina attacks in recent letters.

I knew Julia would remain active as long as she could drag herself to meetings and to picket lines. Shane knew it too. "She always said she'd rather die on a picket line, or at something other than just watching the news or reading. She's made quite a reputation for herself up here already with her letters to the editor, in the small little group they've got up here."[1]

On Monday, February 18, I call Shane. Julia has been released from the hospital, but Shane is very pessimistic, "The visiting nurse was here today and told us to make funeral arrangements." I ask to talk to Julia.

"Now don't say anything to Shane, but I won't be here much longer," she tells me. I decide to go to Alaska.

When I call Shane on Tuesday to say I'll arrive Friday night, he tells me that might be too late. I fly out that evening, arriving in Anchorage at midnight.

The next morning the phone wakes me at 7 A.M. It's Shane. "Julia woke up very early, asking if you're here."

Although fruit trees are blooming in Oregon, it is winter in Alaska. The sidewalks are packed with ice, dirty snow fills the gutters and is banked against the buildings. Only the main streets are bare. It is 7 degrees Fahrenheit. I bundle up for the walk across the parking lot to Shane's pickup. His house is only a few blocks away. Inside, I wait for Julia.

It's nearly four years since I helped her onto the plane in Portland for Alaska. We both knew it might be the last time we saw each other. She was weak then, but still I am surprised when I see her. A tiny, bent old lady moves slowly into the room pushing a walker. Her uncombed hair stands on end. She wears a bathrobe over her pajamas. She looks at me and says, "She still has her wonderful smile." We hug.

I had no idea how much she wanted to see me. I came because *I* needed to see her again. I needed a last visit. She has missed me, and is terribly excited by my presence. She tells me about her heart attack. She naps. I knit. I read.

Julia tells me she is ready to die. There is no pleasure left in life. She can't go anywhere. She can't concentrate enough to read. She isn't strong enough to type. She tells me she has the means (hoarded pills) to die, and soon she will take care of things. "Don't tell Shane," she orders me.

I promise. I tell her I will miss her, but I understand.

"I want my ashes scattered on Maria Raunio's grave. Shane says he won't do it. Will you?"

This was the grave the Red Finns had assigned her to decorate when she lived in Astoria. "Of course," I tell her. She sighs with relief.[2]

Shane has grown into a man Julia can be proud of. When he was twenty-one and working in a plating shop in Portland, he helped to organize the machinists union. In Chignik, Alaska, he helped bring nonunionized workers into the Alaska Fishermen's Union. In Anchorage he was involved in his third big union organizing drive with AFSCME. To him this was the best organizing drive because it involved the largest number of people. Drug addiction has receded into an unhappy memory.

Shane has stayed home from work. While Julia naps, he agrees to be interviewed. He says, "Julia thinks she's a burden. Hell, I owe her so much. I'm glad to do this." And he talks about organizing for AFSCME, how she encouraged him when he got discouraged, and how important her wisdom was to him:

> I probably was the most visible member in responding to the attacks on public employees in writing and that directly came from her. She said, "You have to stand up for yourself and the members. You have to deter-

mine your own public image and identity and not let your opponents do it for you."

And she talked about how important political action was, putting together groups of members in all the precincts and districts, phone banking, for local and statewide and national elections. Money doesn't win elections; it's grass-roots stuff that wins the close races, and she always stressed that. You have to get members motivated to stand up for themselves.[3]

Later that day an aide comes to bathe Julia. Julia asks her what she thinks about the Gulf War. The aide is evasive. Then Julia shares her own opinion in great detail. They disappear into the bathroom. Julia returns dressed, combed, and looking much stronger. "Did you know this woman is Cherokee?" she asks me.

The nurse arrives. She is also asked her position on the war. She too is evasive. When they have both left, Julia tells me how much she likes the aide, "but that nurse is very cold." I wonder if, alone in the bathroom, the aide talked to Julia about the war, while the nurse refused to talk about anything but Julia's health? Or does she prefer the aide because she is Cherokee?

In the privacy of Julia's room, I get out the tape recorder and play Shane saying she is not a burden. She is very touched. "I didn't know he cared so much," she says. Later she will admit this is why she decided not to take her hoarded pills.

Julia grows stronger each day. By Friday, she is nagging Shane to take us to an antiwar demonstration in downtown Anchorage on Saturday. Shane agrees on the condition that Julia stays in the car; the icy ground is treacherous, and the temperature is near zero.

On Saturday morning, Julia naps, saving her strength for the outing. A nurse is due at 10 to give Julia a checkup; we are to leave for the demonstration at noon. The nurse is late. When we have given up on her and are already in our coats and boots, the nurse finally appears. Julia refuses to delay her outing. She tells the nurse (a new one) how she feels about the war, that this demonstration is more important than her checkup. Then we venture out into the cold.

Less than two dozen people are congregated at the small downtown plaza, holding yellow, orange, and white signs: "Cease Fire Now," "No World in War," "Oil Addiction is Our Enemy," "Peace is Patriotic." More signs are poked in the piles of snow alongside the cleared square and sidewalks. Julia reminds me this is a conservative military town.

Shane parks the car across the street where Julia can get a good view, and he and I join the demonstrators. A "Blessed are the Peacemakers" sign hangs from a card table spread with literature from the local SANE chapter. We hold signs for a few minutes and visit with the others. I take a few sheets from the table.

Julia waits patiently in the car. I think about all the demonstrations she attended in Oregon, all the picket lines she walked, all the leaflets she wrote. While she is unable to actively participate in this particular protest, she is nonetheless happy to be here, and more excited than I've seen her since I arrived in Alaska.

My visit is almost over. Julia sleeps most of the afternoon. My plane leaves early the next morning. I stay for dinner, watch TV with her. Then we kiss, hug, and I bundle myself up for the short ride to my hotel, knowing this is finally and really goodbye. I try to permanently memorize her small figure, her red hair ribbons, and her imp's smile.

Julia lived another six weeks. Shane gives me credit for it, and perhaps it's due. He thinks I cheered her with my visit, but I think about the day I played the tape for her with Shane's words of gratitude, and how she set aside her stash of pills after she heard it. Or was her talk of suicide just bravado?

Lois Stranahan called with the news of her death. Julia died on April 5, 1991. My last letter from her arrived the next day; it was dictated to her grandson Jason. I had written her mentioning the discovery that Oregon senator Mark Hatfield, ranking minority member on the Senate Appropriations Committee, had failed to disclose gifts from the University of South Carolina at a time when the university was seeking a $16 million grant (the Senate Ethics Committee rebuked him the next year). Although Hatfield was a Republican, Julia liked him because of his strong stand on peace and his longshoreman father-in-law.

> Dear Sandy,
>   Jason is writing this for me since I can't sit up and type.
>   Don't worry about Hatfield's alleged ethics violations. The ethics committee doesn't give a damn.
>   He is being persecuted for his opposition towards Bush's foreign and domestic policies.
>   Thanks for calling. I'm sorry I was unable to talk longer. For I am too feeble.
>   Love, Peace, & Keep Well
>   Julia
>
>   P.S. She ate a good lunch. I fixed it for her
>   Jason[4]

Epitaph

This is my death, and I shall go
In my own way into the super dark.
And if I choose to type all night
Or protest in the park,
I'm not the only one who's finished so.
Why mortgage my last days to medicos?
It was their chemicals that killed me in the end.
Physicians, like most lawyers, are ghouls
Briefcased in the system, without souls.
There was an Irishman who drank in bars
And scribbled poetry on tavern doors.
(And so might I, if I had half his powers.)
Don't ask me how I am,
Let's talk about the dying in Vietnam
Where men as young as you with years to lose
"Rage, rage against the dying of the light."

I shall go shouting into the black night.
In Potter's Field, inscribe upon my stone:
Died as she lived, shouting the system down.[5]

—Julia Ruuttila, n.d.

ABBREVIATIONS IN NOTES

CLRC	Coast Labor Relations Committee
FHC	Family History Libraries, Church of Jesus Christ of Latter-Day Saints, Portland
ILWU:P	ILWU archives, Portland
ILWU:SF	ILWU archives, San Francisco
JR	Julia Ruuttila papers at Oregon Historical Society
MC	Multnomah County Records Department
NA	National Archives
NYT	*New York Times*
OHS	Oregon Historical Society
OJ	*Oregon Journal*
OSA	Oregon State Archives
Or	*Oregonian*
PDW	*People's Daily World*
RB	Ray Becker papers at Oregon Historical Society
UO	Division of Special Collections and University Archives, University of Oregon Libraries
UW	Mary Farquharson papers at University of Washington Libraries

NOTES

FORWARD

1. Cook, "Female Support Networks and Political Activism: Lillian Wald, Crystal Eastman, Emma Goldman," p. 413.
2. "Wobbly" is a term used to describe members of the Industrial Workers of the World, a radical labor organization founded in 1905.
3. See Nekola and Rabinowitz, eds., *Writing Red, an Anthology of American Women Writers 1930–1940.*
4. Slesinger, "Writers on the Volcano," *Clipper: A Western Review* (June 1941), as quoted in Nekola, "Worlds Unseen: Political Women Journalists and the 1930's," in *Writing Red,* p. 194.
5. See Chateauvert, *Marching Together: Women of the Brotherhood of Sleeping Car Porters* and "A Sister in the Brotherhood: Rosina Corrothers Tucker and the Sleeping Car Porters, 1930–1950"; Pfeffer, "The Women Behind the Union: Halena Wilson, Rosina Tucker and the Ladies' Auxiliary to the Brotherhood of Sleeping Car Porters"; Levine, "Workers' Wives: Gender, Class and Consumerism in the 1920s"; and Lasky, "'Where I was a Person': The Ladies' Auxiliary in the 1934 Minneapolis Teamster's Strikes." For an account of the activities of the women's auxiliary during the 1936–37 sit-down strikes in Flint Michigan, see Dollinger, *Not Automatic: Women and the Left in the Forging of the Auto Workers' Union.*
6. Milkman, ed., *Women, Work & Protest: A Century of U.S. Women's History,* p.181.
7. Ruuttila played this role in both of the auxiliaries to which she belonged. Women radicals played similar roles in both the Flint, Michigan sit-downs of 1937 and the Minneapolis Teamsters' strikes of 1935. See Dollinger, especially chapter 12, and Lasky.
8. Lasky, p. 200.

INTRODUCTION

1. In 1997, the union changed its name to International Longshore and Warehouse Union, but the original name is used here since that was its name during Julia's lifetime.
2. Louis Aragon (1897–1982) was a French writer. During the Nazi occupation of France he was one of the leaders of the resistance writers, directing the work of clandestine publication. These lines are from his poem "C" translated by William Jay Smith, appearing in *Aragon: Poet of Resurgent France,* edited by Hannah Josephson and Malcolm Cowley, London, Pilot Press, 1946, p. 60. (The poem was originally published in Aragon's 1942 book *Les Yeux d'Elsa.*)
3. Russ Farrell, interview by author, tape recording, Portland, Oregon, 24 April 1992, JR.
4. "Good Work Sister! Women Shipyard Workers of World War II," NWHP, Portland, 1981.
5. Precinct Committeemen/Female. Abstract of Votes, Multnomah County Primary, 1938; Abstracts of Votes May 16, 1970, Primary Election, microfilm 1996–131–01/033A, MC;

Roger Auerbach, interview by author, tape recording, Portland, Oregon, 13 March 1992, JR, phone call, 28 November 2002.

6. Portelli, *Death of Luigi Trastulli,* pp. 1–26. Some of the subsequent discussion on memory appears in altered form in my article "Secrets, Lies, and Misremembering: The Perils of Oral History Interviewing," *Frontiers: A Journal of Women Studies* XIX, 3 (1998), copyright 1998 by Frontiers Editorial Collective.

7. Johns, "Discussing War."

8. Neisser, ed., *Memory Observed,* pp. 148, 151–52, 157.

9. Julia also painted Reed College professor Lloyd Reynolds as heroic in his appearance before a congressional committee. He was not. He claimed the Fifth Amendment (see chapter 15). It is possible Julia is confusing him with someone else: Four men were found in contempt during the hearings—they were likely "heroic."

10. Loftus, *Eyewitness Testimony,* pp. 55, 78.

11. Nevins, "Oral History: How and Why It Was Born," pp. 36–7.

12. Julia Ruuttila, to author, 30 April 1989, JR.

13. Gorn, *Mother Jones,* pp. 8, 82.

14. Betty Wollam, interview, tape recording, Portland, Oregon, 21 May 1991, JR.

15. Julia's father's name was John B. Godman, her brother, John R. Godman. John B. was called Jack, her brother goes by John. To avoid confusion I will call the former Jack, as much as possible, and the latter John.

16. John R. Godman, phone interview, 19 November 2001; Cone, *Cone Family,* p. 77.

17. 1840 census M704122 Ky. Pendleton County reel 7831, p. 5; 1850 census Greenup Ky. microfilm roll 0442970, p. 205, dwelling house in order of visitation and family 684; 1850 census Pendleton County reel 442995, p. 369; 1860 census Greenup Ky. microfilm roll 7835, p. 6; Marriages in Greenup Co., vol. 2, 1854–1903, fiche 6101147, #46, FHC.

18. Susan Wheeler, interview, tape recording, Portland, Oregon, 21 March 1992, JR.

19. Clara Fambro, interview, tape recording, Portland, Oregon, 6 May 1991, JR.

20. Cone, p. 77; 1880 and 1900 Ohio census information from e-mail correspondence with Laurel Lynn Demas, genealogical research volunteer, 3–5 November 2002; Polk's Eugene, vol. 4, p. 94.

21. Marietta College information from e-mail correspondence with Linda Showalter, Special Collections, Dawes Memorial Library, Marietta College, 6 November 2002; Spanish War Military Pensions; *Ky. Civil War Rosters;* Oscar Ruuttila was a Navy Seaman First Class, 1942–45, phone call, Willamette National Cemetery, 1 October 2002; Mike joined the service June 1946 and was released in January 1948. May Apgovannon, Veterans Administration counselor, phone call, 19 November 2002. The records do not say which branch Mike served in but his letters from the period are on U.S. Marine Corps stationary and he writes of being in the Marines.

22. Watts tapes and transcripts OHS; Bigelow tapes in collection of Bill Bigelow, Portland; Copeland transcripts at the Tamiment Library, New York University. The interview is part of the Tamiment Library's Oral History of the American Left Collection, Series I.

23. I have incorporated an unpublished manuscript, "Eggs in Baskets," into chapter 1. One talk I made use of was a lecture Julia gave in the summer of 1975 to a political science class at Oregon State University, Corvallis. In the chapter on Ray Becker and the Centralia Tragedy, I use a letter she wrote on 5 January 1971 to accompany the Ray Becker materials she donated to the OHS, JR and RB.

CHAPTER 1

1. John B. Godman served in the First Kentucky Infantry as a private. Compiled Service Records of Volunteer Soldiers, roll 40, FHC.

2. Kornbluh, ed., *Rebel Voices*, p. 13; Dubofsky, *We Shall Be All*, p. 156.
3. Godman, p. 3; Kennedy, *Interracial Intimacies*, p. 258.
4. Jensen, *Lumber and Labor*, pp. 99–100; U.S. Bureau of Census, Thirteenth Census of the United States, Abstract of the Census with Supplement for Oregon, p. 652. In 1909 the timber industry employed 52.4 percent of Oregon industrial workers and accounted for 32.5 percent of the value of manufactured products.
5. Philip S. Foner, *History of the Labor Movement in the United States*, p. 172; Dubofsky, *We Shall Be All*, pp. 173–97.
6. Brissenden, *The IWW*, pp. 262–63, 367; Foner, *Fellow Workers*, p. 12, 15; Dubofsky, *We Shall Be All*, p. 383.
7. Since the job locations of loggers were isolated and far from the cities where the Wobblies had branches, in 1911 they instituted a camp delegate system, a man on the job to recruit and service union members. Howd, *Industrial Relations*, pp. 67–8.
8. "[P]ine logs were cut shorter than the 'long logs' of forty feet or more in the Douglas fir region on the western slopes of the Cascades." Tyler, *Rebels*, p. 92.
9. Ella's grandfather, Charles Cone, was a justice of the peace for 26 years. He also owned a wholesale grocery business and, after some years in Cincinnati, moved to his farm near Marietta. Cone, p. 43.
10. "*Ohio School Reports* . . . in the 1880s and 1890s . . . contain a . . . description of the examination that any teacher had to complete in order to teach. . . . They could be a high school graduate or could have completed the Boxwell Exam." E-mail from Tom Neel, library director, Ohio Genealogical Society, 5 November 2002.
11. After nearly five years of construction, the completion of the line connecting North Bend and Marshfield (Coos Bay) with Eugene was celebrated with a special train from Portland to Coos Bay on 24 August 1916. *OJ*, 24 August 1916, p. 1; *Or*, 25 August 1916, p. 1.
12. Elizabeth Gurley Flynn was the only woman leader of the IWW, traveling around the country organizing and speaking. In the late thirties she joined the Communist Party and in 1961 became its first woman chair. William D. "Big Bill" Haywood first worked as a miner's helper at the age of fifteen. He started organizing for the Western Federation of Miners in Idaho and, in 1905, was one of the original organizers of the IWW. He was also active in the Socialist Party. In 1921, after being convicted and sentenced to 20 years in prison under the Sedition Act with most of the IWW leadership, Big Bill jumped bail and fled to the Soviet Union, where he died in 1928.
13. None of the Socialist Party offices (Lane County, Oregon, and national) have records from this period to verify Ella Godman's position.
14. Though not effective as a contraceptive, Lysol was promoted as such starting in the second decade of the twentieth century and became a popular birth control product. Andrea Tone, *Devices and Desires*, pp. xvi, 170.

CHAPTER 2

1. In May 1916, 100,000 soldiers and civilians marched in New York City. Curti, *Peace or War*, pp. 234–35, 246, 248; Chatfield, *For Peace and Justice*, p. 22.
2. At the very beginning of the war, the IWW came out quite strongly against it, yet the organization soon realized its impotence and devoted little attention to peace mobilization. Once the United States entered the war, they were equivocal on the issue, and most Wobblies registered for the draft and served when called. Foner, *Labor Movement*, p. 555; *Solidarity*, 3 Oct. 1914, p. 4, quoted in Brissenden, *The IWW*, 2d ed., p. 331; Dubofsky, *We Shall Be All*, pp. 349, 354–57; Howd, p. 70; Jensen, p. 124. See also Gambs, *Decline*, pp. 41–2.

3.   Tyler, p. 90; *Final Report and Testimony of the United States Commission on Industrial Relations* (Washington, D.C., 1915), vol. 4, pp. 4236–37, quoted in Dubofsky, *We Shall Be All,* p. 128.

4.   Tyler, pp. 92–6; Jensen, pp. 125–26; Dubofsky, *We Shall Be All,* p. 363, 365, 411; Kornbluh, p. 253.

5.   Tyler, p. 95; Gambs, p. 52; Dubofsky, *We Shall Be All,* pp. 357, 407.

6.   Tyler, pp. 96–7; Dubofsky, *We Shall Be All,* p. 365; Jensen, p. 127; Howd, p. 75.

7.   To join the 4L, employees signed a patriotic pledge and promised "to faithfully perform my duty toward this company by directing my best efforts . . . to the production of logs and lumber for the construction of Army airplanes and ships to be used against our common enemies." Howd, pp. 77–78, citing "The Northwest Front," by W. A. Wolff, in *Collier's,* Apr. 20, 1918, p. 32; Tyler, pp. 101–7; Dubofsky, *We Shall Be All,* pp. 412–13; Kornbluh, p. 255; Thompson, *The IWW,* p. 122.

8.   Lane County real properties record, vol. 101, 412, #4853; vol. 104, 610, #11092; vol. 112, 231, #10975, 7 August 1915.

9.   Since Julia remembered Agnes Thesla Fair visiting the ranch, they must have moved there before the United States entered the war, because Fair died in January 1917. The *Oregonian* reported that Fair was despondent because of ill health. *Or,* 12 January 1917, p. 8; *OJ,* 30 March 1914, p. 1; *Or,* p. 11 January 1917; *Or,* 26 March 1919, p. 1.

10.   John R. Godman to author, 29 May 1992, JR.

11.   While I could find no evidence that either the Fort Lewis or Aberdeen strikes occurred, in 1917 the lumber strike caused a shortage that interfered with the building of Fort Lewis, and shortly after, ship carpenters on Grays Harbor, where Aberdeen is located, refused to handle lumber from ten-hour mills. Jensen, p. 126; Howd, p. 73, citing *Or,* p. 26, July 1917, p. 6, *Seattle Union Record,* 4 August 1917, p. 1, and Washington State Bureau of Labor, Biennial Report, 1917–18, p. 67.

12.   John R. Godman to author, 16 March 1992, JR.

13.   The novel was likely *Freelands,* published in 1915, in which tenant farmers attempt to unite and take collective action against oppressive landowners.

14.   Swaggart, ed., *The Eugenean,* pp. 125–26.

15.   Information obtained from Registrar's Office, University of Oregon, Eugene.

16.   The results of the first Harper Intercollegiate Literary Contest were announced in the August 1926 issue. Julia Godman, of the University of Oregon, was the first listed winner of an honorable mention. *Harper's Monthly Magazine* 153 (August 1926), p. 395.

17.   Williams, "The Late, Great, Mt. June Flume Company."

18.   John R. Godman to author, 10 September 1993, JR.

19.   Dubofsky, *We Shall Be All,* pp. 443–44.

20.   Ibid., pp. 444, 466–67.

CHAPTER 3

1.   Dr. Thomas N. Sample founded the Sample Sanitarium around 1910. It became the Sequoia Hospital after his death. *California U.S. Gen Project* <http://www.cagenweb.com/~cpl/sumbios4.htm> (February 20, 2003), citing Charles W. Clough, William B. Secrest, Bobbye Sisk Temple, *Fresno County, the Pioneer Years: From the beginning to 1900,* Fresno, Cal.: Panorama West Books, 1984.

2.   Bertram, "The Wolf at the Door," p. 156, JR.

3.   The title of the poem is "I Have Been a Spendthrift."

4.   John B. Godman died on 22 September 1926. Oregon Death Index, 1921–1930, Record 2395.

5.   Ella B. Godman filed on 18 November 1926. Veterans Administration Pension Index File, reel 2262, FHC.

6. Perhaps a married woman would not have been hired as a live-in maid.
7. While the Colorado coal-mine strike did not begin until October of 1927, two months after Julia and Butch left the state, the IWW was organizing in the Colorado fields that summer. Gambs, pp. 143–45.

    Surely Julia would have lost her job. She might also have feared what her former employer might do. On 29 August 1927, Will Dietrich wrote Julia saying it was a good thing she had left because someone thought her former employer had "put a dick on your trail," JR.
8. Chicago City Directory and Supplement, *Chicago*, p. 802.

CHAPTER 4

1. For a detailed account of organized employer opposition to unions in the 1920s, see Bernstein, *Lean Years*, chapter 3.
2. *Oregon Blue Book, 1935–1936*, "Oregon Timber Resources," p. 127.
3. During her first marriage, to William Bowen.
4. *Crow's Pacific Coast Lumber Digest* was an industry publication. Lembcke and Tattam, *One Union in Wood*, p. 38.
5. This story is surprising because Julia always insisted she was terrible at mathematics. Unfortunately, I was unable to ask her about this discrepancy because this incident was not relayed to me but to Elizabeth Patapoff, a producer at KOAP-TV in Portland, in 1976 during an exploratory interview. I did not discover the audiotaped interview until after Julia's death, JR.
6. Inman-Poulsen was in southeast Portland, not St. Johns.
7. ILA Union <www.ilaunion.org/history_creation>; Nelson, *Workers on the Waterfront*, pp. 52, 120–21; Buchanan, pp. 15–29, 37.
8. This account is based on several sources, including: Buhle, Buhle, and Georgakas, pp. 672–74; Frank Young, Neighborhood History Project under the auspices of the Portland Parks Department, interview by Susan Kristof, tape recording, 10 August 1979, tape 1. OHS; Egan, "That's Why Organizing Was So Good," pp. 66, 81, 93; Hinckle, *Big Strike*, pp. 15–6.
9. Julia is correct that two men died; however, the official body count was 32 wounded by gunfire and 75 seriously hurt. Mike Quin points out in his book on the strike that these figures include only those who went to the hospitals. Hinckle, p. 60; Quin, *Big Strike*, p. 116. For an account of the Portland events by union organizer Matt Meehan and others, see Hardy, "The 1934 Portland Longshoremen's Strike."
10. Bernstein, *Turbulent Years*, 355; Zieger and Gall, *American Workers*, pp. 72–3.
11. Bernstein, *Turbulent Years*, pp. 359, 624; Jensen, p. 205.
12. Jensen, pp. 164–85.
13. Jensen, p. 176.
14. Paragraph 2 of the original 1905 preamble said: "Between these two classes a struggle must go on until all the toilers come together on the political, as well as on the industrial field, and take and hold that which they produce by their labor, through an economic organization of the working class without affiliation with any political party." Paragraph 2 of the 1908 revised IWW preamble reads, "Between these two classes a struggle must go on until the workers of the world organize as a class, take possession of the earth and the machinery of production, and abolish the wage system." Kornbluh, pp. 12–3.
15. The Loyal Legion of Loggers and Lumbermen. See chapter 2.

CHAPTER 5

1. "John L. Lewis—Industrial Unionism, Unsound and Destructive," MS., container 5, Frey Papers, Library of Congress, quoted in Morris, *Conflict Within the AFL*, p. 4.

2. Bernstein, *Turbulent Years,* pp. 356, 400.

3. For greater detail on the split, see Bernstein, *Turbulent Years,* chapters 8, 9, and Morris, chapters 8, 9.

4. This account relies heavily on both Jensen, chapter 11, and Lembcke and Tattam.

5. NLRB report in Formal and Informal Unfair Labor Practices and Representative Case Files, 1935–37, RG 25 NLRB, NA.

6. Hardy, p. 204.

7. Folsom, *Impatient Armies,* p. 415; Rosenweig, "Socialism in Our Time," pp. 486, 499–506.

8. Hardy, pp. 72, 78–9.

9. Julia had a further comment about Trent Phillips, "The last time I saw Trent Phillips, the Oregon Workers' Alliance had gone under and he was working in some restaurant and pool hall with a broom. I don't know what happened to him after that. But he was a smart man."

10. Affidavit of Julia Eaton, 28 February 1947, sworn as part of a struggle by maritime and lumber unions opposing the appointment of Joseph K. Carson (Carson had been the mayor of Portland at the time of the lockout) to the U.S. Maritime Commission, JR.

11. The Sunshine Division, a nonprofit volunteer organization founded in 1923 connected to the Portland Police Bureau, assists Portlanders with emergency allotments of food, clothing, and bedding.

12. After the lumber has been cut and trimmed, it "moves on out of the mill on transfer chains into sorting sheds, commonly referred to as the 'green chains.' . . . Green-chain men are stationed at short intervals along the chains to pull off the lumber and load it onto trucks or carriers," Howd, p. 35.

13. Official Report of Proceedings before the National Labor Relations Board, Case no. XIX-C–329, 13, 16, 22, 29 June 1938, pp. 1413, 1691, 2247, 2925–28, NA; *Timber Worker,* 20 August 1938, p. 2, International Woodworkers Association Records (Box 199), UO.

14. Those mills at which the IWA lost remained in the AFL in the Lumber and Sawmill Workers' Union along with locals in other parts of the Northwest that had refused to leave the AFL in 1937. As a result, there remain two unions representing woodworkers. In 1994 the IWA merged with the International Association of Machinists and Aerospace Workers and is now the Woodworkers Division of IAMAW. The Lumber and Sawmill Workers' Union is now part of the Western Council of Industrial Workers. Julia wrote: "The rift between the IWA and the L&SMW, now the Lumber Production & Industrial Workers, was years in healing. But finally the two unions began to coordinate contract demands and contract expiration dates. And now, of course, they are members, with the ILWU, the AWPPW [Association of Western Pulp and Paper Workers], and the Inland Boatmen, which has since affiliated with ILWU, of the Federation of Tidewater Organizations." Julia Ruuttila, "Why Unions?" p. 14, JR.

15. Levenstein, *Communism, Anticommunism, and the CIO,* pp. 40–1; Zieger and Gall, p. 55.

16. Lembcke and Tattam, pp. 45, 63.

17. Ibid., p. 63; Bernstein, *Turbulent Years,* p. 630.

18. Julia added, "But after the Canadians began to have a growing part in the union, the IWA learned from its bitter mistakes of that period and they yanked that out of the constitution. The present international president of the union, Keith Johnson, is a Canadian. The whole union changed and began to be like it was in the old days."

    A resolution banning Communist Party members from the union was passed in 1941. It was revoked in 1973, the same year Keith Johnson was elected president. Lembcke and Tattam, pp. 100, 174.

19. Georgakas, "Taft-Hartley Loyalty Oath," Buhle, Buhle, and Georgakas, p. 767.

CHAPTER 6

1. Brecher, *Strike!* p. 104; Copeland, *Centralia Tragedy,* 41. I have relied heavily on Copeland for my account of the events in Centralia on 11 November 1919 and following.
2. Copeland, p. 37.
3. *Centralia Chronicle,* 21 October 1919, as quoted in McClelland, *Wobbly War,* p. 59.
4. There has always been controversy over this point. Some historians and investigators at the time have taken a position that it is unclear whether the legionnaires had attacked the hall when the shooting began. From my reading of the documents and literature, I take the position stated here, in agreement with Julia.
5. Affidavits: Etta Patterson, 20 October 1936; J. M. Eubanks, 10 June 1936; Charles Carey, 24 April 1937; Clyde Tisdale, 1 July 1939; Vernon O'Reilly, 16 July 1936, RB; Federal Council of Churches of Christ in America, *Centralia Case,* p. 43.
6. Juror affidavits: G. Robinson, 29 January 1936; P. V. Johnson, 9 May 1936; Carl C. Hulten, 20 July 1936; W. E. Inmon and E. E. Sweitzer, 15 May 1922, RB.
    The charges against one man had earlier been dismissed. Lawyer Elmer Smith was one of the two found not guilty. Smith worked tirelessly for the freedom of the remaining imprisoned men until his death in 1932. Loren Roberts was found insane. He was released in 1930.
7. Juror affidavit, W. E. Inmon, 3 July 1936, RB.
8. Gunns, "Ray Becker," pp. 90–2, 95; Copeland, p. 185.
9. Julia Bertram to Mary Farquharson, 28 Sept. 1936, Mary Farquharson Papers, UW.
10. Bertram, "Review of Becker Case Plea of Portland Local," *Timber Worker,* 28 August 1936, p. 3, UO.
11. Affidavit, 16 August 1936, RB.
12. Morgan's paranoia presumably stemmed from the IWW's contempt for him. Affidavit, Julia Bertram, 11 March 1937, RB.
13. Juror affidavit, 9 May 1936, RB.
14. Gunns, "Ray Becker," p. 94; Oregon Military Department, Communist Intelligence Reports, Accession no. 89A–012, Box 56, folder 12, 2–3 February 1936, OSA.
15. Irvin Goodman to Ray Becker, 22 April 1936, RB.
16. Ray Becker to Julia Bertram, 11 August 1936, 31 May 1937, RB.
17. Julia Bertram to Ray Becker, 2 June 1937; Ray Becker to Julia Bertram, 26 October 1937, RB.
18. Gunns, "Ray Becker," p. 92; Mary Farquharson to Roger Baldwin, 24 September 1939, UW.
19. Robertson Trowbridge published two books, *Forty-eight Years,* and *Thirty Sonnets, 1919–1929* (New York: The Harbor Press, 1929). In *Forty-eight Years* he tells that he opposed the Spanish-American War, became involved in the Sacco-Vanzetti defense, and believed in Tom Mooney's innocence, but does not mention Becker, pp. 63, 208–16. In 1928, he signed a letter written by Jane Addams to President Calvin Coolidge asking for restoration of citizenship to those convicted under the espionage act during World War I. *Chicago Metro History Fair,* <http://www.uic.edu/jaddams/hull/Addams_PetitiontoPresidentCoolidge.html>.

CHAPTER 7

1. The murder had occurred in 1923. He had been identified by fingerprints after his arrest for disorderly conduct. *Or,* 25 February 1943, p. 10.
2. Mike McDonald to Julia Eaton, 28 July 1946, 7 June 1952, JR; State of Oregon Death Index, 1971–1980, certificate 75–06158.

3. Multnomah County Circuit Court, film file 718, case 173483.
4. Mary (Equi Jr.) McCloskey, interview, Santa Rosa, Calif., 12 March 1980. Notes in author's possession.
5. Rickie Solinger (author of *The Abortionist: A Woman Against the Law*) e-mail to author, 18 September 1996.
6. Ben Eaton died in Portland, Oregon, 21 December 1976. He was 71 years old, unmarried, and a retired building inspector for the City of Portland. State of Oregon Death Index, certificate 76–20004.

CHAPTER 8

1. Still in 1937, 95 percent of Americans asked "If another war like the World War develops in Europe, should America take part again?" responded "No." Wittner, *Rebels Against War*, pp. 1–20.
2. Fraser, *Blood of Spain*, p. 127.
3. Sam Sills, "Abraham Lincoln Brigade," in Buhle, Buhle, and Georgakas, p. 2.
4. Jay Allen lost his job at the conservative *Chicago Tribune* due to his reports from the Spanish front. Cook, *Eleanor Roosevelt*, p. 504.
5. Only a few priests outside of the Basque provinces supported the republic. The Basque priests and laity were exceptions because their autonomist aspirations were supported by the republic. Sánchez, *Spanish Civil War*, p. 70.
6. Wittner, pp. 23–24; Howe and Coser, *American Communist Party*, p. 394.
7. Schrecker, *Many Are the Crimes*, pp. 91, 208–9; *NYT*, 3 September 1942, reprinted in Rovere and Brown, *Loyalty and Security*, p. 101.
8. FBI report, 29 December 1942, JR.
9. Special Agent H. I. Bobbitt, Portland, to the Director of the FBI re: Mrs. Julia Eaton, 25 July 1946, JR.
10. Mike was eighteen when he enlisted in the Marines. The baptismal record must have been for either the shipyards or the Merchant Marine. See chapter 14.

CHAPTER 9

1. Miriam Kolkin, news editor, to Kathleen Cronin, 30 March 1946; Kathleen Cronin to Allan Fletcher [February, 1947], facsimiles, JR.
2. Sauvies Island is only ten miles from Portland's city center.
3. Kathleen Cronin, "Portland Peonage Bared," *PDW*, May 7, 1946, p. 3.
4. *PDW*, 7 May 1946, pp. 1, 3; *Or*, 22 September 1946, p. 17; Oregon Bar Association, p. 43; Frank Pozzi, interview, tape recording, Portland, Oregon, 10 June 1992, JR; *OJ*, 16 September 1949, pp. 1, 3.
5. U.S. Bureau of Census, *16th Census of the United States*, Table 36, p. 1042; City Club of Portland, "The Negro in Portland," *City Club Bulletin* 26, p. 52.
6. For this account of Vanport, I have relied heavily on Maben, *Vanport*.
7. An Open Letter to the Vanport Flood Victims from The Citizen's Committee [for Flood Disaster], 17 June 1948, JR; Vanport Flood Evacuees Schedule Placard Parade, *Or*, [28?] June 1948; "'Demonstration' Halts Hearing of Flood Group," *OJ*, 30 June 1948.
8. "Another Commie Front Exposed!" [Editorial] *Oregon Labor Press*, 2 July 1948.
9. *Or*, 15 July 1948, sec. 2, p. 4.
10. The Housing Authority successfully pleaded governmental immunity for all claims. Maben, pp. 130–31.
11. One of the stories, entitled "Flood Victims Get Pitiful Dole," appeared in the *PDW* on 28 June 1948, pp. 1–2.

12. In 1941 the *Oregon Labor Press,* with S. Eugene Allen as editor, published "The Enemy Within," a vilifying pamphlet on Communist influences in the labor movement. It named Julia Bertram as a member of the "contributions committee" for the 30 August, 1–2 September 1940 Peace Mobilization Conference in Chicago and referred to her as the "energetic little local lady journalist for the Commie-controlled *Timber Worker,*" p. 27.
13. AFSCME does not have records from this period. Mike Sayan, Oregon AFSCME, phone call, 22 November 2002; Susan Holleran, National AFSCME, e-mail, 3 December 2002.
14. The chairman of the Julia Eaton (Kathleen Cronin) Defense Committee was Matt Meehan. Murnane was secretary. Other members included several attorneys, a professor, a photographer, a writer, a doctor, a minister, the chairman of the IWA auxiliary, the chairman and vice chairman of the Citizen Disaster Committee, and many union officers and members, both AFL and CIO. Statement of the Julia Eaton (Kathleen Cronin) Defense Committee, n.d., facsimile, JR.
15. "Witnesses for Mrs. Eaton Claim Dismissal for 'Political Reasons,'" *OJ,* 25 August 1948, p. 2.
    The Progressive Party was formed in July 1948 in opposition to President Harry Truman's Cold War policies and the anticommunist, antilabor, and anti-civil liberties campaigns of the Truman administration. Former vicepresident Henry Wallace was the party's presidential candidate.
16. Ron Moxness, "Attendance at Demonstrations Considered in Eaton Firing," *Or,* 26 August 1948, p. 17.

CHAPTER 10

1. Editorial, *Or,* 9 September 1946, p. 6.
2. City Club of Portland, "The Negro in Portland," *Bulletin* 26, pp. 62–3.
3. Julia is referring to the brotherhoods for the railroad jobs held exclusively by whites. The Brotherhood of Sleeping Car Porters was the only black railroad brotherhood. Though it was first organized in 1925, it did not sign its first contract until 1937. Only then was it recognized by the AFL. Evan Stark, "Randolph, A. Philip," in Buhle, Buhle, and Georgakas, p. 643.
4. *Or,* 23 February 1950, p. 1; *OJ,* 9 March 1950, p. 1; *OJ,* 23 March 1950, p. 5; Abstracts of Votes, Multnomah County, 1950, roll 2 of 2; Election Precincts as Established by the City Court, January 1950, MC.
5. A fair employments practices law was enacted in 1949 (after a defeat in 1947) by the Oregon legislature, prohibiting discrimination in employment because of race, religion, color, or national origin. A public accommodation law was passed by the Oregon legislature in 1953. The same year saw the deletion of the word "white" from the state constitution with respect to reapportionment, which was previously based on white population only. City Club of Portland, "[T]he Negro in Portland," *Bulletin* 37, p. 357.

CHAPTER 11

1. Larrowe, *Harry Bridges,* pp. 293–99.
2. Hardy, pp. 179–80.
3. After nearly five months, the union settled for an immediate 14-cent raise with another 7 cents in five months. *NYT,* 9 May 1949, p. 16, 7 October 1949, p. 1.
4. Frank Pozzi, interview, tape recording, Portland, Oregon, 26 December 1990, JR.
5. *Dispatcher,* 3 August 1951, p. 1; 8 June 1956, p. 1; 6 July 1956, pp. 1, 3; *NYT,* 4 July 1956, p. 36; *ILWU v. Hawaiian Pineapple Co. Ltd., Hawaiian Pineapple Co. Ltd. v. Martin E. Aden et al.* 226 F. 2d 875, 1955 <web.lexis-nexis.com> (23 November 2002).

6. Larrowe, pp. 327–31.
7. Gladstein was prevented from defending Bridges in his 1949–50 perjury trial because he was serving a six-month sentence for contempt of court when Bridges' trial began in November 1949. *NYT,* 15 Oct 1949, pp. 1, 3.
8. Urban League of Portland, "News Roundup," p. 6.
9. Julia remembered, "A few years later, the Longshoremen were picketing some scab operation that they were trying to shut down, and I was over there writing that up and he was there, and he was taking a good position, so we spoke to each other."
10. The front-page story in the *Dispatcher* on November 19, 1943, was the awarding of honorary lifetime memberships in the ILWU to actor-singer Paul Robeson and artist Rockwell Kent at a luncheon in their honor on 12 November 1943.
11. For a discussion of the history of black membership in ILWU locals, see Nelson, *Divided We Stand,* chapter 3, especially pp. 94–101.
12. Although the international leadership was committed to racial equality, it was difficult to impose it because the union also embraced local autonomy and rank-and-file democracy. Ibid., pp. 93, 99–100.
13. Minutes of Meeting of the CLRC, meeting no. 3, 31 January 1967, ILWU:P.
14. Minutes of Meeting of the CLRC, 7 May 1968, ILWU:P.
15. Minutes of Meeting of the CLRC, meeting no. 12, 15 August 1968, ILWU:P.
16. Minutes of Special Meeting of the Portland Joint Longshore Labor Relations Committee for Registration, no. 41, 20 August 1968, no. 45, ILWU:P; Complaint for Injunctive and Affirmative Relief and Damages under Title VII of the Civil Rights Act of 1964 in the United States District Court for the District of Oregon, civil no. 68–608, filed 29 October 1968, facsimile, JR.
17. *Linell Hill, et al, v. Local 8, ILWU, et al,* civil no. 68–608, 6 December 1968, transcript of proceedings, pp. 3–4, facsimile, JR.
18. Shane Ruuttila, interview by author, tape recording, Anchorage, Alaska, 20 February 1991, JR.

CHAPTER 12

1. "Woman's Attempt At Suicide Fails," *Or,* 6 November, 1950, p. 19.
2. On 3 January 1951, the *Oregonian* reported that the Building Services Employees Local 49, AFL, had "been picketing Emanuel hospital for many weeks in an effort to get a union contract," p. 1.
3. Ruuttila, *This Is My Shadow,* p. 50.

CHAPTER 13

1. Julia was released from the hospital 26 November 1950. Emanuel Hospital records department personnel, telephone conversation, 2 April 1991.
2. Nordhoff, *Nordhoff's West Coast,* p. 210. Nordhoff was coauthor, with James Norman Hall, of *Mutiny on the Bounty.*
3. Hummasti, *Finnish Radicals,* p. 7.
4. Ibid., p. 3. In 1905, Astoria's population was 11,045, of whom 2,027 were Finns. *Morning Astorian,* 26 August 1905, as cited in Hummasti, *Finnish Radicals,* p. 31. In 1950, Portland, with a population of 704,829, had 964 Finnish-born residents and 1820 U.S.-born people of Finnish parentage. Astoria was too small to be listed in this second breakdown, but assuming a similar ratio of descendants to immigrants, its Finnish-identified population would have been about 2700, or nearly 22 percent of the town. U.S. Bureau of Census, *U.S. Census of Population: 1950,* vol. II, part 37, pp. 12, 51, 52, and vol. 14, Special

Reports, part 3, chapter A, pp. 77, 80; Hummasti, "Ethnicity and Radicalism," pp. 362, 367.

5. Ross, *The Finn Factor,* pp. 36–37, 69, 162–64. Immigration figures from Reino Kero, *Migration from Finland to North America in the Years between the Civil War and the First World War* (Turku, Finland: Institute for Migration, 1974), pp. 91–92, cited in Ross, p. 59.

6. Hummasti, *Finnish Radicals,* pp. 7, 41–2, 50, 70, 235.

7. Ibid., pp. 70–3, 235.

8. Ibid., p. 59.

9. The Communists built another hall in 1936, Columbia Hall, though much smaller and with a much less ambitious program. The ASSK became the ASTK, Astorian Suomalainen Työläisten Klubi, when the Finnish Socialists affiliated with the Communist Party in 1926. Hummasti, *Finnish Radicals,* pp. 176, 221–22, 296–98.

10. They were married 3 January 1951. The marriage license is listed in the *Evening Astorian-Budget* of the next day on page 2, Oscar Andrew Ruuttila, 313 Alameda, Astoria, and Julia G. Eaton, Portland.

11. Betty Wollam, interview, 21 May 1991, JR.

12. Julia asked me to add a footnote that "today there are Blacks on the Portland docks, and a young black member of Local 8, Robert Fambro, is Secretary of the ILWU Columbia River District Council, which includes 4 locals in Portland, and locals in Astoria, Newport and North Bend. Fambro's mother, Clara Fambro, is president of ILWU Women's Auxiliary 5 and also President of the Federated Auxiliaries, which has groups in California, Oregon, Washington and British Columbia." Julia Ruuttila, to author, 14 November 1990, JR.

13. None of the daily bulletins survive among Julia's papers, but she did save a handbill explaining the strike to the public, lauding the cannery workers and launchmen for refusing to cross the picket line, and thanking the "home town people for their support."

14. The packers sued the union (Julia was one of the named defendants). The decision, handed down on 13 March 1953, disallowed the packers' claim for damages but ordered the union to be "forever enjoined and restrained from . . . causing to be established or maintained any pickets . . . or in any manner unlawfully interfering with the plaintiff's conduct and operation of its business." *Columbia River Packers Association v. Columbia River Fishermen's Protective Union,* 21560 OR 20371 (1953).

15. While Democrats did increase their voting power in Astoria and Clatsop County, there is no evidence of Republicans switching party affiliation. Voter pamphlets from the period have not survived. *Evening Astorian-Budget,* 8 November 1950, pp. 1–2; 3 November 1954, p. 1; 7 November 1956, p. 1; 5 November 1958, p. 1.

16. Ward, *Ancient Lowly.*

17. Betty Wollam, interview, 21 May 1991, JR.

18. Uppertown is on the east end. Its population was predominantly Scandinavian, but some Finns settled there as well. Ruby Hammarstrom, "The Finnish Settlement in Astoria, Oregon" [honor's thesis, University of Oregon, 1912], p. 2, cited by Hummasti, *Finnish Radicals,* p. 32.

19. In Astoria, Raunio became the first editor of the left-wing women's newspaper *Toveritar* in 1911. She produced eight issues before her death from an overdose of sleeping pills. Hummasti, *Finnish Radicals,* p. 51, citing *Toveritar,* 3 May 1927, p. 1, and *Toveri kymmenvuotias,* p. 10.

20. Finland was part of Tsarist Russia from 1809 and was dependent on Russia for grain. In 1917, the combination of political upheavals disrupting trade and a poor harvest caused food shortages close to famine in some parts of the country. Singleton, *History of Finland,* pp. 1, 107, 114; Wuorinen, *History of Finland,* p. 223.

21. After the Communists came to power in Russia, Finland, supported by Lenin, declared its independence on 6 December 1917. In January 1918, civil war broke out. By February the south was under Red control and the north under White. Victory followed in May for the Whites after Germany entered the war on their side. Many Reds fled to Russia and others were imprisoned, many dying of starvation and neglect. Singleton, pp. 99, 110–14.

CHAPTER 14

1. Much of my information about Mike's World War II years is from his letters to Julia and one to his grandmother Ella. The letters, often undated, start sometime in 1945 (probably summer) and continue fairly regularly until September of 1947. There are two other letters dated 10 May 1952 and 7 June 1952. Also a letter to Senator John A. Carroll from Julia, 19 October 1958, facsimiles, JR.
2. Shane Ruuttila, interview, 20 February 1991, JR, and phone call 26 November 2001.
3. See chapter 15. HUAC refers to the House Committee on Un-American Activities, popularly called the House Un-American Activities Committee, hence the order of the letters in the acronym.
4. Shane Ruuttila, interview, 20 February 1991, JR.
5. Julia Ruuttila to U.S. Veterans Service, Astoria, Oregon, 18 October 1958; Julia Ruuttila to John A. Carroll, Astoria, Oregon, 19 October 1958, JR; Shane Ruuttila, phone call, 10 October 2002, JR.
6. The adoption decree was signed on 29 November 1963. Shane was fourteen. Decree number 2706, Judge Charles M. Johnson, JR.

CHAPTER 15

1. R. J. Keenan [Julia Ruuttila], "What's Behind the Screen?" [part 1], *March of Labor* (April 1952), p. 21, JR.
2. Frank Pozzi, interview, 10 June 1992, JR.
3. Enclosed with a letter from James M. Donahue, chairman, Local Appeal Board, to Oscar Andrew Ruuttila, Seattle, Washington, 13 April 1954, JR.
4. Keenan, "What's Behind the Screen?" [part 1], p. 22; [part 2], (May 1952), p. 23, JR.
5. According to their defense literature, the correct spellings of two of the defendants' names are Hamish Scott MacKay and John Stenson. However, the other two defendants' names are spelled differently in two pieces of defense literature. In a 1953 pamphlet, they are Casimiro B. Absolor and Karolina Halverson, but are Casimoro Absolar and Caroline Halverson on a 1950 leaflet issued by the Committee for Defense of Four of Oregon's Foreign Born. U.S. House Committee on Un-American Activities, *Communist Political Subversion,* House Report 1182, 16 August 1957, pp. 86, 87 and 81, cited in FBI report, 2 July 1963, JR.
6. The official name of the boilermakers' union is the International Brotherhood of Boilermakers, Iron Ship Builders, Blacksmiths, Forgers and Helpers.
7. Julia's surprise stemmed from the fact that the carpenters union was a conservative AFL union.
8. In 1980, the Inlandboatmen's Union of the Pacific (IBU) affiliated with the ILWU. In 1987, ILWU Local 37, the Alaska Cannery Workers' Union, representing nonresident Alaskan seafood processing workers, affiliated with the IBU to become Region 37. International Longshoremen's and Warehousemen's Union, *The ILWU Story,* pp. 2, 56.
9. Though labor was never able to repeal the act outright, it remained the subject of continuing revision and debate. Dubofsky, *State and Labor,* pp. 209–12.
10. Dubofsky, *State and Labor,* p. 204.
11. [Ruuttila], "CRDC Debates the Cost Of Junketing Solons," *Dispatcher,* 12 October 1956, p. 10; Cronin, "Those Junkets at Public Expense; Taxpayers tired picking up tab," *PDW,* 2 November 1956.
12. "Demos up strength in Astoria," *Evening Astorian-Budget,* 7 November 1956, p. 1.
13. "Six Oregon Residents Called Briefly Before Un-American Activities Group," *Or,* 15 December 1956; "3 More Oregon Residents Balk at Seattle Hearings," *OJ,* 15 December

1956, p. 3; U.S. House of Representatives, *Communist Political Subversion,* 84th Cong., 2nd sess., 1956.

14. According to the *Seattle Post Intelligencer,* Bert Nelson was the Washington State Communist Party chairman. 14 December 1956, p. 7.

15. Pozzi explained why Julia asked reporters not to take pictures. "In those days, you could be on television or not, and it was your choice, some court had held you didn't have to. . . . Julia chose not to . . . because they were making a spectacle out of it for their own aggrandizement." Interview, 26 December 1990, JR.

16. Jim Running, "3 More Oregon Residents Balk at Seattle Hearing; Astoria Woman Surprise Witness," *OJ,* 15 December 1956, p. 1B.

17. U.S. House of Representatives, *Communist Political Subversion,* 1956, p. 7025.

18. Ibid., pp. 7032–7033; Frank Pozzi, interview, 26 December 1990, JR.

19. *Evening Astorian-Budget,* 15 December 1956, p. 1. A related story appeared on page 2.

20. Matt Meehan to the editor of the *Evening Astorian-Budget,* 26 December 1956, p. 4.

21. Arthur Spencer, interview, tape recording, Portland, Oregon, 15 October 1992, JR.

22. Shane Ruuttila, interview, 20 February 1991, JR.

CHAPTER 16

1. Ruuttila, *This Is My Shadow,* p. 83.

2. Shane Ruuttila, interview, 20 February 1991, JR.

3. Julia Ruuttila to Amanda, George, and Einar Ruuttila, 20 December 1962, JR.

4. Shane Ruuttila, interview, 20 February 1991, JR.

5. Julia added, "'Course, its different now. The grandchildren have become quite progressive and radical. After I moved up here to Portland, I went to a meeting of the Finnish left wingers in Astoria. It was interesting to see that some of the grandchildren had gone the other way again and took a different view of things. They were no longer intimidated."

6. Julia's FBI file contains a memo written on 26 July 1965 reporting her move from Astoria to Portland "on or about June 9, 1965," JR.

7. Bettina Aptheker was the founder of the Student Mobilization Committee to End the War in Vietnam, originally formed to organize student support for the 15 April 1967 Spring Mobilization to End the War in Vietnam marches in San Francisco and New York. The daughter of prominent American Communist and historian Herbert Aptheker, in 1966 she was also a member of the Communist Party.

8. Shane Ruuttila, interview, 20 February 1991, JR.

9. Ibid.

10. Shane recalls that he was given his diploma two weeks early and told not to come back because of bad behavior. Shane Ruuttila, telephone call, 10 October 2002.

CHAPTER 17

1. Lois and Jesse Stranahan, interview, tape recording, Portland, Oregon, 8 August 1991, JR.

2. Federated Auxiliary ILWU Minutes/Proceedings, 16–20 June 1969, ILWU:SF.

3. Larrowe, p. 382.

4. Ibid., p. 386.

5. *Dispatcher,* 12 October 1973, pp. 3, 10.

6. The International Transport Workers Federation, London, to Harry Bridges 13 December 1973, facsimile, JR.

7. Clara Fambro, interview, 6 May 1991, JR.

8. Ibid.

9. Sid Roger, interview, tape recording, Mill Valley, California, 9 December 1991; telephone call, 10 December 1991; telephone tape recording, 5 May 1992, JR.

CHAPTER 18

1. FBI report PD 100–5640, 14 July 1967, JR.
2. Ibid.
3. Shane Ruuttila, interview, 20 February 1991, JR.
4. Julia Ruuttila to Valerie Taylor, 28 September 1996, facsimile, JR.
5. *NYT,* 1 January 1966, p. 1; *NYT,* 13 January 1966, p. 1; *NYT,* 2 March 1966, p. 63.
6. "Ray's letters" probably refers to the Free Ray Becker Committee papers that Julia donated to the Oregon Historical Society 5 January 1971. University archivists had been negotiating with her for them since at least 1965. Receipt from OHS; Julia Ruuttila to Richard C. Berner, custodian of manuscripts, UW, 30 May 1965, JR.
7. Julia Ruuttila to Valerie Taylor, [26 March 1967], facsimile, JR.
8. FBI report, 30 April 1968, JR; *OJ,* 12 January 1968; *Or,* 13 January 1968.
9. Two more students were killed by police at Jackson State College in Mississippi, 15 May 1970.
10. Lois Stranahan, interview, 8 August 1991, JR.
11. *NYT,* 13 November 1969, p. 33; *NYT,* 16 November 1969, p. 1.
12. Lois Stranahan, interview, 8 August 1991, JR.

CHAPTER 19

1. Lois Stranahan, interview, 8 August 1991, JR.
2. Martina Curl, interview, tape recording, Portland, Oregon, 30 December 1990, JR.
3. Ibid.
4. Lois Stranahan, interview, 8 August 1991; *Or,* 2 April 1975, p. A26.
5. Russ, Lorine, and Sharron Farrell, interview, tape recording, Portland, Oregon, 24 April 1992; Sandra Ford, interview, tape recording, Portland, Oregon, 17 January 1992, JR.

CHAPTER 20

1. Julia Ruuttila to Valerie Taylor, 14 November 1966, facsimile, JR.
2. Letter from Julia to Valerie Taylor [26 March 1967], facsimile, JR; Shane Ruuttila, interview, phone call, 10 October 2002.
3. Shane Ruuttila, interview, 20 February 1991, JR.
4. Ibid.
5. Ibid.

CHAPTER 21

1. Ruuttila, *This Is My Shadow,* p. 116.
2. Roger Auerbach, interview, 13 March 1992, JR.
3. "Time, Injuries Fail to Mellow Activist," by Lynda Lesowski, *The Neighbor* (Portland, Oregon), January 1985, pp. 1, 4, JR.
4. James W. Overgaard, executive administrator, Union Labor Retirement Association, to Julia Ruuttila, January 15, 1985, JR.

5. Shane Ruuttila, interview, 20 February 1991, JR.
6. They have to have lived in the state for one year prior to January 1, 1997. *Division of Alaska Longevity Programs* <http://www.state.ak.us/admin/alp/bonus.htm> (27 November 2002); *MyFlorida.com Dept. of Elder Affairs* <http://www.myflorida.com/doea/healthfamily> (12 November, 2002); Shane Ruuttila, telephone interview, tape recording, 21 August 1994, JR.
7. Ibid.
8. Julia Ruuttila to author, 14 June 1987, JR.
9. Ibid., 9 September 1988, JR.
10. Ibid., 14 November 1990, JR.

AFTERWORD

1. Shane Ruuttila, interview, 20 February 1991, JR.
2. See chapter 13.
3. Shane Ruuttila, interview, 20 February 1991, 21 August 1994, JR.
4. Julia and Jason Ruuttila to author, 1 April 1991, JR.
5. Ruuttila, *This Is My Shadow,* p. 62.

BIBLIOGRAPHY AND SOURCES

INTERVIEWS

All interviews were tape recorded in person by the author in Portland, Oregon, unless otherwise indicated.

LeRoy Adolphson, 20 September 1993, Astoria, Ore.

Joan Allen, 22 August 1992 (phone)

Roger Auerbach, 13 March 1992

Emilia Bohm, 16 March 1991, Astoria, Ore.

Bob Boyer, 2 April 1992

Mary Jane Brewster, 12 July 1991

Doreen Labby Carey, 18 January 2002

Lee Coe, 12 December 1991, Berkeley, Calif.

Hank Curl, 13 March 1991

Martina Curl, 30 December 1990

Clara Fambro, 6 May 1991

Robert Fambro Sr., 25 February 1994

James "Jimmy" and Charlotte Fantz, 11 June 1992

Russell, Lorine, and Sharron Farrell, 24 April 1992

Sandra Ford, 17 January 1992

George Gates, 29 August 1995

John R. Godman, 19 November 2001 (phone); 10 December 2001 (phone)

Linell Hill, 1 March 1994

Ruth (Correia) Hill, 22 October 1993

Theophulis T. Jermany, 13 June 1994

Helmi Kortes-Erkkila, 8 March 1992, Vancouver, Wash.

Mary McCloskey, 12 March 1980, Santa Rosa, Calif.

Paul R. Meyer, 21 March 1994

Evelyn Murray, 19 March 1992

G. "Johnny" Parks, 13 May 1992

Frank Pozzi, 26 December 1990, 29 March 1994, 10 June 1992 (phone)

Sid Roger, 9 December 1991, Mill Valley, Calif.; 10 December 1991 (phone), 5 May 1992 (phone)

Jim Running, 18 May 1993

Jason Ruuttila, 21 February 1991, Anchorage, Ala.

Julia Ruuttila, 9 March 1983; 1, 8, December 1983; 5, 19, 26 January 1984; 9, 16 February 1984; 1, 8, 29 March 1984; 11 October 1985; 19 March 1987, 16 April 1987, Portland, Ore.; 21–23 February 1991, Anchorage, Ala.

Ryan Ruuttila, 26 March 1992

Shane Ruuttila, 20 February 1991, Anchorage, Ala.; 21 August 1994 (phone); 9 December 1995 (phone); 19, 26 November 2001 (phone); 12 December 2001 (phone); 10 October 2002 (phone)

Rhys Scholes, 22 November 1993
Lawrence Sefton, 12 April 1994
Francis "Scotty" and Helen Sinclair, 8 March 1992, Vancouver, Wash.
Arthur Spencer, 15 October 1992
Jesse and Lois Stranahan, 8 August 1991
Valerie Taylor, 19 August 1991, North Bend, Ore.
Susan Wheeler, 21 March 1992
Dick Wise, 21 November 1991
Margaret Wisser, 12 March 1992
Don and Betty Wollam, 21 May 1991
At ILWU Convention in Seattle, 3–4 June 1991:
Danny Beagle, James D. Foster, Joan Fox, Henry Lunde, Dick Moork, Miriam Moork, Glen Ramiskey, Ken Rohar
Other interviews with Julia Ruuttila were recorded by the following:
Bill Bigelow, 27 October 1977, in the possession of Bill Bigelow, Portland, Oregon; Elizabeth Patapoff 1976, JR; Tom Copeland, 7 September 1972, transcripts at Tamiment Library, New York; Roberta Watts, OHS
Interviews with others:
Frank Young, Neighborhood History Project, under the auspices of the Portland Parks Department, interview by Susan Kristof, tape recording, 10 August 1979, tape 1

ARCHIVES

Family History Centers, Church of Jesus Christ of Latter-day Saints, Portland
    Census records
    Compiled Service Records of Volunteer Soldiers
    Veterans Administration Pension Index
The Genealogical Forum of Oregon Inc., Portland
    Census records
ILWU, Local 8, Portland
    CLRC Minutes
    Dispatcher
    Portland Joint Longshore Labor Relations Committee for Registration Minutes
ILWU, San Francisco
    Federated Auxiliary ILWU Minutes/Proceedings
International Woodworkers of America, Clackamas, Ore.
    Timber Worker
Multnomah County Records Department, Portland
    Abstract of Votes
    Democratic Precinct Committeewomen
    Election Precincts
    Election Records
    Voter registration cards
National Archives, Washington, D.C.
    NLRB report in Formal and Informal Unfair Labor Practices and Representative Case Files, 1935–37, RG 25 NLRB, NA
    Official Report of Proceedings before the National Labor Relations Board, case no. XIX-C–329, June 13, 16, 22, 29, 1938, NA
Oregon Historical Society, Portland
    Ray Becker Papers
    Julia Ruuttila Papers/vertical file

Oregon State Archives, Salem
    Communist Activity Intelligence Reports
Portland City Archives
    Red Squad Files
Southern California Library for Social Studies and Research, Los Angeles
    People's World
Tamiment Library, New York University
    Oral History Collection
University of Oregon, Eugene
    Timber Worker
    Student Records
University of Washington Libraries, Seattle
    Mary Farquharson Papers

BOOKS AND ARTICLES

Allen, S. Eugene, ed. *The Enemy Within*. Portland: Oregon Labor Press, 1941.

Bennett, Marion T. *American Immigration Policies: A History*. Washington, D.C.: Public Affairs Press, 1963.

Bernstein, Irving. *The Lean Years: A History of the American Worker, 1920–1933*. Boston: Houghton Mifflin, 1960.

———. *Turbulent Years: A History of the American Worker, 1933–1941*. Boston: Houghton Mifflin, 1971.

Bertram, Julia. "The Wolf at the Door." Manuscript.

Boyer, Richard O., and Herbert M. Morais. *Labor's Untold Story*. 3d ed. New York: United Electrical, Radio and Machine Workers of America, 1986.

Brecher, Jeremy. *Strike!* Reprint, with a new introduction. Boston: South End, 1977.

Brissenden, Paul. F. *The I.W.W.: A Study of American Syndicalism*. 2d ed. New York: Russell & Russell, 1957.

Buchanan, Roger B. *Dock Strike; History of the 1934 Waterfront Strike in Portland, Oregon*. Everett, Wash.: Working Press, 1975.

Buhle, Mari Jo, Paul Buhle, and Dan Georgakas, eds. *Encyclopedia of the American Left*. Urbana: University of Illinois Press, 1992.

Chaplin, Ralph. *The Centralia Conspiracy*, 3rd ed., revised. Chicago: General Defense Committee, 1924. Reprinted in *The Centralia Case: Three Views of the Armistice Day Tragedy at Centralia, Washington, November 11, 1919*. New York: Da Capo Press, 1971. Published by the IWW as part of the ongoing defense.

Chateauvert, Melinda. *Marching Together: Women of the Brotherhood of Sleeping Car Porters*. Champaign: University of Illinois Press, 1998.

———. "A Sister in the Brotherhood: Rosina Corrothers Tucker and the Sleeping Car Porters, 1930–1950." In Harley and the Black Women and Work Collective, *Sister Circle: Black Women and Work*. New Brunswick, N.J.: Rutgers University Press, 2002.

Chatfield, Charles. *For Peace and Justice: Pacifism in America, 1914–1941*. Knoxville: University of Tennessee Press, 1971.

Chicago City Directory and Supplement. *Chicago: The Great Central Market*. Chicago: R. L. Polk, 1923.

Churchill, Thomas. *Centralia Dead March*. Willimantic, Conn.: Curbstone Press, 1980.

City Club of Portland. "The Negro in Portland," *Portland City Club Bulletin* 26 (July 20, 1945).

City Club of Portland. "Report on the Negro in Portland: A Progress Report, 1945–57," *Portland City Club Bulletin* 37, no. 46 (April 19, 1957).

Cone, William Whitney. *Some Account of the Cone Family in America, Principally of the Descendants of Daniel Cone, Who Settled in Haddam, Connecticut, in 1662*. Topeka, Kans.: Crane & Co., 1903.

Cook, Blanche Wiesen. *Eleanor Roosevelt,* vol. 2, *The Defining Years, 1933–1938.* New York: Viking, 1999.

———. "Female Support Networks and Political Activism: Lillian Wald, Crystal Eastman, Emma Goldman." In Cott and Pleck, eds., *A Heritage of Her Own: Toward a New Social History of American Women.* New York: Simon & Schuster, 1979.

Copeland, Tom. *The Centralia Tragedy of 1919: Elmer Smith and the Wobblies.* Seattle: University of Washington Press, 1993.

Curti, Merle. *Peace or War: The American Struggle, 1636–1936.* New York: W. W. Norton & Co., 1936.

Dollinger, Sol, and Genora Johnson Dollinger. *Not Automatic: Women and the Left in the Forging of the Auto Workers' Union.* New York: Monthly Review Press, 1999.

Dubofsky, Melvyn. *The State and Labor in Modern America.* Chapel Hill: University of North Carolina Press, 1994.

———. *We Shall Be All: A History of the Industrial Workers of the World.* 2d ed. Urbana: University of Illinois Press, 1988.

Egan, Michael. "'That's Why Organizing Was So Good,' The Portland Longshoremen, 1934: An Oral History." Bachelor's dissertation, Reed College, 1975.

Federal Council of Churches of Christ in America. *The Centralia Case: A Joint Report on the Armistice Day Tragedy at Centralia, Washington, November 11, 1919.* New York, Baltimore, Washington, D.C.: Department of Research and Education of the Federal Council of the Churches of Christ in America, the Social Action Department of the National Catholic Welfare Conference, and the Social Justice Commission of the Central Conference of American Rabbis, 1930. Reprinted in *The Centralia Case: Three Views of the Armistice Day Tragedy.* The most objective and moderate report.

Folsom, Franklin. *Impatient Armies of the Poor: The Story of Collective Action of the Unemployed, 1808–1942.* Niwot: University Press of Colorado, 1991.

Foner, Philip S. *History of the Labor Movement in the United States,* vol. 4, *The Industrial Workers of the World, 1905–1917.* New York: International Publishers, 1965.

———. ed. *Fellow Workers and Friends; I.W.W. Free-Speech Fights as Told by Participants.* Westport, Conn.: Greenwood Press, 1981.

Fraser, Ronald. *Blood of Spain: An Oral History of the Spanish Civil War.* New York: Pantheon, 1986.

Gambs, John S. *The Decline of the I.W.W.* New York: Columbia University Press, 1932.

Geiger, Robert. "Solidarity in the 1934 Portland Waterfront Strike." Bachelor's dissertation, Reed College, 1984.

Godman, John Robert. *Some Account of the Godman Family in America and Their Connections,* vol. 1, *The Decedents of Zachariah B. Godman of Pendleton County, Kentucky.* Huntsville, Ala.: Privately published, 1998.

Golding, Anne. "The Oregon Anti-Picketing Act." Bachelor's dissertation, Reed College, 1941.

Gorn, Elliott J. *Mother Jones: The Most Dangerous Woman in America,* New York: Hill and Wang, 2001.

Gornick, Vivian. *The Romance of American Communism.* New York: Basic Books, 1977.

Grele, Ronald J. *Envelopes of Sound: The Art of Oral History,* 2d. ed., revised and enlarged. Chicago: Precedent Publishing, 1985.

Gunns, Albert F. *Civil Liberties in Crisis: The Pacific Northwest, 1917–1940.* New York: Garland, 1983.

———. "Ray Becker, the Last Centralia Prisoner," *Pacific Northwest Quarterly,* April 1968.

Hardy, David Robert. "The 1934 Portland Longshoremen's Strike." Bachelor's dissertation, Reed College, 1971.

Healey, Dorothy Ray, and Maurice Isserman. *Dorothy Healey Remembers: A Life in the American Communist Party.* New York: Oxford University Press, 1990. Also published under the title *California Red: A Life in the American Communist Party.* Urbana: University of Illinois Press, 1993.

Hinckle, Warren. *The Big Strike: A Pictorial History of the 1934 San Francisco General Strike.* Virginia City, Nev.: Silver Dollar Books, 1985.

Hoffman, Alice M., and Howard S. *Archives of Memory: A Soldier Recalls World War II,* Lexington: University Press of Kentucky, 1990.

Howd, Cloice. *Industrial Relations in the West Coast Lumber Industry.* Bulletin of the U.S. Bureau of Labor Statistics 349. Washington, D.C., 1923.

Howe, Irving, and Lewis Coser. *The American Communist Party: A Critical History.* 2d ed. New York: Frederick A. Praeger, 1962.

Hummasti, Paul George. "Ethnicity and Radicalism: The Finns of Astoria and the *Toveri,* 1890–1930," *Oregon Historical Quarterly* 96, no. 4 (1995–96).

———. *Finnish Radicals in Astoria, Oregon, 1904–1940: A Study in Immigrant Socialism.* New York: Arno Press, 1979.

International Longshoremen's and Warehousemen's Union. *The ILWU Story: Six Decades of Militant Unionism.* San Francisco: International Longshoremen's and Warehousemen's Union, 1997.

Jensen, Vernon H. *Lumber and Labor.* New York: Farrar & Rinehart, 1945.

Johns, Michael. "Discussing War and Postwar Memories in Austria." Paper presented at the annual meeting of the Oral History Association, Anchorage, Alaska, October 1999.

Keenan, R. J. [Julia Ruuttila], "What's Behind the Screen?" *March of Labor* (April and May 1952).

Kennedy, Randall, *Interracial Intimacies: Sex, Marriage, Identity, and Adoption.* New York: Pantheon, 2003.

Klehr, Harvey, and John Earl Haynes. *The American Communist Movement: Storming Heaven Itself.* New York: Twayne Publishers, 1992.

Kornbluh, Joyce L., ed. *Rebel Voices; an IWW Anthology.* Expanded edition, with a new introduction and an updated bibliography by Fred Thompson. Chicago: Charles H. Kerr, 1988.

Lampman, Ben Hur. *Centralia: Tragedy and Trial.* Centralia and Tacoma, Wash.: American Legion, 1920. Reprinted in *The Centralia Case: Three Views of the Armistice Day Tragedy.*

Larrowe, Charles P. *Harry Bridges; The Rise and Fall of Radical Labor in the United States.* New York: Lawrence Hill, 1972.

Lasky, Marjorie Penn. "'Where I Was a Person': The Ladies' Auxiliary in the 1934 Minneapolis Teamsters' Strikes." In Milkman, ed., *Women, Work and Protest: A Century of U.S. Women's Labor History.* London and New York: Routledge & Kegan Paul, 1985.

Lembcke, Jerry, and William M. Tattam. *One Union in Wood: A Political History of the International Woodworkers of America.* Madeira Park, B.C.: Harbour Publishing; New York: International, 1984.

Levenstein, Harvey A. *Communism, Anticommunism, and the CIO.* Westport, Conn.: Greenwood Press, 1981.

Levine, Susan. "Workers' Wives: Gender, Class and Consumerism in the 1920s United States," *Gender and History* 3 (spring 1991).

Liebman, Joshua Loth. *Peace of Mind.* New York: Simon & Schuster, 1946.

Litwack, Leon. *The American Labor Movement.* Englewood Cliffs, N.J.: Prentice-Hall, 1962.

Loftus, Elizabeth. *Eyewitness Testimony.* Cambridge, Mass.: Harvard University Press, 1979.

Maben, Manly. *Vanport.* Portland: Oregon Historical Society Press, 1987.

McClelland, Jr., John. *Wobbly War: The Centralia Story.* Tacoma: Washington State Historical Society, 1987.

McLagan, Elizabeth. *A Peculiar Paradise: A History of Blacks in Oregon, 1788–1940.* Portland: Georgian Press, 1980.

Menninger, Karl. *Man Against Himself.* New York: Harcourt, Brace, 1938.

Milkman, Ruth, ed. *Women, Work, and Protest, A Century of U.S. Women's Labor History.* London and New York: Routledge and Kegan Paul, 1985.

Morris, James O. *Conflict Within the AFL: A Study of Craft Versus Industrial Unionism, 1901–1938.* Ithaca, N.Y.: Cornell University, 1958.

Murray, Robert K. *Red Scare: A Study in National Hysteria, 1919–1920.* Reprint, New York: Mc-Graw-Hill, 1964. Original edition Minneapolis: University of Minnesota Press, 1955.

National Industrial Recovery Act of 1933. U.S. Statutes at Large 48.

National Labor Relations Act of 1935. U.S. Statutes at Large 49.

Navasky, Victor S. *Naming Names.* New York: Viking Press, 1980.

Neisser, Ulric, ed. *Memory Observed: Remembering in Natural Contexts.* San Francisco: W. H. Freeman, 1982.

Nekola, Charlotte. "Worlds Unseen: Political Women Journalists and the 1930's." In Nekola and Rabinowitz, eds., *Writing Red.* Quoting Tess Slesinger. "Writers on the Volcano," *Clipper: A Western Review* (June 1941).

Nekola, Charlotte, and Paula Rabinowitz, eds. *Writing Red: an Anthology of American Women Writers, 1930–1940.* New York: Feminist Press at CUNY, 1987.

Nelson, Bruce. "Class and Race in the Cresent City: The ILWU, from San Francisco to New Orleans." In Rosswurm, *The CIO's Left-Led Unions.*

———. *Divided We Stand: American Workers and the Struggle for Black Equality.* Princeton, N.J.: Princeton University Press, 2001.

———. *Workers on the Waterfront: Seamen, Longshoremen, and Unionism in the 1930s.* Urbana: University of Illinois Press, 1990.

Nevins, Allan. "Oral History: How and Why It Was Born." In Dunaway and Baum, eds., *Oral History: An Interdisciplinary Anthology.* 2d. ed. Walnut Creek, Calif.: AltaMira Press, 1984.

Nordhoff, Charles. *Nordhoff's West Coast: California, Oregon and Hawaii.* 1874, 1875; reprint, 2 vols. in 1: *California for Health, Pleasure and Residence* and *Northern California, Oregon and the Sandwich Islands,* with an introduction by Kaori O'Connor. London: KPI, 1987.

Oregon. *Compiled Laws, Annotated,* annotated by Bryan Goodenough (1940).

Oregon. *Laws and Resolutions Enacted and Adopted by the Legislative Assembly* (1969).

Oregon. *Revised Statutes* (1989).

Oregon Bar Association. *Twelfth Annual Meeting of the Oregon Bar Association: Committee Reports.* [Salem]: State Printing Dept., 1946.

Oregon Blue Book, 1935–1936. Salem: State Printing Dept., 1935.

Perks, Robert, and Alistair Thomson, eds. *The Oral History Reader.* London and New York: Routledge, 1998.

Pfeffer, Paula. "The Women Behind the Union: Halena Wilson, Rosina Tucker and the Ladies' Auxiliary to the Brotherhood of Sleeping Car Porters," *Labor History* 36 (fall 1995).

Pilcher, William W. *The Portland Longshoremen: A Dispersed Urban Community.* New York: Holt, Rinehart and Winston, 1972.

Polk's Eugene City and Lane County Directory, vol. 4, Portland: R. L. Polk, 1907.

Portelli, Alessandro. *The Death of Luigi Trastulli and Other Stories: Form and Meaning in Oral History.* SUNY Series in Oral and Public History. Albany: State University of New York Press, 1991.

Portland. Election Precincts as Established by the City Court, January 1950. Portland: Bushong & Co., 1950.

Preston, Jr., William. *Aliens and Dissenters: Federal Suppression of Radicals, 1903–1933.* Cambridge, Mass.: Harvard University Press, 1963.

Quin, Mike. *The Big Strike.* Olema, Calif.: Olema Publishing, 1949.

Renshaw, Patrick. *The Wobblies: The Story of Syndicalism in the United States.* Garden City, N.Y.: Doubleday, 1967.

Richmond, Al. *A Long View from the Left: Memoirs of an American Revolutionary.* Boston: Houghton Mifflin, 1973.

Rosenzweig, Roy. "'Socialism in Our Time': The Socialist Party and the Unemployed, 1929–1936," *Labor History* 20, no. 4 (fall 1979).

Ross, Carl. *The Finn Factor in American Labor, Culture and Society.* New York Mills, Minn.: Parta Printers Inc., 1977.

Rosswurm, Steve, ed. *The CIO's Left-led Unions*. New Brunswick, N.J.: Rutgers University Press, 1992.

Rovere, Richard H., and Gene Brown, eds. *Loyalty and Security in a Democratic State*. New York: Arno, 1977.

Rowan, James. *The I.W.W. in the Lumber Industry*. [1919]. Seattle: Shorey Book Store, 1969.

Rubin, Lester. *The Negro in the Longshore Industry*. The Racial Policies of American Industry, report no. 29. Philadelphia: Industrial Research Unit, the Wharton School, University of Pennsylvania, 1974.

Ruuttila, Julia. *This Is My Shadow*. [Anchorage]: Privately printed, n.d.

———. "Why Unions? The Labor Movement in the Northwest," manuscript for speech, 198?.

Sánchez, Jóse M. *The Spanish Civil War as a Religious Tragedy*. Notre Dame, Ind.: University of Notre Dame Press, 1987.

Schneider, Betty V. H., and Abraham Siegel. *Industrial Relations in the Pacific Coast Longshore Industry*. West Coast Collective Bargaining Systems. Berkeley, Calif.: Institute of Industrial Relations, University of California, 1956.

Schrecker, Ellen. *Many Are the Crimes: McCarthyism in America*. Boston: Little, Brown, 1998.

Singleton, Fred. *A Short History of Finland*. Cambridge and New York: Cambridge University Press, 1989.

Smith, Walker C. *Was It Murder? The Truth About Centralia*. Centralia, Wash.: Centralia Publicity Committee, n.d. Published 1922 or later.

Solinger, Rickie. *The Abortionist: A Woman Against the Law*. New York: Free Press, 1994.

Stetson, Dorothy McBride, ed. *Abortion Politics, Women's Movements, and the Democratic State: A Comparative Study of State Feminism*. Oxford and New York: Oxford University Press, 2001.

Swaggart, Lester, ed. *The Eugenean*. Eugene, Ore.: Eugene High School Student Body, 1924.

Thompson, Fred, and Patrick Murfin. *The I.W.W., Its First Seventy Years (1905–1975): The History of an Effort to Organize the Working Class*. Chicago: I.W.W., 1976. A corrected facsimile of Thompson's *The I.W.W., Its First Fifty Years* (1955) with an appendix listing sources on IWW history published since 1955.

Tomlins, Christopher L. "AFL Unions in the 1930s: Their Performance in Historical Perspective," *Journal of American History* 65, no. 4 (1979).

Tone, Andrea. *Devices and Desires: A History of Contraceptives in America*. New York: Hill and Wang, 2001.

Trowbridge, Robertson. *Forty-Eight Years: Anecdotes and Other Oddments Collected from Original Sources, 1884–1932, With which are incorporated some excerpts from The Little Book of Pleasures*. New York: Privately printed, 1937.

Tyler, Robert L. *Rebels of the Woods: The I.W.W. in the Pacific Northwest*. Eugene: University of Oregon Books, 1967.

U.S. Bureau of Census, *13th Census of the United States, 1910, Abstract of the Census with Supplement for Oregon*. Washington, D.C.: 1913.

———. *16th Census of the United States, 1940, Population*, vol. II, *Characteristics of the Population, New York-Oregon*. Washington, D.C.: 1943.

———. *U.S. Census of Population: 1950*, vol. II, *Characteristics of the Population*, part 37, *Oregon*, vol. 14. Washington, D.C.: 1952.

———. *U.S. Census of Population: 1950*, vol. 14, *Special Reports*, part 3, chapter A. Washington, D.C.: 1954.

U.S. House of Representatives. Committee on Un-American Activities. *Investigation of Communist Activities in the Pacific Northwest Area—Part 10 (Portland)*. 83 Cong. 2 sess. 1954.

———. *Communist Political Subversion, Part 1*. 84 Cong. 2 sess. 1956.

U.S. National Labor Relations Board, Official Report of Proceedings before the National Labor Relations Board, case no. XIX-C–329, 13, 16, 22, 29 June 1938.

Urban League of Portland. "News Roundup." Portland: December 1961.

Ward, C. Osborne. *The Ancient Lowly: A History of the Ancient Working People from the Earliest Known Period to the Adoption of Christianity by Constantine.* 2 vols. Chicago: Charles Kerr, 1888–1900.

Williams, Jerold. "The Late, Great, Mt. June Flume Company," *Lane County Historian* 21, no. 2 (winter 1976).

Wittner, Lawrence S. *Rebels Against War: The American Peace Movement, 1933–1983.* Revised. Philadelphia: Temple University Press, 1984. Originally published as *Rebels Against War: The American Peace Movement, 1941–1960.* New York: Columbia University Press, 1969.

Wuorinen, John H. *A History of Finland.* New York: published for the American-Scandinavian Foundation by Columbia University Press, 1965.

Zieger, Robert H., and Gilbert J. Gall. *American Workers, American Unions: The Twentieth Century.* 3d ed. Baltimore: John Hopkins University Press, 2002. The extensive U.S. labor history bibliographic essay found in the first two editions (1986, 1994) does not appear in this edition but can be found on the website www.pressjhu.edu/press/books/

E-MAIL CORRESPONDENCE

Laurel Lynn Demas, genealogical research volunteer, 3–5 November 2002.
Tom Neel, Library Director, Ohio Genealogical Society, 5 November 2002.
Linda Showalter, Special Collections, Dawes Memorial Library, Marietta College, 6 November 2002.
Ricki Solinger, 18 September 1996.

WEBSITES

California U.S. Gen Project <http://www.cagenweb.com/~cpl/sumbios4.htm> (February 20, 2003).

Chicago Metro History Fair, Citizenship for All: Jane Addams and the Hull-House Settlement, Documents for Hull-House "History Teacher's Workshop." <http://www.uic.edu/jaddams/hull/Addams_PetitiontoPresidentCoolidge.html> (18 December 2002). Petition of Jane Addams et al. to President Calvin Coolidge, regarding the restoration of civil rights to American citizens convicted of espionage during World War I, 16 November 1928. Herbert Hoover Presidential Library, West Branch, Iowa, in JAMC (reel 20–0533–0534), Special Collections, University Library, University of Illinois at Chicago.

Division of Alaska Longevity Programs <http://www.state.ak.us/admin/alp/bonus.htm> (27 November 2002).

ILA Union <www.ilaunion.org> (21 February 2003).

Ky. Civil War Rosters, Twenty-second Kentucky Infantry <http://www.rootsweb.com/~kymercer/CivilWar/Union> (18 November 2002).

LexisNexis ILWU v. Hawaiian Pineapple Co. Ltd., Hawaiian Pineapple Co. Ltd. v. Martin E. Aden et al. 226 F. 2d 875, 1955 <web.lexis-nexis.com> (23 November 2002).

MyFlorida.com Dept. of Elder Affairs <http://www.myflorida.com/doea/healthfamily> (12 November 2002).

MICROFILM AND FICHE

Abstracts of votes, 16 May 1970, Primary Election, microfilm 1996–131–01/033A, MC.
Abstracts of Votes, Multnomah County, 1950, roll 2 of 2, MC.
1850 census Greenup Ky. microfilm roll 0442970; Pendleton County reel 442995, FHC.

1840 census M704122 Ky. Pendleton County reel 7831, FHC.

1860 census Greenup Ky. microfilm roll 7835, FHC.

General Index to Compiled Service Records of Volunteer Soldiers who served during the War with Spain, National Archives Microfilm Publication 871. Washington, D.C., General Service Administration, 1971. Roll 40. FHC.

Lane County real properties record, vol. 101, 412, #4853; vol. 104, 610, #11092; vol. 112, 231, #10975, August 7, 1915.

Marriages in Greenup Co. vol. 2, 1854–1903 fiche 6101147, FHC.

Multnomah County Circuit Court, film file 718, case 173483.

Oregon Death Index, 1921–1930 A–2 microfilm reel 4, OHS.

Spanish War Military Pensions, GL-GO, Film 0540934.

Veterans Administration Pension Index File (Washington, D.C.: VA Pub. Service. 1953), microfilm reel 2262, FHC.

NEWSPAPERS AND MAGAZINES

Dispatcher (San Francisco)

Evening Astorian-Budget

Harper's Monthly Magazine

March of Labor (New York?)

Morning Astorian

The Neighbor (Portland, Oregon)

New York Times

"News Roundup" (Urban League of Portland, Oregon)

Oregon Journal (Portland)

Oregon Labor Press (Portland)

Oregonian (Portland)

People's Daily World (San Francisco)

Seattle Union Record

Timber Worker (Seattle)

CORRESPONDENCE

Julia's correspondence is in the Julia Ruuttila papers at OHS; however, her letters to Valerie Taylor are in the possession of Valerie Taylor. Copies of some of these letters are at OHS. The originals of Julia's correspondence with Federated Press are in the possession of Miriam Kelber. Mike McDonald's letters are in the possession of Shane Ruuttila. Copies of both collections are at OHS. Copies of the portions of Julia's FBI files released to me are in her papers at OHS as well.

INDEX